POST CARD

Foster & Reynolds, 1 Madison Avenue, New York

This side for the Address

Miss Betty Blake
Rogers
Ark.

WILL

ROGERS

Courtship and Correspondence 1900-1915

BY REBA COLLINS

WITH COMMENTS BY

JAMES BLAKE ROGERS AND WILL ROGERS, JR.

NEIGHBORS AND QUAID, INC. OKLAHOMA CITY

PUBLISHED BY
NEIGHBORS AND QUAID, INC.
1600 SUNSET LANE
OKLAHOMA CITY, OK 73127

DISTRIBUTED BY
PUBLISHERS DISTRIBUTION SERVICE
121 EAST FRONT STREET
TRAVERSE CITY, MI 49684
(800) 345-0096

DESIGNED BY CAROL HARALSON

DUST JACKET PHOTOGRAPH BY STEVE FRITZ
BOOK PRINTED BY TAYLOR PUBLISHING COMPANY, DALLAS, TEXAS
ARCHIVAL MATERIAL AND PHOTOGRAPHS COURTESY OF THE WILL ROGERS MEMORIAL,
CLAREMORE, OKLAHOMA

International Standard Book Number 0-9632882-0-2

Manufactured in the United States of America

To the memory of Mary Amelia Rogers Brooks,
daughter of Will and Betty Rogers,
with love

Contents

The Letters

The raw material for this book—love letters, family correspondence, signed contracts, vaudeville programs, clippings and Will's unpublished notes—survived because of several miracles. Only Betty Blake Rogers knew of their existence for many years. Will wouldn't have taken the time to sift through such things and the children had other irons in the fire.

Betty was by nature a keeper. Even Will's first letters to her, which he asked her to destroy, she kept. Later Will would stuff things in his pockets and she would sort them from the jumble on his dresser and keep them. So she was the original "savior" of this invaluable material. It was stored first in boxes at the Rogers home and later in a vault in the Rogers Company office in Beverly Hills. After her death in 1944, the office was maintained by the Rogers children for various transactions such as matters that involved rights to their father's films, photographs, writings and memorabilia. Will Rogers, Jr., handled family affairs for many years. As he neared the age of seventy-five, he turned them over to his younger brother James Rogers.

Mary Rogers Brooks, only daughter of Will and Betty, lived abroad most of the years following her divorce from millionaire Walter Brooks in the 1950s until a year or so before her death in 1990. But she was always consulted on important matters. The Rogers children knew about the love letters and other correspondence because Betty Rogers used selections from them when she wrote her book *Will Rogers: The Story of His Life Told by His Wife,* published in 1941. Then all the material was put back in the vault. But that's getting ahead of my story, as Will would say.

In 1965 I was working to complete a dissertation at Oklahoma State University for my doctorate in Journalism for Higher Education. My research topic—one of those nose-counting jobs that become obsolete and begin gathering dust on a shelf almost as soon as they are tabulated—was boring me, so I took time out in August to travel to Washington, D.C., and the World's Fair in New York City.

In the nation's capitol we saw the larger-than-life statue of Will Rogers, located where he could "keep an eye on Congress," and the guide told us it was the most popular statue there. His bronze toes were rubbed shiny by those who wanted just to touch him—for luck or out of love for Will's memory.

The Oklahoma booth at the Fair featured Will Rogers. Long lines waited to hear his voice on records. As I waited my turn, I heard chuckles and comments about Will's humor and I was amazed at the love in the voices of visitors as they shared memories about him. Then it was my turn and I learned why.

We started back toward Edmond and Central State University (now University of

Tall and slender, with arm and chest muscles trained to manipulate a heavy 90-foot rope into a "wedding ring," or the "big crinoline," as Will called it, "The Greatest Catch in Vaudeville" had hundreds of cards made up. He sent handsful home to his family and passed them out generously to friends. The title suited him. It was used by newspapers and magazines dozens of times between 1905 and 1910.

The Greatest Catch in Vaudeville

Manipulating 90 ft of Rope.

COMPLIMENTS OF **WILL ROGERS** THE LARIET EXPERT

Central Oklahoma), where after seven years on the journalism faculty I was head of public relations. As we traveled through northeastern Oklahoma on the Will Rogers Turnpike we saw a lone sign pointing to the Will Rogers Memorial in Claremore.

Needing lunch anyway, we decided to stop and see what was there.

The awesome statue in the foyer makes you catch your breath. It's a twin to the one in Washington, but it is somehow much more moving to look up into Will's rugged, friendly face in the stillness of the Memorial. We saw the vast collection of his personal effects on display—the recordings, the film clips and finally the collection of his newspaper and magazine articles, which kept us there until closing time.

As we drove toward home, Will haunted me. Especially his writings. His comments are the kind that cause you to say, "I wish *I'd* said that!" and make you chuckle hours later.

"Literature!" I thought, as I recalled the definition of the term I'd learned in "English Lit 103." Something that reaches a wide range of people and lasts a long time.

"If I were just doing my dissertation in literature..." Then it hit me. Why not "Will Rogers, Writer and Journalist?"

It cost me an extra year—a year of exciting discoveries. It must be sinful to enjoy a dissertation as much as I did. I heard Will's actor friend and protégé Joel McCrea say, "Everything Will Rogers touched, he added a little glory to." True in spades in my case.

Early in my research I contacted Paula McSpadden Love—daughter of Will's eldest sister Sallie McSpadden—who had been curator of the Will Rogers Memorial in Claremore since it opened in 1938. She was extremely cautious about sharing Will's materials—and rightfully so, considering their value. But we hit if off right away. She saw my joy in reading Will's writings, appreciated my nose for research, and realized how much I wanted to share his philosophy and his laughter with others by publishing his material.

One day when she trusted me enough she showed me her most secret cache. It was in boxes, locked in a broom closet off the foyer. She had acquired it by rather devious means—for the Memorial, of course, not for herself—and wanted my help.

She had assumed Will's personal correspondence was destroyed after Betty's death, she told me. She evidently did not know about the vault in the Beverly Hills office. An author in New York had managed to borrow the correspondence, along with some of Will's typed articles, in the 1960s. When he was unsuccessful in contacting Will, Jr., to get permission to use them, he wrote the Memorial staff to see if they could tell him something about them.

"I had been searching all over the world for Uncle Will's things," Paula said. "Even though I wasn't sure exactly what he had, I told him that if he showed them to me I would see what I could do. But when they got here and I saw what they were, I decided to lock them up and tell him they were lost in shipping!"

Later she took the letters to her house on the Memorial grounds and hid them under the bed. At night she would pull them out one by one and read them in privacy. She knew they should be published, but she wanted to be involved in the publication to insure its accuracy. I was the one she wanted to do the book with her.

Swearing me to secrecy until the time was right and she had cleared it with the Rogers family, she said she would photocopy the letters and mail them to me. Then it was my turn to be astounded.

Unfolding before my eyes were answers to my questions: What made Will Rogers a "national treasure?" What motivated him? Where did he gain such understanding of the world and its people? How did his Indian heritage affect him? How about his family? Why did his father exclaim to the Oklahoma constitutional chairman and later Oklahoma governor William Murray, "What am I going to do with that damn kid now!" Where did Will get such a sense of humor? What drove him so hard to succeed? Who taught him to write, to speak? How did he become "the greatest communicator America has ever produced," as the late Dr. Laurence Peter (the *Peter Principle* author) called him?

Why did Betty Blake refuse Will's pleas for eight years, and why did he continue his pursuit while girls around the globe chased him? Why did the whole world come to a standstill when he died, and why did newspapers around the globe scream the tragedy: *WILL ROGERS KILLED.*

This period of his life—from 1900 to 1915—is the time frame in which to seek answers to those questions. The letters he wrote to Betty and his family on his travels around the world, as he entered into Wild West shows and later into vaudeville, as his family life began—reveal how it all happened. The keys to understanding him are in his letters.

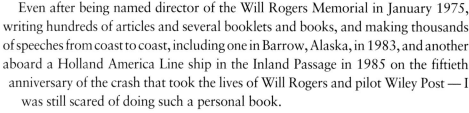

Even after being named director of the Will Rogers Memorial in January 1975, writing hundreds of articles and several booklets and books, and making thousands of speeches from coast to coast, including one in Barrow, Alaska, in 1983, and another aboard a Holland America Line ship in the Inland Passage in 1985 on the fiftieth anniversary of the crash that took the lives of Will Rogers and pilot Wiley Post — I was still scared of doing such a personal book.

But I did decide that Paula had been right about the format of the book. I had written a narrative of Will's life in 1968-69, using the letters as needed to tell the story. Paula wanted the letters to be used in their entirety, with only enough narration to help the reader make sense out of them. The manuscript of the book that I did "my way" sat on the shelf. When Paula passed away unexpectedly in 1973, I was too heartsick to start over. Now, twenty years later, I have discovered she was right! The letters do need to be published "as is." And so they are.

The spelling, grammar and punctuation are Will's own. Always careless of the rules, he wrote fast and let the commas fall where they would. He often failed to use periods and never discovered semicolons. Where such punctuation is needed for clarity, we have left spaces for the reader's benefit.

Ordinarily brackets would be used to correct the original writings, but in these boisterous, sometimes hurried and rambling letters, so many brackets would be required that they would distract readers instead of helping them. So brackets are used sparingly.

Will's contractions are the same ones he used throughout his life, from the time he was in the fourth grade until his later years when he was America's most widely read newspaper columnist. Instead of *hadn't* he wrote *hadent*. Rather than *didn't*, he wrote *dident*, etc. Soon one gets used to the pattern and wonders why the practice never caught on. These we have left alone.

Will said of his first syndicated columns for the papers: "Let it go as it lays. I don't care if the printer has to get drunk to set the type." As to editing, he disavowed that too. He said he was getting paid "writing wages," not for reading the stuff. For the most part, we have "let it go," too. Spacing approximates that used in the original letters.

Included in the pages that follow are all the existing letters written by Will Rogers to Betty Blake between January 1900 and their marriage on November 25, 1908, plus additional letters written from the road after their marriage, letters that Betty wrote home during the early years of her marriage, and selected letters from Will's friends and family. All are printed here as they were written. No major deletions or changes have been made. Only a few of the shorter notes Will wrote to his father have been combined to save space.

Will's letters, private, written on the go in lonely nights in stark hotel rooms or on long afternoons between shows, reveal Will Rogers' true feelings and help us to understand what drove him to greatness. Through them, we can find some keys to his success.

When I asked Will's sons, Will Rogers, Jr., and James Rogers about co-authoring the book, Will, Jr., said he wanted me to write it, and he wanted it done now. If not, many of the people close to the immediate family would not be alive. And it would be a long time before someone else spent as many years as I had seeking the truth of this great man. Bill and Jim Rogers agreed to go over the material and to provide comments for the margins if I would do the remainder of the writing.

I spent several weeks in Arizona working with Will, Jr., reading him all the letters, plus the reviews, clippings, etc., and we recorded our conversations. Then I sent all the letters and most of my notes to Jim Rogers in California and he made comments on the telephone and on paper, as well as during a visit to my home. This capped the thousands of hours I had spent querying them about their parents, and the few hours I had had with Will's daughter Mary Rogers before her death.

We all owe a debt of gratitude to Betty Rogers for keeping the letters, preserving them for others even after she completed her book.

It was Paula Love who first introduced me to the vast storehouse of material at the Will Rogers Memorial in 1965 and encouraged me to complete my doctoral dissertation "Will Rogers, Writer and Journalist." Pat Lowe, Greg Malak, and Elwyn Isaacs, keepers of the material on file at the Memorial, have helped me through the years to find elusive references and to verify facts. My sister Wanda Voss introduced me to the computer that enabled me to do the final manuscript, and she did the first complete typing of the letters, helping to decipher the often difficult writing. Publishers Tom Quaid and enthusiastic and creative Gloria Quaid helped me to produce the final manuscript and get this work in print. William Hubbard, former manager of the Will Rogers Ranch and my personal friend, took care of finances and other details of our everyday lives, enabling me to continue this work.

The Rogers family made the book possible by permitting use of the personal letters and by encouraging me to continue when I would have faltered. My debt to them for their love and understanding is more than I can ever repay. Printed comments in the margins are those written and spoken by Will Rogers, Jr., and James Blake Rogers for this publication. The memory of my long telephone conversations with Mary Rogers Brooks, first from her home in Athens, Greece, and later from California where she fought and almost won her long battle with cancer, meanwhile giving me daily pep talks as I struggled with the same malady, assures me that her blessings are upon this project. Clippings and photos are from holdings in the Rogers Collection—material collected by Will himself, then preserved by Betty—now in the Will Rogers Memorial in Claremore, Oklahoma. My gratitude goes to the Will Rogers Memorial Commission, chaired by James C. Leake; to Joseph Carter, who replaced me as director and enabled me to spend more time writing; and to the entire staff of the Memorial.

We sincerely feel that the material presented here will prove invaluable to later scholars—helping to explain the magic, charisma and eloquence that earned Will Rogers a unique place in literature, in entertainment, in philosophy, and in history.

So, with great humbleness yet with great expectations, we present to you, dear readers, *Will Rogers: Courtship and Correspondence 1900-1915.*

Dr. Reba Collins
Director Emeritus, Will Rogers Memorial
Edmond, Oklahoma 1992

At left: This famous vaudeville photo of "The Cherokee Kid" shows a large hole in the left knee of his chaps. Later photos show he continued to wear the torn chaps as the hole got bigger. But his twinkling blue eyes and big grin stayed the same.

NEW AMSTERDAM THEATRE

42ᴰ ST. WEST OF BROADWAY

NEWAM THEATRE CORPORATION

ERLANGER, DILLINGHAM & ZIEGFELD

DIRECTORS

At the Station, Oologah

Will Rogers' letters to Betty Blake, the blond, blue-eyed city girl from Rogers, Arkansas, began shortly after the "Injun Cowboy" saw her for the first time at the railroad depot in Oologah, Indian Territory, in the waning weeks of the nineteenth century.

Both were twenty years old. Both enjoyed popularity in their respective social circles. Both loved laughing, music, parties and traveling. Each had lost one parent—Will's mother, Mary Schrimsher Rogers, had died when he was ten and Betty's father, James Wyeth Blake, before she was three. Will was the youngest of eight children born to Captain Clement Vann Rogers and his wife Mary. Betty was the seventh child in a family of seven girls and two boys. Betty's older brother, John Blake, was killed in a railroad accident in 1889. Three of Will's siblings had died in infancy and an older brother, Robert, died from typhoid at seventeen, leaving Will the only son.

Their homes were only about 100 miles apart as the crow flies. One of Betty's sisters married a pharmacist. One of Will's sisters did too. Each grew up in a two-story white house.

From Indian Territory to the New York stage was a long way, but Will would travel that road and many others before he and Betty Blake were married. At left, Will Rogers' childhood home in the Cherokee Nation, Indian Territory—which he affectionately called the "White House on the Verdigris" River. On the facing page is the cover of a 1925 program for a Follies performance that featured Will Rogers and his act.

NAME

William Penn Adair Rogers, named for Colonel William Penn Adair, C.S.A., commanding officer of Captain C.V. Rogers in the Civil War.

PARENTS

Clement Vann Rogers and Mary America Schrimsher Rogers.

BIRTHDATE

4 November 1879

BIRTHPLACE

Cooweescoowee District, Cherokee Nation, Indian Territory, four miles northeast of present Oologah, Oklahoma, in Rogers County.

MARRIAGE

25 November 1908 in Rogers, Arkansas, to Betty Blake (born Benton County, 9 September 1879 to James Wyeth and Amelia Crowder Blake).

DIED

15 August 1935 near Barrow, Alaska, in a plane crash with pilot Wiley Post. Buried at Will Rogers Memorial, Claremore, Oklahoma, beside his wife Betty who died in Santa Monica, California, 21 June 1944, their baby son Fred, and daughter Mary Rogers Brooks.

ISSUE

~Will Rogers, Jr., born 20 October 1911 in New York City.

~Mary Amelia Rogers, born 18 May 1913 in Rogers, Arkansas; died December 1990.

~James B. Rogers, born 25 July 1915 in New York City.

~Fred Rogers, born 15 July 1918 in New York City; died 17 June 1920 in Los Angeles of diptheria.

But their ethnic backgrounds — hers Anglo-Saxon and his Cherokee — separated them by generations of prejudice.

Betty had come to the tiny railroad town of Oologah, Indian Territory, in fall of 1899 to visit her sister Cora, wife of station agent Will Marshall. Hers was a "railroading" family. At one time or another every one of the Blakes worked for the railroad. James ("Sandy") Blake served as a station master in various towns, including some in the Indian Territory. Betty herself worked as a telegrapher and as a clerk — once taking over the entire operation of the station at Jenny Lind, Arkansas, when her brother Sandy was on vacation.

Located a few blocks from the bustling commercial center of Rogers, Arkansas (population just over 2,000), the home of Amelia Crowder Blake, an attractive widow, and her seven daughters was alive with activity — comings and goings, giggles and tears, music and secrets, cooking and sewing, the swapping of bows and beaux, the clatter of screen doors slamming and feet pounding up the stairs or the soft padding of slippers as someone sneaked into the kitchen for a late-night snack.

The "white house on the Verdigris" River where Will spent his early childhood had once known equal gaiety when his dark-eyed little mother Mary played the piano for square dancing in the big dining room, when young Willie played pranks on the boyfriends of his three older sisters — Sallie, Maud and May — and when his father Clem Rogers discussed territorial affairs with his fellow tribal officers around the dining room table.

But Will had begun to notice a change. He heard bits of conversations that boded no good. His mother's gay voice was quieter. Something evil was in the air.

White farmers crouched along the Kansas border, waiting impatiently for the federal government to let them into the fertile fields of the Indian Territory. The

Cherokee men vowed to fight to keep their land free from intruders, knowing that, sooner or later, change was inevitable. The red men always lost. Will sensed the tension in the voices of visitors who discussed the impending doom with Clem Rogers.

Then in 1890 fate dealt a terrible, sudden blow to Clem and his family. During a typhoid epidemic, Mary Rogers died. It was the beginning of the end of life as young Willie knew and loved it.

Will's older sister Sallie had married Tom McSpadden in 1885. A year after Mary Rogers' death, Maud married Cap Lane and moved to Chelsea, I.T. In 1892, the youngest Rogers girl, May, married Matt Yocum and moved to Oologah. Then in January 1893, Clem Rogers married again. The bride was Mary Bibles, a local Cherokee girl who had helped with the housekeeping, and was young enough to be Clem's daughter. The newlyweds moved from the banks of the Verdigris River into a new house in Claremore, a dozen miles to the south.

In three years, Will's life changed completely. No laughing mother and older sisters to look after him, no ranchland to ride across, no bunkhouse cowboys to rope and to laugh with, no home with parties and good times, and, as far as he was concerned, no father who cared about him anymore. As outsiders threatened to take over the "Beautiful Indian Territory," it's little wonder that Will's identity too was threatened.

At age sixteen, Will was sent to Scarritt College, a Methodist school in Neosho, Missouri. As a Cherokee Indian, he was in the "minority" there, a new experience for him and one he little understood. Will had been taught that Cherokees were among the best people on earth, and he had no reason to doubt it. When his schoolmates "looked down on him," he did not know why. Trying to be part of the group, he joined some of the young men at a local wine maker's establishment, but the expedition cost him. Afterwards when he asked pretty Maggie Nay to attend a party with him she refused him on the orders of her mother, who had heard about the boys' escapade. It hurt him deeply.

Practicing with his ropes and showing off for his classmates at Scarritt, Will roped a mare and caused her to bolt across campus and "tear up some scenery," as he later described it. That prank and others boosted him out of the Neosho school and back into the Territory.

Exasperated with his erring son who "would not take advantage of his opportunities," Clem decided that what he needed most was discipline and so in January 1897, he sent him to Kemper Military Academy in Boonville, Missouri. Warned not to take his ropes along, Will smuggled them into the school in plain view, disguised as bindings to secure his baggage. He was prepared not to like the place but he learned fast in spite of his rebellious spirit and made good grades in the subjects he liked. However, demerits piled up. At age eighteen, Will bor-

Facing page, at top: Will and Betty were married 25 November 1908 at the Blake home in downtown Rogers. A historical marker later pointed to the home but in the early 1970s it was demolished and replaced with a parking lot. In the inset photo, Betty is dressed in a new cape and muff; she had this photo taken for Will in 1906-07.

Below: Will at Kemper. Of his days there, Will said, "I was at Kemper two years, one year in the guardhouse and the other in the fourth grade. One was about as bad as another."

*Sixteen-year-old Will wrote to Maggie Nay after she refused his invitation to a party on her mother's instruction. He writes, "My Dearest Friend if you can not be my Sweetheart / I received the note a little bit ago and was more than glad to hear from you but was sorry to hear my fate. I did not think of getting such a note but it is all right of course I am as sorry as can be but then if your mother does not want you to go with me why it is all right. I would hate to do anything contrary to her will. I know I drink and am a wild and bad boy and all that but then you know that Marvin is a model boy. he never did anything in his life he is as good as an angel I am an outcast I suppose so of course dont do anything that will get you with a drunkard as I am . . . "
The letter continued for several pages in the same half-sarcastic, half-apologetic tone, obviously the words of one experiencing the true pain of exclusion.*

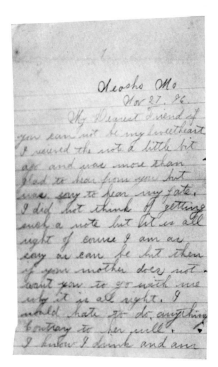 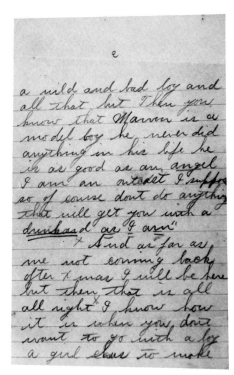

rowed twenty dollars from his sisters and bought a railway ticket. Writing about it in later years, Will said he went to "old man Ewings ranch on the Canadian River near Higgins, Texas," and found a job on a working ranch.

The Spanish American War had started by this time, and Will went to Amarillo where he tried to join Teddy Roosevelt's cavalry. He was turned down. Humiliated, he took a job driving cattle to Kansas. Later he went to Deming, New Mexico, to work on a ranch, and in the winter of 1899, he went to San Luis Obispo with a load of cattle for the Hearst Ranch. Once it was delivered, the cowboys went on to San Francisco to see the sights. Will shared a hotel room with a cowboy friend. They came home late one night and blew out the light, one different from the kerosene lamps they were accustomed to using. With the flame blown out, the gas continued to pour into the room, and by morning the boys were almost dead. As soon as he was able, Will returned to Claremore and Clem sent him on to Hot Springs, Arkansas, to take the mineral baths and recuperate.

Everything he did seemed to turn out wrong. He was glad to be home and to see all his friends, but he just didn't belong anymore. His heart was in the Indian Territory as long as he lived, and from time to time, he returned. But never again was Will able to settle down and make it his home.

Perhaps he found in Betty Blake the warmth and sparkle and love which he sensed more than remembered from his own mother and the home he once knew in the big white house on the Verdigris River. Whatever the attraction, it had a powerful pull.

As the year 1900 opened, he began to write to the beautiful girl he had first seen the previous autumn on the train platform in Oologah.

And that's where our story begins.

"YOUR TRUE FRIEND AND INJUN COWBOY"

As the century ended, Will was on the move and so was the whole country.

As folks learned to write the year 1900 instead of 1899 on their letters and checks, this country of nearly 76 million Americans was on the move.

In January 1900, the first "autostage"—an electric bus that seated eight inside and four outside—was seen on Fifth Avenue in New York. Fare was five cents. At an organized auto race in New Jersey an electric car won—doing fifty miles in two hours and three minutes. Horses still pulled streetcars, and livery stables were everywhere. Not ten miles of concrete roads existed in the nation.

Railroads sprang up like dandelions. Mail went by train from New York to San Francisco in 102 hours.

Republicans meeting in Philadelphia in June nominated William McKinley for president and Theodore Roosevelt for vice president. The next month, William Jennings Bryan was nominated by the Democrats.

Woodrow Wilson was still a professor at Princeton. Herbert Hoover, twenty-five, was just five years out of Stanford. Coolidge was a small-town lawyer in New England.

The nation's strong suit was the freedom of opportunity to "make it." Living examples were Andrew Carnegie, Thomas A. Edison, John D. Rockefeller, Mark Twain and Joseph Pulitzer.

Construction workers in Chicago struck for an eight-hour day. A turkey dinner cost twenty cents, breakfast fifteen cents. Price of a hotel room was one dollar. In Los Angeles a male clerk-bookkeeper made $110 a month.

A hurricane destroyed Galveston, Texas, in September.

Pop music included ragtime and the cakewalk. Both forms derived from black music—this, thirty-five years after the Civil War. *David Harum* was a popular novel.

In Arkansas as elsewhere, women wore shirtwaists tucked into long skirts that neatly covered the "Cuban" heels on their hightop shoes. A bill was signed to make Hawaii a territory—like Oklahoma, New Mexico and Arizona.

Clement Vann Rogers (1839-1911), Confederate captain, judge, senator of Cooweescoowee District, rancher, cattleman and banker, was named for his mother's people, the Vann family. Will's mother Mary Amelia Schrimsher Rogers (1839-1890) was from a family that came over the Trail of Tears.

Seven sisters, all in a row, as they liked to be seen: Cora, Anna, Waite, Theda, Betty, Virginia and Zuleki. Although the youngest was fathered by Amelia Blake's short-term second husband J. O. Boyd, she grew up just one of the Blake sisters.

In Indian Territory—most of the eastern half of what is now Oklahoma—there was street corner talk of opening the area to white settlers. The Indian tribes had been warned following the Civil War that their penalty for supporting the Confederacy would cost them their territory, and they grudgingly prepared to divide up the land. Clem Rogers was one of those chosen to evaluate the holdings of "intruders" so they could be bought out before the land was divided among the Cherokees.

"Clem V. Rogers, 61," was listed as a quarter-blood on the Cherokee rolls in 1900. His son was listed "William Penn Adair Rogers/ No. 11,384, Age 20/ 1/4 Cherokee." Will would be twenty-one on November 4.

Leaving young Will to look after the ranch—when he wasn't shipping his horse and saddle by train and entering roping contests from St. Louis to San Antonio and a dozen other places—Clem built a fine home in town and installed a system of lights that burned "bright and steady," the Claremore *Progress* reported. One

small jet lit a whole room, and the seven lights could burn every night for a full year for fifteen dollars.

Tribal schools, seminaries, churches, courthouses and social life equalled or surpassed those of the "Oklahoma Territory," the middle part of the state which had been opened for settlement by a "run" in 1889. Telephones came to the Cherokee Nation.

Trains came down from Coffeyville, Kansas, through Talala, Oologah and on to Claremore, connecting with the Frisco that ran from St. Louis to Vinita and Tulsa, that "new town" west of Claremore. It was at the train station in Oologah that Will met Betty.

Pretty as a picture, with a smile that sent boys into a tailspin, she startled Will when he swung down from the train and went inside to pick up a package, a banjo he'd purchased on a trip to Kansas City. Overwhelmed by shyness and suddenly tongue-tied, he left without waiting to see if it arrived.

The next evening, the Ellis family, including daughters Lil and Kate, invited him to dinner at the hotel across the road from the depot. They also invited Betty who was staying with her sister Cora Marshall and Cora's husband, Will Marshall, railroad station master at Oologah.

Will was soon telling what was going on in Kansas City and making everyone laugh as they pulled taffy and made music after dinner.

Betty and the Ellis sisters were eager to see the sheet music Will had brought home with him. And to his delight, Betty could play the tunes on the piano and lead the singing. Later he brought out his new banjo, and Betty showed him how to string and tune it. Then she played it, too!

We had one of the old roller pianos and we would stand around and listen. Dad tried to play the ukulele. But none of us was really musical. I can't recall ever standing around the piano and singing while mother played. But the piano was always there, so she must have played it sometime. Or maybe she had Mary take lessons. . .
~Will Rogers, Jr.

Acting the part of serious suitor long before he became one, Will joined his cousin Spi Trent (right) in entertaining the two McClellan sisters, Mary (left) and Pearl.

It was the music that first brought Will and Betty together. Perhaps she reminded him of his mother whom he had adored. Mary Rogers had played the piano at the Methodist church as well as at the dances in their home on Saturday nights and had let Will stand by her side and sing while turning the pages for her. Her death when Will was ten left a void in his heart which he would never fill.

"If you had an old-fashioned mother and her name was Mary, you didn't have to say anything else. Everyone knew already," Will said later. And, as Betty later wrote in a book about her famous husband, he never spoke his mother's name without a tear in his voice as long as he lived.

Before Christmas, Betty returned to Rogers, Arkansas, and the big bustling house where she grew up. For her, the curious episode out among the Indians was over—good for a chuckle as friends teased her about her would-be sweetheart, Will Rogers. An Indian!

On January 5, 1900, Will sat down to write his first love letter to Betty Blake.

Oolagah. I.T. Jan. 5th 1900

Miss Bettie Blake

Rogers Ark

My Dear Friend

No doubt you will be madly surprised on receipt of this Epistle But never the less I could not resist the temptation and I hope if you cannot do me the great favor of droping me a few lines you will at least excuse me for this for I <u>cant</u> help it.

Well I know you are having a great time after being out among the "Wild Tribe" so long. Well I have had a great time this Xmas myself have not been at home three night in a month taken in every Ball in the Territory and everything else I hear of.

I was in Fort Gibson again last week to Masque Ball I had a time but the Ball came near being a failure it was managed by Sidney Hagood which accounts for it.

I see Sandy and the other folks real often. Kate is still as pretty as ever and going with Doctor Place. Lil is just the cutest girl I know and I am as silly about her as ever.

Say you people never did come out home as you said you would and see us "Wooly Cowboys" rope a wild Steer I have some pictures of it I think and if you want them I will send them to you if you will send me some of those Kodak Pictures you had up here of yourself and all those girls Now <u>isent that</u> a "mamoth inducement for you" To have your pictures in lovely "Indian Wigwam"

I never have had that Swell Ball that we talked of when you were here But if you had staid we would of had it but you would not stay long enough for us to show you a hot time we were just getting acquainted good when you left

If you will only come back up here we will endevor to do all that we can to make you have a time all kinds of late songs but I know they are old to you there. dances. Skating. Sleigh Riding. Horse Back Riding of which you are an expert, and in fact every kind of amusement on the face of Gods footpiece

Well I guess you have had ample suffiency of my nonsence so I will stop. Hoping you will take pity on this poor heart broken Cowpealer and haveing him rejoiceing over these ball prairies on receipt of a few words from you I remain Your True friend and Injun Cowboy

  W P Rogers.
  Oolagah I.T.

Will used whatever writing paper was available. Likely he found this Indian Service letterhead in Clem's desk at home. The elder Rogers was hired by the federal government to appraise property held by "white intruders" in the Indian Territory. The plan was for the government to buy out the intruders' improvements, then send them packing so the total property in the Indian Territory could be divided equitably among the Cherokees.

There is no doubt but what he [Will] knew Betty Blake was the wife for him from their very first meeting.

~James Blake Rogers

Somehow, it doesn't seem quite fair. The only way we know what Mother said was what he wrote back to her—his interpretation. But she wrote her book on dad after he was killed, so I guess she had the last word, after all.

~Will Rogers, Jr.

Everyone said the Blake girls were like stair steps, or, in this case, "rungs on the ladder." From the youngest, Zuleki, just a year or two old when this photo was taken, are Virginia, Betty, Theda, Waite, Anna and Cora. Spellings for the girls' names vary as the sisters changed the spellings of their names as the notion struck them—and there was no Social Security card or other reason to stop them. The family Bible at the Will Rogers Memorial lists Waitie, Thedia, Bettie, Virgie, Zulika (or Zulica) as variations. Census records varied, too. Betty simplified the spelling of her name as she grew older—or maybe as fashion dictated. Theda preferred "Dick" in the days when girls liked to take boys' names. "Watie," "Waitie," and "Waitey" were all pronounced the same. The record shows that Betty was born 9 September 1879—just two months before the birth of Will Rogers on November 4 of the same year. Betty never told him she was older—he would have teased her unmercifully!

Relating his social activities to let Betty know what she had missed by going home for the holidays, Will enthusiastically wrote of both ordinary and special happenings—a style he refined in his later years as a newspaper columnist and radio commentator.

"All those girls" meant the Blake girls—Cora, Anna, Waite, Theda, Betty, Virginia and Zuleki—plus their female friends in Rogers. "Sandy" was Betty's brother, James K. Blake. Sandy held various positions with railroads in Arkansas as well as in the Territory. He evidently knew and liked Will Rogers.

Newspaper writers, ministers and politicians at that time called Indians "savages" or worse in Benton County, Arkansas, less than 100 miles from Claremore.

Betty's sister Theda (called "Dick" by the family) admitted in a taped interview years later that the Blakes were shocked at the thought of Betty's new beau. Even though Betty's mother, Amelia Crowder Blake, took in sewing and all the family worked, they were considered one of *the* families in Benton County. Betty's grandfather, Larkin Blake, was a medical doctor, one uncle was sheriff of Benton County and her Uncle Bo Y. Blake graduated West Point and was a hero in the Boer War. The family was highly respected.

Dr. Edgar Pleas—pronounced Place, as Will wrote it—was a local physician who graduated from an Arkansas medical school and in 1892 came to Oologah where he boarded at the hotel.

Steer roping by the "wooly cowboys" took place in local pastures, often with some betting on the side. It was also called "pot roping" because participants put money in a pot from which winnings were paid.

The Rogers ranch home—preserved and maintained by the State of Oklahoma and known as "Will Rogers' Birthplace" and the "Dog Iron Ranch" as this book is published—was far from being a "wigwam." It was one of the finest in the Cherokee Nation. Built by C.V. Rogers for his wife following the Civil War, it was originally two sturdy log buildings separated by a "dog trot." Then the two-story "White House on the Verdigris," as Will sometimes called it, was enlarged and the logs covered with siding. Inside, walls were plastered and covered with colorful wallpaper. Axminster rugs covered the floors. Completed by 1875, it had four fireplaces, two large upstairs bedrooms and a sleeping porch, and a state-of-the-art kitchen. Downstairs were two bedrooms, a living room and large dining room where the furniture could be shoved back and the rug rolled up for dancing.

Will was born in the southeast bedroom. He often claimed he was born in a lowly log cabin but by 1879 the logs were well hidden!

In spite of young Will's shyness with the bright city girl from Arkansas, his parents had been educated at the Cherokee seminaries. They had fine china and silver for entertaining and one of the earliest pianos in the Territory. Will himself had about the same amount of education as had Betty Blake. But he put Betty Blake on a pedestal and kept her there for the remainder of his life. She knew which fork to use, how to spell and use correct grammar, how to be a lady, how to sing and play the music he loved.

She was the Indian-Cowboy's dream girl.

Before he did anything else, however, his father kept telling him he had to "make something out of himself . . . take advantage of his opportunities." Life could not be all fun and games.

Clem urged Will to stay on the ranch or else move into town and take over one of his businesses—the livery stable, or perhaps the New York Hardware store he had bought that year. But Will was not cut out for "town work."

Will half-heartedly tried to run the ranch. But parties and ropings were so much more fun. By March he had probably given up on hearing from Betty Blake. Then came her reply.

Her letters to him do not exist, but she must have indicated that she would at least permit him to write. They could be pen pals, but nothing more.

[March 14, 1900]
Oologah, I.T.
My Dear Bettie.

Now for me to attempt to express my delight for your sweet letter received would be utterly impossib[l]e so will just put it mild and say I was very very much pleased.

I was also surprised for I thought you had forgotten your Cowbow (for I am yours as far as I am concerned)

Well I am still in the Land of the Broncho and the Texas Steer   have not gone to New Mexico yet   dont know that I will go now for my Father is back and he dont much want me to go   I hope that I wont now for I can live in hopes of seeing you some day   I do wish you could come out this Spring   I will do everything in my power to make you have a good time even if the company was not so enjoyable.

I know you had a fine time when your Sweetheart was down to see you. Oh! how I envy him for I would give all I possessed if I only knew that you cared something for me for Bettie you may not believe it or care any thing about it   but you do not know that you have made life miserable for one poor boy out in the B.I.T   but never the less you did for I think of you all the time and just wish that you might always have a remembrance of me for I know that I cant expect to be your sweetheart for I am not "smoothe" like boys you have for sweethearts   But I know you have not one that will think any more of you than I do although I know they may profess to   Now   Bettie I know you will think me a Big fool (which I am) but please consider that you are the one that has done it   but I know you did not mean to and I ought not to have got so broken up over you   but I could not help it   so if you do not see fit to answer this please do not say a word about it to any one for the sake of a broken hearted Cherokee Cowboy

Now Bettie if you should stoop so low as to answer this please tell me the plain truth for that is what you should do and not flirt with me for I would not be smoothe enough to detect it.

I have some New Songs to send you   also those pictures I promised   I was very glad to get   your pictures and thank you very much for them   I have had lots of compliments on them especially yours.

I am going to Fort Smith some time soon and if you will permit I can probaly come up but I know it would be a slam on your Society career to have it known that you even knew an ignorant Indian Cowboy.

He's certainly defensive about his Indian heritage. . . . You know, growing up we didn't hear anything about Indians, not that I can remember. I'm sure we never considered ourselves to be Indians. It was many years later that I discovered I was eligible for membership in the Cherokee tribe. Now I am very proud of my Cherokee card and I'll whip it out to identify myself with pleasure.
Now that I have read Dad's writings and paid more attention, I realize that he mentioned his Cherokee heritage many times and really championed the Indians, at a time when it was not very popular to do so.
~Will Rogers, Jr.

I think it was Maud who said, "There's a lot of mule in Willie."
~James Blake Rogers

You know, I remember something about Deming, New Mexico . . . about him saying he'd always wanted to go back there and buy a ranch. I had no idea he'd planned to go there when he was so young.
~Will Rogers, Jr.

I still have lots of pretty ponies here if you will come out I will let you pick the herd

Well Bettie please burn this up for my sake   Hopeing you will consider what I have told you in my undignified way and if not to please never say anything about it and burn this up

I am yours with love

Will Rogers.

Oolagah Indian Territory
March, fourteenth, ninteen Hundred.
"Headqarters Dog Iron Ranch"
"Hillside Navy"

Betty changed the spelling of her name at will. She rarely used her middle name, but once in a society story in the Rogers newspaper she was listed as "Bettie Beatrice Blake."

"Cowbow" may be Will's spelling error—he had plenty of them, as Betty reminded him. Or he may have meant to coin a word: "Cow Beau."

The Blakes around 1905. From left, Zuleki Blake Stroud, Maxine Marshall, Grandmother Emiline Crowder, Amelia Crowder Blake, Cora Blake Marshall, Will Marshall, Betty Blake, Anna Blake Adamson, Lee Adamson, Waite Blake, Theda Blake, James Blake, Bruce Quisenberry, Virginia Blake Quisenberry.

There seems to be little reason for Will's wanting to see Betty so much, yet failing to hop on the train for a few hours' trip to her home town. He had the money and the time. But he needed reassurance from her that he would be welcomed, an assurance she could not give her suitor at this time.

Perhaps she was serious about someone else, but in any case it is evident she did not answer this letter. Will was crushed. As usual, when he was hurt, he increased his frenetic pace. In June he gave a big party and dance at the old Rogers ranch with an imported band. His older sister Maud served as hostess. Guests came from as far away as Fort Gibson. To his disappointment, Betty was not among them.

He attended a social hop at the Opera House in Claremore with a large crowd of friends. The next month he went to Oklahoma City to attend the Rough Riders reunion, entering roping contests with Lucille Mulhall, the attractive young daughter of Colonel Zack Mulhall, for whom the term "cowgirl" was coined.

It was not his first encounter with the determined but charming girl. Even though she was only thirteen or fourteen at the time, she looked like a woman and rode and roped like a man. Will enjoyed teaching her some of his rope tricks and she warmed him with her smile.

Papers told of his attending "Texas Steer Ropings" at Vinita and Pryor. The Pocahontas Club—organized by Cherokee girls to give the young people something to do in the summertime—took their cameras to Kephart's Springs for "Kodaking," a picnic and a swimming party. They rode home by moonlight. Willie was there. When his sisters entertained in Chelsea, Will was there.

He went to Springfield, Missouri, for the fair with thirty-nine other contestants, including Lucille and her two sisters. Her older sister Agnes, called Bossie, was claimed by Tom Mix as "his girl."

After Will returned from Hot Springs where he had gone to recover from the near-fatal accident with the gas jet, he went back to the ranch, and by that time Clem had put some sharecroppers on it. He had begun to wonder if his son would ever amount to anything.

Later that month, newspapers reported that Will and a young lady friend had won a cakewalk contest and that he had entertained the party with a "home talent minstrel" solo.

In May he talked his father into trusting him to take a load of cattle to Kansas City to see if he could deal with the buyers there. How he came out on the financial deal was of little importance to him. He learned of a Confederate veterans' convention to be held in Memphis and he went home by way of that city to work out plans for a roping contest for the Cherokee cowboys.

In Hamilton Park in Memphis the first of June, Jim Hopkins broke the world record, roping and tying a steer in eighteen and one-half seconds. He was riding Will's favorite horse Comanche. Will had his fun too, though. He and a few of his friends entertained the huge crowds with fancy roping on horseback. How he loved to make folks laugh!

In July 1901, he won third in roping to get a split of the $100 purse. He went to Carthage, Missouri, to rope and in September to Springfield, Missouri, for a big roping contest at the Elks Street Fair. There he saw Betty again briefly.

The famous Mexican roper Vincente Oropeza was performing and Will saw him

The home of Will's sister Maud and her prosperous druggist husband C. L. Lane in Chelsea, I.T., had a room with a separate entrance set aside for Will.

Wonder what C.V. thought about his son clowning around in a headdress and making war whoops?

~Will Rogers, Jr.

for the second time. He had first seen him in 1893 when Clem took him to the Chicago World's Fair where Oropeza had appeared with Buffalo Bill's Wild West show. Seeing Oropeza again solidified Will's promise to himself that he could one day do all those same rope tricks.

He took second money at the steer roping. Jim Hopkins was first. Again, about a dozen of the boys dressed up and gave an old-fashioned Indian stomp dance and sent all the cowboys home laughing.

Back home, he did the same dances and sang several songs for his Cherokee friends, to the delight of the Pocahontas Club members. It was two o'clock A.M. when the party broke up and guests were taken home in a "wagonette."

With nutting parties and gypsy teas, possum hunts and table tennis at his sisters' homes in Chelsea, along with all the traveling and roping—he was in Des Moines for the World Championship contest and in St. Louis for the Pan American Exposition in October—he had little chance to be lonely for Betty. At least it didn't show.

AFTER TRAVELING 34,000 MILES, HE IS "STILL THE SAME OLD WILL"

oung Mr. William P. Rogers did nothing in 1902 to prepare himself for the future, or so his father thought, and nothing to further his courtship with Betty Blake, or so she thought. But he did find romance of another sort, and it would lead him toward a future beyond his wildest dreams.

Meanwhile, he believed that, as in a song lyric from the period, "People there all say, 'Oh, he is no account. . . . ' " It was time to get away.

Adventure was the name of the game that year, and it takes a calendar to follow Will's trail. The year started with him still in Oologah—trying once again to become a rancher as his father had always planned he should. But as usual he was on the go. Local newspapers kept up with his social life. He attended weddings of his friends, dated local girls, and wondered if his time would come.

Clem Rogers turned sixty-three on January 11, and the family celebrated with him at the Frisco restaurant; that night "W.P. Rogers of Oologah" attended a "jolly party" with friends. Later that month he went to a "musical entertainment." On Valentine's Day, he went to a party at "Pool's Hall" in Chelsea where eligible young ladies smiled upon the catch of the county.

Will Rogers had itchy feet and read all he could find on the opportunities in the Argentine. He didn't want to go alone, so he worked on his roping buddy, Dick Parris, to get him in the mood to go along. Will would pay the way.

Clem Rogers sold one of his old ranches northwest of Oologah to get cash to buy Will's cattle from him so his restless son could strike out for the highly touted ranch country in South America. The elder Rogers then went to Hot Springs again for his health. Will went there to get the money, but instead of giving it to him, Clem sent it to New Orleans where the boys could pick it up before sailing southward.

Claremore, I.T., March 13, 1902
Dear Willie

Hot Spring. My Health continues good. We had a good rain here Monday night & Tuesday All day & it is nice & warm today. Willie we sent you your money to day to the Commercial Bank at New Orleans. $1300.00 I also sent you a Telegram about sending the money to the Commercial Bank at New Orleans, La. Keep the Telegram & this letter & you wont have any trouble about being identified at the Bank there. Sallie Maude & May & all the children are well, Write when you can

Your Pa. C. V. Rogers.

New Orleans, La.
March 18, 1902
My Dear Sisters and Folks.

Well We are here arrived Sunday Night and find that we can not get a boat direct from here but you can get a ticket from here via New York for Bueanos Ayers for about 150 apiece that is first class there is no second class just first and the steerage.

We leave here in the Morning (Wednesday) at 9 o'clock on the steamship Comus. and it is due to arrive in New York on Next Monday Morning and then will have to wait probaly several days before we can get a boat out of there

We have seen most all of New Orleans been down to the wharf most all day seeing them unload and load the big ships.

Went to see Julia Marlowe in When Knighthood was in Flower. last Night it was simply fine.

We sent our baggage aboard this eve consisting of a big trunk of mine which has both our saddles and all our outfits in it and some of our clothes and we each have a grip with the rest of our togs in them.

It is regular spring down here grass is away up and trees are all green and everything is as pretty as can be.

I will write you a long letter while on the boat and mail to you when we get to N.Y. I guess if I am not to sick.

This seems an offul long way but it is the way they all go from here to that far down in S.A. It will take about 25 days from N.Y. to B.A.

We are in good Spirits and feeling fine.

I dont have time and there is no use to write to each of you I will write to both in one so this is for all. give all the children Uncle E. love and tell them I will have lots to tell them when I see them.

I cant tell you where to write to for I dont know where I will be so I will write as often as possible.

Southampton. England
April 4th. 1902.
My Dearest Sisters and All.

Well Old <u>Dunker Dee</u> Landed after Eight long days of heaving forth every thing he looked at. got on the boat at 10 oclock   ate a big dinner and then the thing come off   went to my little 1½ by 5 and did not arise till the <u>Engineer</u> squalled out Southampton   then I sallied out   looked like a freak. after that dinner on Wednesday could not look towards anything not even water till Monday   then after various attempts got a lemon and an orange that never managed to find the way back. Now I want to chirp to you now that if they would of been any turning back there I would of took out a small stack   for when you hear people say you get over it in a day or so you put it down that they have been taking foolish powders   for I and lots of the rest of them was all out on the whole trip   then when I could eat the last two days they dident have anything I could eat. Dick was only sick about one day   O how I did think about all the good beans and good things we ever did have to eat at home. But now I feel good   we got in Wednesday Night at 10 oclock. they search your baggage for <u>Spirits</u> and <u>Tobacco</u>. dident find any in mine for I dident chew and my Spirits had all left me on that boat if I had any at all I contributed them to the <u>big blue</u> before I met them. I dont know but what we may have to pay something on our saddles in S.A. for I think they ride bareback. then we took a "<u>handsome</u>" not a Lady. but a kind of a dog cart and went to a hotel. We got a nice room almost papered with pictures of Queen Victoria who certainly had a stand in with the Photographer   We pay 2 shillings for both (now search out your Almanac and see what that is)   I've tried to learn the measly stuff till I am blue in the face   the penny is the principal thing and the half penny   the penny looks about like our $20 gold pieces   I think I have got a great lot of coin and feel in my geans and when I go to pay for any thing its only a pipe dream for it takes them all for an apple or orange   they are the only familiar Characters Ive met.

Every time We eat or get any thing they speal out what its worth   I just hand them a pound   that is all I know   which is about a five spot over there   and trust to the lord that they will take pity on my ignorance and do me half way right   anyway they'll hand me back a double hand full of something and strut off   I have got enough money in <u>bulk</u> to start in some kind of business. but when I count it (or if some one else did) there would not be enough there to make the first payment on a soda cracker.

That Machine [Victrola] Maud has got there that talks so fast aint one. two. three. with the slowest creature over here. why they would make it "<u>go</u> <u>to</u> <u>the</u> <u>rear</u> <u>and</u> <u>find</u> <u>a</u> <u>damp</u> <u>place</u> <u>and</u> <u>fade</u> <u>away</u>" Our English must be a kind of a slow process. I went up to a Man for some information yesterday and he throwed open the throttle and broke out on one of those chained lightning speeches and I flagged him at the first quarter and asked him (in my speediest tone   which by the way he seemed tire of before I got done) that I was perfectly willing to pay him for his over time if he would kindly relate it over again as though he were speaking of some of his poor or dead relation.

WILL'S ITINERARY, 1902

MARCH 13
Claremore to Hot Springs, Arkansas, with Dick Parris

MARCH 16
New Orleans

MARCH 19
Took steamship COMUS *to New York*

MARCH 24
Arrived New York

MARCH 26
Left New York on steamer PHILADELPHIA

APRIL 2
Arrived Southampton, England

APRIL 3
London, England

APRIL 16
Sailed on royal mail steamer DANUBE

APRIL 16
St. Vincent, Cape Verde Island, across the Equator

APRIL 24
Pernambuco, Brazil

APRIL 28
Arrived in Rio de Janeiro; there 36 hours

MAY 1
Montevideo, Uruguay

MAY 5
Arrived Buenos Aires; quarantined two days on board ship

MAY 8
Started for interior, 500 miles by rail, then overland

MAY 24
Dick Parris leaves for home

JULY 4
Aboard U.S. battleship ATLANTIC; *sang for the sailors*

AUGUST 5
Left Buenos Aires for South Africa on a cattle steamer

AUGUST 22
Arrived Capetown, South Africa

SEPTEMBER 11
Mooi River Station, Natal, South Africa

NOVEMBER 4
Will's 23rd birthday

NOVEMBER 17
Durban, Natal; in Ladysmith

DECEMBER 5
Joined Texas Jack's Wild West Show

DECEMBER 25
Saw ball game in Canadian soldier's camp

DECEMBER 28
Standenton, Transvaal, with Texas Jack's show

Their dress is about the same as ours all but the shoes   and you couldent imagine anything half so big and clumsy   why those old buckle plow shoes over home would be "dancing pumps" over here   all of them Dukes. Dudes, Earls and hod-carriers.

And this <u>food</u> over here is altogeather different by name and by nature. Oh I am almost starved for something cooked over in America.

We are only 40 miles from London and as we cant get out from here till a week from today we will go up there and spend a few days as it is just as cheap living We will see some great sites there I suppose but we are prepared for the worst.

We may call on his Royal Nibs the king.

Our boat leaves here on the 12th for Buenos Aeyers   will be 20 or 25 days on that trip   I tell Dick he has got to get me drunk to get me on another boat   we go by Rio Janerio and Montivideo. and then B.A.

I just sent Dick out to hunt the post office and he is back saying all the letters have to be weighed and then he stamps them and you pay

This information I am putting you next to is quite a weighty matter and I look to have to draw on my inside pocket to send this.

But By By will write you from London or here after being there   before we sail Lots of Love to all. I am fast regaining my lost flesh for the next episode Your Loving Bro and Uncle

   E.

Nowhere In Particular
Southampton, Eng., Apr. 13, 1902.
Dear Sisters and All:

Well Dick and I have visited London and find it the biggest case of a town it has ever been my misfortune to see.

We visited the House of Parliament where all the great doings of state are carried on, also Buckingham Palace where the king and queen will reside during the "big blow-out." Then we went to West Minster Abbey where all the great men of England have monuments erected to their memory and dull as I am I felt a curious sort of sensation creep over me while looking at this, although I knew very few of the men personally. Here all the old armour, chains and crowns worn by all the English sovereigns are kept, but the one that opens your eye lashes most is the one that King Edward will be topped with.

The whole city is being torn up and rebuilt for the cornation. I think they are going to stop up the Thames to make more room for the people. You have dreamed of the great London bridge. Well, I was on that bridge as well as visited the London Tower. On every street corner is a monument to some brave, heroic old man who met his death on the field. What a pity they haven't some of that old stock left to make a stand for them now in South Africa.

The work here seems all to be done by girls. All the ushers in the theaters, the bartenders, waiters and all are girls. They are real pretty, but all look alike and talk so fast I don't know what they are saying.

There is no end of theaters in London but they are not up to the Americans in either tragedy or comedy. The only advantage I have seen over our American cities, is that here they have large parks or play grounds all through the city for the children, and you see thousands of them playing there all the time.

We passed some very beautiful places between Southampton and London. All so well improved, but not a vacant foot of land on the way. We leave here tomorrow for Buenos Ayres and I'll have a long letter to mail you at the first point at which we touch land, which I think will be a port above Rio Janerio, then on by Montevedio, so don't be uneasy if you don't hear from me for a month or six weeks.

Lovingly,
Willie.

19 Apr '02
My Dear Sisters:

Well as we are steaming into St. Vincent, on one of the Cape Verde Islands and will be here all day   I'll have a chance to write and let you know how I am. This place is just north of the equator and is very warm, but the nights are cool. Of course it is much warmer on the land. We have about 200 Portugese and Spanish emigrants on board, all third class or steerage passengers that are going to Brazil. There seems to be every kind of woolie in the world on this boat. I can't understand a soul but Dick, and he is getting so he talks just like some of these folks.

We have very good food. Our six o'clock dinner is splendid, we have five different courses. This morning they gave a practice exhibition of letting down all the life boats. It was a fine sight. They blew a whistle and there were men running from every little hole to their places. The boats were lowered in just a few seconds. You see there are about 500 men employed on the boat. You would think there were only about 100. Then there are 300 passengers. It is one of the largest boats.

It is a sight to see how all these ports are garrisoned, and the vast expense it takes to fix them up. Of course New York has the finest lay out.

These Islands belong to the French and there is a French Man-of-War here. We saw all the Portugese war fleet in the Lisbon harbor. We stopped at Vigo, which is a lovely place, last Sunday evening. At all these places we anchor in the harbor and the small boats come to us, and there are so many fruit peddlers come with all kinds of fruit that is very cheap.

I hope you are all as well as when I left, for I can't get to hear from you. It has been just two months ago today since I left home and will be two more weeks before we reach Buenos Ayres. When we go home we will go up the west coast.

I will write you again from Pernambuco, our next stop. Lots of love to each of you.

Willie

A "woolie" is a derogatory term, designating a sheep or a person who works with sheep. Cowboys and cattlemen did not like sheep. The word also had to do with the smell, and to some extent meant a person who was somewhat "dirty."
~James Blake Rogers

"I CAN'T UNDERSTAND A SOUL BUT DICK, AND HE IS GETTING SO HE TALKS JUST LIKE SOME OF THESE FOLKS."

Pernambuco, Brazil.
April 24, 1902.
My Dearest Sisters:

I will now state you a few more facts about the country in which we do not live. I wrote you a card from Lisbon and a letter from St. Vincent, on an island we passed Saturday. Oh, what a horrible place that was, it was so hot and all the people were negroes and didn't wear enough clothes to cover a postage stamp. It was a dry, sandy desert. There were hundreds of little negro boys who swam around the boat and when the passengers would throw coins in the water they would dive to the bottom of water 100 feet deep for them. They were the finest divers and swimmers I ever saw. We now see the South American coast, for in a few hours we will be at Pernambuco, but we will not be allowed to go ashore nor can any one come aboard for they have the Bubonic Plague there. Our next stop will be at Rio de Janerio and then to Beunos Ayres on the 4th of May.

We crossed the equator yesterday at 4 o'clock. It was very hot, but has been raining ever since and is now quite cool. This trip is getting just a bit old and we will be glad to land.

We learn there are very few Americans in Argentina so Dick and I will have to learn to talk Spanish. You must look over this writing for the boat is trying to "turn a cat." There are lots of sharks following us, some 50 and 75 feet long. We have discovered two Americans among the first class passengers. We enjoy our long talks with them. They are very wealthy. Most of the other first class passengers are English. Well, I will write again from Rio de Janerio, as we get there in four more days.—

Give my love to all,

Willie.

Will was an experienced cowhand from his years on ranches in Texas and New Mexico as well as at home. No one could accuse him of being a "drugstore cowboy."

Bunos Ayres, [Argentina]
May 7, 1902.
My Dear Sisters:

Well we are here at last, got here on the 5th of May. We were quarantined for two days on board, before we were allowed to land.

This is a beautiful country and a very fine city, the prettiest I ever saw. There are about one million inhabitants. We are stopping at an English hotel, "The Phoenix," where English is spoken. We start for the interior tomorrow, by rail for about 500 miles, then we will get us some horses and see if we can get a job, although wages are almost nothing, but we want to learn how they handle cattle here, which is very different from what it is in the United States, then, we want to learn the language too.

The cities here are built something on the order of San Antionio, Tex. All the houses are on the Spanish plan, with lots of openings through the roof, and court where they have all kinds of palms and flowers.

They have an abundance of fruit here. I dont know what half of it is. I guess Clem [McSpadden] will be at home by the time this reaches you. I hope he got through all right and covered himself with glory like his old uncle did.

Some high official died here and was buried to-day. It was a state funeral and of course the grandest I ever saw.

Such a fine hearse with 10 fine black horses. The police and soldiers were all mounted and presented a splendid appearance. The police here are always mounted on very fine horses, though they are small.

Hoping you are all well I am

Lovingly

Willie.

"THE CITIES HERE ARE BUILT SOMETHING ON THE ORDER OF SAN ANTIONIO, TEX."

Will is kidding about "covering himself with glory" at Kemper Military school. He ran away to take a job on a Texas ranch before he graduated. The Clem McSpadden mentioned in the letter was the son of Sallie and Tom. Another of Sallie and Tom's children, Herb McSpadden, had a son whom he named Clem after his brother; that Clem McSpadden—Sallie and Tom's grandson—became a state senator and a U. S. congressman.

This letter to the *Progress* is Will's first travel article written for the purpose of publication.

"Strike a lay" refers to a potential good deal, a "pat hand." "Pipe," below, probably means a pipe dream.

Buenos Ayres, Rep. S.A.,
May 7th, 1902.
READERS OF THE [Claremore] PROGRESS:—
Hello, comrades!

We have at last landed in South America after an exceedingly hard struggle. There may be places farther away than this, but it is a "pipe" they are no harder to get to.

On arriving in New Orleans we found that there were no boats to Buenos Ayres, but that from New York we could go direct. So we went forth on our first voyage on anything bigger than the Verdigris. Well old hands, it is not what its cracked up to be. Five days to New York and then we happened to another spasm of hard luck. No boat for B.A. for three weeks, but found we could go by way of England for the same price and quicker as they were faster boats. We stayed in New York for three days, and then were off for South Hampton, England, on the steamer Philadelphia. I only lasted on deck to see the big guns at Sandy Hook and it was "up" with me. I went to my bunk and didn't get out until we were tied to the dock at South Hampton. I thought die I would. Any time an old nestor tells you sea sickness is not bad, he hasn't been on anything larger than Dog Creek. I couldn't eat a thing for six days with any success, (you know friends that Willie is sick when he can't eat). We were eight days and had very rough weather.

We were in England twelve days; up to London, which is a great place, but its not got a "look in" with New York for speed. No electric cars and no street cars at all in the main squeeze of town. Hitch a thrasher engine to a string of covered wagons and you have an English train, as fast, as comfortable, and as handsome. If you call that prosperity, excuse me.

We saw the Houses of Parliment, London Tower and all the places of interest, the chair where his royal highness will be crowned in. All the crowns of his "decestors," and all the royal jewelry and finery. It looked pretty good.

We saw his big Nibs at a distance. Don't think he recognized us though.

We sailed on the eleventh of April on the royal mail steamer Danube, which called in at several different ports for cargo and passengers. We would get to go to ashore for several hours. First in Rupert, France; then Vigo, Spain. Saw what was left of the Spanish navy. Lisbon, Portugal, which is a beautiful place; by the Canary Islands, to the Cape Verde at St. Vincent, crossed the equator the twenty-second of April, and it was good and hot, but got cooler soon. Then to Penambuco, on the northeast coast of Brazil; Bahia, and then Rio De Janerio, where we stopped for thirty-six hours. It is a city of 800,000 inhabitants and has the finest harbor in the world. It is a great fruit growing country. We next stopped at Montivideo, which is the cleanest and healthiest city in South America; then to Sanata, thirty-five miles from Buenos Ayres. Large boats cannot go clear up the river. We were quarantined for two days before we could land. Republics are quarantined against each other all the time.

We then went by rail to Buenos Ayres. We landed the fifth day of May after a twenty-five days trip from England, seven thousand miles. I never got so I would not get sick when it got rough. It would be "up" to the ocean with me. Those boats do everything but rare up and fall back.

Buenos Ayres is the prettiest place I ever saw. Houses are all built on the Spanish plan, with an open court clear to the roof. The street cars, trains and almost everything is on the United States plan. Much more like it than England. It has one million population and is the largest city in South America.

As I want to tell the cow men of the country, I went to see Mr. Newbrey, the United States Consul, who has been here for twenty-five years, and is a land and cattle owner. He has made a great deal of money here, and says there are fortunes

"WE WERE
QUARANTINED
FOR TWO DAYS
BEFORE WE
COULD LAND."

to be made by persons who have capital to buy land which is actually advancing one hundred per cent a year, and will continue to do so for a time. It is practically a new country and lots of foreign capital is coming in. The export of cattle almost doubles each year, the surplus being shipped to the various foreign countries on foot and frozen. The seasons are exactly the reverse of yours, for it is now fall here. July and August are the coldest months, but not so cold as home, only in the south and the mountains.

They are breeding up the herds here now and are getting more good cattle.

They figure on a fifty per cent increase when they do not feed at all. Only the very best cattle are fed. There are no diseases in the south or west. Taxes are very low. In parts they raise lots of Alfalfa and it is a great wheat country.

There are lands here they will give to a person if he will live on them and become an Argentine citizen. It is also a great sheep country.

They are expecting a war with Chili any day, but the consul says that will not have any effect on conditions. You can't buy land from the government, but have to deal with some individual. There is certainly money in it for the man able to buy it. We start for the interior to-morrow to try and strike a lay on some of the big ranches. We go about five hundred miles by rail and then overland to our destination. Wages are very low. We are trying to learn Spanish, as that is the only language.

I will be able perhaps to tell you of the ranches and cattle and how they handle them, in another letter.

We have not heard a word from home since we left. They are very few Americans in this country, but quite number of Englishmen.

Hoping you are all having a tim [time] I am as ever yours.

Will Rogers.

Buenos Aires, A.R.S.A.
May 23. 1902.
My Dear Folks

As Dick is going to go back to America I have some things to send to you [Maud] and Sallie.

I went up into the Interior about 800 miles and looked around for a few days but was not able to strike anything   but am not in the least discouraged for I am going out west from here in a few days. Dick has decided to go to Texas so he leaves in the morning for N.Y. has to go back the same way we came I am liable to show up at any minute so look out   I send you these pieces of lace   they are considered very rare   are made by the Native Indians of the Republic of Paraguay. are very expensive even here   and a large duty on them   but Dick will see that they are not found   there is one for you, [and] Sallie. and May   send hers to her please.

That fierce looking corn knife in there is for Papa   I did not know what would interest him so I will send the most common thing here   for everybody carries the biggest knives you ever saw   but are not so <u>bad</u>. tell him to put that with his Curios.

The story that's been told about Dad being scared of guns because of the accident with his rifle from Kemper—when he demonstrated it for a friend back home and it went off, creasing his head—is just not true. He was not a person who ran from danger. I've seen him get thrown off a horse and have it roll over on him, and damn near kill him. He'd get up and keep going. He was really a very tough man. He had to be for the steer roping and other things that he did. And he did keep a set of pistols at home. I now have them at my house.
~James Blake Rogers

The goards and silver Bombillars things are for you and Sallie   they put the Tea in them and then suck it up with the other   they are used by the Natives of this country.

I have a little collection of coins of each country I have been in and got each one in their respectave countrys   I will put in for one of you   their are ten with the old penny I have carried the rounds. You see I am making so much money I have to send it home on the installment plan.

Tell the children that I will try and bring them something   it will not be much unless business picks up   but it may be something.

You see this is no place to make money unless you have at least $10,000 or more and then you may do some good   but still if it had a lot of Americans here it would be good   but Lord there is none at all. Lots of all kinds of people but Americans   the biggest part of the capital is English but I do hate them   and you dont have any Idea how jealous they are of Americans   they wont hire an American.

I have seen them on the Ranches   I was out at the biggest one in S.A. when I was up North they work all Natives   only the head men are English. I have not seen an American Cattle Man and as for American Cow Boys I guess I am the only one here   they all go back   These Natives are bad looking but are not so bad I dont think if you treat them good   and they are very cowardly   I will send you some views of the camp pictures so you can see how they dress and what kind of Saddles they ride. All wear those big pants and carry corn knives   I carry a pistol they are afraid of a pistol.

This is a beautiful place and has a lovely level country all around it. it is winter here but it is like Spring at home

Please write to May and Papa when you get this and tell them I am allright and will write to them at once but wont have time just now

Did you get the address Dick sent to papa hope you did and have written   I will perhaps hear from you by the Middle of July   hope you are all well.

I am trying to learn Spanish   I think I can say 6 words   did know 7 and forgot one   there is very little English spoken down here.

Well you must write all the news you ever did know   for remember I havent heard a word since I left   Address the same place as before

With lots of love to all   I am as ever your loving

Brother

Willie

Will gave nearly all his remaining money to Dick for a return ticket, evidently confident he could make out somehow on his own. But he must have been homesick when he saw Dick leave.

The lace collars he sent his sisters were treasured for years. One collar (probably Maud's) still exists in an old scrapbook which now belongs to the Will Rogers Memorial.

Buenos Ayres, Argentenia, S.A.
June 9, 1902.
My Dear Sisters:

I expected to write to you sooner, but did not so will write now. Did you receive the package I sent by Dick? He left here for home on the 24th of May. I have been in B.A. most of the time, except what time I was in the country. I was on one of the biggest ranches in South America; but find ranch life here different from what it is at home.

Our cowboys cant stand to work with the Peons or natives, for you have no place to sleep and only get beef, bread and a native kind of tea as diet. So many Americans come here with a small capital, but they can do no good, for the government has no land for sale and it takes a huge piece of land to keep a bunch of cattle or sheep on. Oh it is nothing like North America. I tell you, you don't know what a good country you have till you see others. After seeing this country all of our people who have money enough go home and those who do not, work till they have saved up money enough for their home passage. Winter is coming on and it is getting quite cold here now. We find the language a great drawback.

It is almost absolutely necessary that you speak Spanish if you are to go into business or to work for wages. Then the manners and customs of the people are so very different from ours. Here you are shoulder to shoulder with every nation on the globe, for every ship brings in four or five hundred passengers that are to live by labor alone. A few with capital. It is almost impossible to get a paying position for there are hundreds waiting even with a pull, to take every vacancy. As for working with cattle, we cant begin to compete with the natives here for we can't speak Spanish, we don't know the country, we can't live on their diet, we can't endure the hardships nor work for from $5 to $8 per month in our American money. In hiring you, you are expected to work the first year for nothing. The only work that we understand how to do is done by the head men who are all or nearly all English.

As I now see things I don't expect to make any money here, but I would not take a fortune for my trip. Here is a bit of advice for my old comrades. "Just stay where you are boys, that is the best country on the globe for a person who was raised there. There you are among people while here you are with every kind of old "Nestor" in the world.

Marry and stay at home boys, for this country is overrated.

My health is good and I feel fine but I do wish I could hear from you all, but I guess it will be the middle of July before I can get your letters. I may stay here some time yet and I may turn up at home at any time. But don't be alarmed about me. Write me long letters and give all the boys and my friends my love. Write at once.

Lovingly Yr. bro.
Willie.

"JUST STAY WHERE YOU ARE BOYS, THAT IS THE BEST COUNTRY ON THE GLOBE. . ."

Claremore, I.T., June 17th, 1902.

Dear Willie.

Buenos Aires S.A.

We have got all the card & letters you have sent back home to me & the Girls, including the letter on May the 1st & May 7th

My Health have been good every since you left. The Girls & their children all are well. Clem [McSpadden] came out at Boonville all OK. Tom, Sallie, Cap, Bessie Schrimsher & me all went up to see him finish. He is now at home. Claremore have now 2 good Brick Hotels. I still keep my same rooms. your 2 poneys are fat & nice up at Home. No one have ever rode them   Them & old Minnie run in the North Pasture.

Good crops on my old Home place   Wheat, Corn, & Oats. Wheat is all cut. They are cutting oats now. Corn is sure fine up here. Hay crop will be good. Cap & Maude are now in their new house. Tom & Sallie had their house fixed up Stine & May are still at the Ta.la.la. Hotel yet. Spi is still at Okmulgee. They like him fine. Bunt Schrimsher married a Kansas man by the name of Robinson. They live here in Claremore. Earnest S. [Schrimsher] & Willie Musgrove are still around Town here but the Girls dont seam to pay any attention to them. Crops are sure good in this country   wheat, corn, oats, cotton, & Hay.

Living at Hotel is sure fine   Frakes & wife run it. The Lindell Hotel here this old Bank building is pretty good. Gibbs & wife run it. I stop here with them. My stone stables is finished but I havent got it Rented yet. It is sure a nice building. Crutchfields stable is about finished. It is built out of Rock also. Dr. Bushyhead have been in St Louis going to school about one month. His wife & children & Aunt Eliza is going to California next week & spend the summer. I will go up Home tomorrow to look after my crops. Alf is still got his cattle in your pasture. He hasent paid the last $200.00 yet. but I will try & get it in time to pay your insurance policy which is due about the latter part of August. Mine comes due about that time also. To day Claremore had a good rain, which will very near make corn. I saw Sallie, Maude & Clem, at Pryor Creek yesterday   they will go back home tomorrow. Joe LeHay & me drove over there yesterday & come back the same day. My stone livery barn cost me about $4000.00. To day I wrote to Miss Miller at Vinita to send me your Ring that she has of yours. Kates got a letter from you & will publish it in his Paper this week & I will send you & Dick several copies. Write when you can is the wish of your Pa.

C.V. Rogers.

Clem Rogers lived alone in rooms over the bank in downtown Claremore after his wife died. He kept the old home ranch and continued to dream that his son would take it over one day.

Cap and Maud Lane built a fine new home in Chelsea, but right after the final coat of paint was put on, it burned. They rebuilt, however, and the beautiful white frame home is still standing.

May Rogers with each of her two husbands—Matt Yocum and later his cousin Frank Stine—tried various vocations. They lived for a time at the Rogers ranch, but failed to prosper. C.V. set them up in business managing the Divan hotel in Claremore, then a hotel in Talala, a little town on the Mo-Pac railroad six miles north of Oologah. No luck again. They had a butcher shop, then an ice cream store. Nothing seemed to work for long.

While Will's two older sisters lived full, productive lives, everyone said, "Poor May," including Will. She was not healthy, nor were some of her children. Her first husband had been killed by a shot in the dark through the window while he was in the bedroom and she sat rocking one of the children.

Later a man she dated was shot one night as he started home after bringing her back from an evening out. Even at that time—when men wore guns and violence was not rare—the murders created quite a stir because of the prominence of the Rogers family. One newspaperman got carried away and sent a story to the *Kansas City Star* indicating that C.V. was involved in some way and speculating that Will also might have been.

But no one who knew Clem Rogers could believe he shot an unarmed man in the dark, in the back, and from outside the house. And he certainly would not have sent his son or anyone else to do it for him, even if he had wanted to see the man dead.

If Clem had felt that his daughter was being mistreated, he would have faced Matt in broad daylight, roared out his rage, and might even have gunned him down. But nothing of the sort happened.

However, Clem Rogers' integrity was without question and he could not let the matter go unanswered. He sued for libel and won. Though the judge granted him only one dollar, he was vindicated.

Although popular opinion was that a jilted lover or a suitor of May was responsible for both killings, a black man named William Rogers was first suspected of killing Matt Yocum. The fact that his name was the same as Clem's son's caused confusion for the out-of-town newspapers but the black William Rogers had a valid alibi and was released. Neither murder was ever solved.

May was a beauty with many friends and the loyal support of her family. She nevertheless missed many of the fruits of prosperity. Poor May, indeed.

On the same day Clem wrote his letter, Will was writing to his father.

[As published in the *Progress* August 1, 1902]
Buenos Aires.
June 17. 1902.
My Dear Father.

I will write you again and tell you that I am getting along alright and well.

I have been out into the interior about 800 miles and seen the country which looks like a good cattle and farming country

The work and cattle business here is nothing like it is at home   they have big ranches but they do not use the judgement in handleing them that is used at home the head men are men that have had no experience at all and it is all left to the Peons or Natives who get about 5 dollars amonth in our money and have to live like dogs. There is hundreds of men to every job of work   there is no American Men much handleing cattle here   it is all English.

It is no place for a man that hasent got plenty of money to buy his land and his cattle also   for the cowman it is alright but for the cowboy it is no good unless he has the job with an American before he comes.

There is hundreds of people coming in on every boat from every country in the world   you hear hundreds of different languages spoken all the time.

I have been well paid for my trip for I have learned lots on the trip. You dont know how good your country is till you get away from it   just tell all of those boys that want to come here to stay right there   that is good enough.

Dick went back about a month ago   I think he was going to Texas to work   I dont think there is much use of me staying here and I may start home any time.

"If Comanche isn't there, I'm not ever coming home," Will wrote his family from South Africa. Everyone in Cooweescoowee District knew of his fondness for the dun-colored pony that had helped steer ropers set records in pasture contests even before the turn of the century. But he didn't want anyone to ride him till he got back.

They are trying to get a bill through the congress to have the Argentine Government lease or sell land to any one who wants it   that will probably pass in a month or so   then a man with money can make something if he knows where to buy.

But after all the Territory is the best I guess even to invest in land.

It is getting a little cold here as it is winter

There is lots of cattle horses and Sheep shipped from here every day on all the boats for South Africa as they dont let them ship live cattle to England now from this country.

I guess you got Dicks letter telling you where to write to me at. And that I should hear from you before long.

I guess you can probably collect enough that is owed me up there to pay my insurance which comes due the 10th of September.

Earnest Schrimpsher owes me $20 besides what the other boys do. Please see that they take good care of my ponies and dont let any one use them.

Well I will close   write all the news. I do hope you all are as well as when I left I may not be here to get the letter but then I might

I guess you are in the new hotel and have your fine barn done and all by now

Give all who might ask of me my best regards   I will write the paper a letter about the country in a few days and tell all the boys to stay at home for that is the best place in the land for them.

I do hope this will find you well and dont worry about me for I will be alright and I am in fine health and will write more often from now on. I may see you soon though

I will close with all my love to a Dear Father   I am your loving son   Willie

June 26 1902 [Oologah, I.T.]
Friend Willie

As uncle Jim is writeing I will tell you how my white face calf is getting a long she is just as fat as she can be and has got to be nearly a cow and I am so proud of her   old Comancha is just as fat as he can be   he comes up evry night and I think he is looking for you but dont see you   I go out to the fince and rub him and kill horse flies off of him and pet him a little   the colt is fine   has grode lots   Wee mis you verry much

Wee are caning Blackberies and when you come home I will make you a cobler Papa and mama send thair best wishes to you

I will close by asking you to answer soon

I remain as ever your little friend
Pearl Yocum

Chelsea, Ind. Ter
July 2, 1902
My Dear, Dear Willie:

Every single day we think of and talk about love you and want oh, so badly to see you.

Every one enjoys reading your letters very much. I have been having them

"I GO OUT TO THE FINCE AND RUB HIM AND KILL HORSE FLIES OFF OF HIM. . . "

printed in the Chelsea Reporter and that keeps all your friends posted. Maud is still in Texas. Expects to return Saturday. The children stay with me all day and go home at night. My children take it time about going home with them.

Papa was up Saturday and stayed till Monday. Herbie and Gunter [Herbie was Sallie's son, Gunter was Maud's son and Johnny was May's son] went back with him . Papa fitted them out with new clothes. He had Johnnie [Yocum] there also. Oh, papa has the loveliest Wilton velvet carpet you ever saw. It is an Indian design. He has had his room all renovated, papered and bought him a wardrobe. It looks so much better. Tom has gone out to see about the thresher. You know we always have to cook for them so, on the "glorious fourth" we will be threshing wheat.

We have a very good crop this year. Corn is fine. Lots of fruit, I mean strawberries, cherries, black and huckle berries and peaches, and not quite so many apples, still a great abundance for our family use. I am putting up some kind of fruit every day for we expect you home for Christmas, sure. We raised so many chickens and turkeys and I have been trying to fill Gunter up on fried chicken before his mama comes home, for she has to buy all her chickens. We had such a very nice trip to Boonville. Cap enjoyed meeting the Cols. [Colonel's] family, and we all took dinner at Kemper. We were treated royally, sure.

With lots of love from every one and the sincere hope of seeing you soon   I am
Your affectionate
Sister Sallie

BROWN DRUG CO.
PRESCRIPTION DRUGGISTS
TAHLEQUAH, IND. TER.

July 4, 1902
My Dear Old Pard

Well here I am at last back home after a hell of a Voyage   say kid you must sure come back cause there aint no place like home.

I arrived on the 3rd of July and they were going to have a dance that night Well

Everybody is well up at your place. and everything is allright. the people all want to see you very bad   there is no news hardly at all   nothing you would care to hear none of them old girls married yet but some of them has got to tell Parris no or he is going to tie up with some of them and that very quick

Well I dont want to ever see that country again and hope you will be back all right in a few months

Well Ill ring off for this time so Write soon and tell me all the news
Your Pard
Dick Parris

Bill
Opened this by mistake, also to put in smaller envelope. Say that damed old kid put on a two cent stamp   durned if these dagas here didn't tax me for 40¢ on account of it, double postage.   Myer

Buenos Ayres, S.A.
July 7, 1902.

I have been here over two months and have made two trips into the country of about eight hundred miles each, and been on some of the big ranches and seen considerable country, but a very small part of what is here, as Argentine alone is half as large as the United States.

I don't think from what I have seen and heard that the unsatisfactory conditions of the country are in the land, climate or natural resources, as the land is generally good and they raise most every thing, but the fault is in the people especially the governing class.

It is supposed to be the same kind of government as the United States, but the men who are in control are always the worst in the country, and it is said to be the most corrupt and unstable of any government in the world.

There is no get-up or energy in the natives, and they of course, are the ones in power. They only think of dressing and showing off to the extent of their means. The country is very deep in debt, and a dollar of their money is worth only forty-three cents and they vary all the time. The laws in regard to law breakers and criminals are never enforced.

All the trading enterprises are owned and managed by foreigners but they risk their money where a war or revolution will take it all for they have no protection whatever. There has been a big war scare on with Chilli, but that has quieted down, but they do not know how long it will remain so. There are very few North Americans as it is said they get disgusted with the conditions and go back. There are a few in the town but none in the country. There are thousands of every other kind of people under the sun here. The most of the capital is English and there are lots of that nationality here, but an Englishman's and an American's ways are altogether different. There is more land to the amount of people than any country I ever struck. The government will not sell land, but they will give you about fifteen hundred acres if you will become a citizen of the country, but it will be away back where you can't get a way out with what you raise and they will tax you to death. You will have to serve in the army and fight in case of war. The American counsul is now trying to have a law passed to sell anyone land and let them pick it where they please and pay for it yearly. That would give a cow man a chance.

The most of immigrants that come can't make a living and starve out. They can't pay the exhorbitant taxes and they go back. There are a lot of Boers coming over here now to settle but it is said they will not stay.

As to the stock business it pays pretty well, but now that the English ports are closed against this cattle it is busting the trade. This country supplies south Africa Only enough are killed here to supply this country. There are no packing houses here.

This is a great sheep country, but I think the hog business would beat them all, for a hog is worth more here than a cow or horse and are very scarce. Cattle and horses are worth about what they are at home.

The wads on the ranches here are no more like America than anything. A man with a pot though he be English, city bred, will come here and go to managing a big ranch. Probably he will not know how to ride, but here they don't think it takes any experience to manage a ranch; and it does not the way they manage it. They don't know what it is to use any judgement or common sense in handling a bunch of cattle. The head men consider that the hands (that is the Peons or natives) know all about it and it is not necessary for them to know anything.

I was on one of the big ranches here for several days and here are a few of the things that I actually witnessed. They will give you an idea how far behind the times they are. It is disgusting for anyone from America, and that is why they will not stay. They drive the cattle in a run and I asked the boss if it did not run too much of the fat off, and he gave me the horse laugh and said: "Why, they fill right up again." In cutting out there are from three to five men to each animal and no one to hold the herd until they get out two or three, then they all go. They would not begin to believe that a horse knew enough to cut out a cow without guiding and one man to the head.

They have good fat horses and plenty of them, but they are never learned anything. They are not very tall but are short and very very heavy made. They do not pitch near as bad as you see them there. They don't think of rounding up a herd of cattle with less than thirty men. There is no such thing as a "chuck wagon." Your grub is tied onto your saddle as it can be made into a regular "carry all." It is two pieces of wood the length of our saddle skirts and fastened together across the front and back and lays long ways on the back, then it is covered over with sheep skin, old sacks or any old thing that strikes their fancy, and it is just a big pack, right flat all over and about a foot and a half wide. The stirrups are little round things like our race stirrup, as they can only just get the tip of their toe in.

There is not a man who would think of putting his feet into a stirrup. The stirrups are fastened by a small piece of leather to an old frame and no fenders. Your whole leg dont hang down, only from the knee hangs over the edge of the pack. The rope is fastened into a ring that is put behind right where our back cinch is. My saddle and all have been a big show ever since they seen it. As for roping, riding or any old thing they cant teach the "punchers" in America. They all use a raw hide rope and are doing well to catch one out of three and always run him at the least one hundred yards, slowing him up. They are not at all reckless.

They are cowardly lot. They all carry knives in their belt from a foot and a half to two feet and very few have guns, if a man points a gun at a whole bunch he can put them all to flight.

They pay the men about eight and ten dollars per month in American money. A boss about twenty five dollars and managers on some of the ranches from forty to fifty dollars.

All the Americans I have met here are only living to get back to America. Any part of the states is better for a man without lots of money, than this place, and the beauty of it is you are among 'people,' and not a lot of 'dagoes' from all over the world and all having a different Lingo. It would be all right for a man with a lot of money to bring down an American outfit and run a ranch on the American plan, he can get rich for these dagoes would give his American cow punchers a wide berth, and they would have things all their own way. Here you are not allowed to put a brand on a brute any larger than your hand and it is almost impossible to read it, but they do not pay any attention to brands as each outfit is supposed to know their own animals by the flesh marks and the brands are only looked for in case of dispute.

It is the middle of winter here now. It is not very cold but always damp and rainy. The Fourth of July passed off quietly here. Once in a while you would see an American flag, but no "roping contests."

Well I must shove off, and my parting words are for all of your people to fight shy of this part of the globe. You never know a country until you leave it, and so stay where you are.

Adue and my best wishes to all.

Will Rogers.

Buenos Ayres, S.A., July 21, 02
Mrs. May Stine, Talala, I.T.
My Dear Sister:

I will write you again as I want to tell you where to write to me. I will shake this land between August 1 and 10 and sail for South Africa on a big cattle boat in care of cattle, and will not come back to this point. It is no good for an American.

There is an old Texas "punch" going with me. Tell all the boys there is nothing doing down here.

I have not heard a word from anyone and you must write me all the news.

I didn't get to rope any on the Fourth of July, as these dagoes don't know what a contest is. They are the greenest and hardest lot I have ever seen. I have been out on lots of the ranches and been with them but did not go to work for them. They only pay seven or eight dollars a month and nothing to eat.

It will take about 18 or 20 days to go to Cape Town from here. If I don't like it there I may come home.

Tell old Cain and Keys my address and tell any of those old boys to write.

There is nothing doing, so I will close with my best wishes.

Yours lovingly, Will Rogers.

Buenos Aires, S.A.
July 21, 1902
My Dear Father

I will write you again   I wrote to the paper a few days ago and that is why I did not write to you also as I knew you would know that I was alright.

Well I have been out in the country and am now back in Beunos Aires   there is no show for a person here unless he has a good big capital but still I have got a lot of learning and experience out of this trip.

I am going from here over to South Africa between the first and 10 of August and you can address my letters to me in care of the American Consul. at Capetown.

I am going with a ship load of stock   horses mules and cattle.

There is lots of stock goes from here   it is about 4500 miles and it takes about 18 to 20 days on a cattle boat   they send from 500 to 1000 head on one boat and about 20 to 30 men to care for them.

You have to have a lot of money before they will let you land but the man that

owns this lot of stock promised me to land me and I will work for him.

It is lots better place than this for they all speak English and there is lots more Americans there.

I may come back to the U.S. from there   I think I will go to work for Halsell and stay there when I get back

I am feeling fine and in the best of health

It is tolerably cold here now and lots of rain

I have not heard a line from any one yet   guess I havent had time quite

I dont hear any news only from New York as they are the only papers we get after they are 5 weeks old. but no news about our country in them.

Well there is nothing of interest to tell you so I will close. have Uncle Jim take good care of my ponies. write me soon and a long letter and tell any one that might feel an interest in me to write me at

       Capetown
         South Africa

Care of the "American Consul."

  Lots of love to all from your loving son
         Willie.

W.E. Halsell was a wealthy Texas and Oklahoma rancher and businessman as well as a long-time friend of Clem Rogers. "Our country" refers to the Cherokee Nation.

Buenos Aires

July 21. 1902.

My Dear Folks at Home

Well I will pen you a small document to keep you posted on my where are you. I am now back from a second "cruise" into the plains of the Goucho. havent been able to do any one out of any considerable sum of colateral but am living in perfect ease. picking up a few unthought of facts but no loose change.

I never felt better or lighter hearted in all the days of my Persimonhood   a dollar dont look any bigger to me than it ever did

Well I put from this land sometime between the 1st and the 10th of August for Capetown South Africa with a ship load of stock   I dont know just when we will start   the boat will be here tomorrow and it takes some time to clean up and load her full cargo   I dont know what the biggest part of the cargo is   I guess all kinds of live stock.

It takes about 18 to 20 days to the cape. ships generally carry from 500 to 1000 head of stock and about 20 to 30 Peons or men to feed and care for them. I am a full fledged Peon.

You see a man cannot land in South Africa according to the law unless he has 100 Pounds or $500 in our coin   but this man wants some men to work for him and he will land me and I will Probaly work for him   you get 2 pounds or $10.00 for going over and 4 pounds if you come back   you see they use them cleaning out the ship   I will stay for they say it is a pretty good place. you see they speak English and there is lots of Americans there

This is a bum land for any one that hasent got the coin but there is lots to be made if a man had the <u>mon</u>.

I just begin to see what a little I did know about this world   I know 10 times more about my own country than I did before I left   I will get all the information I can for that is all I will have when I again approach the B.I.T.

I wish you people had a little of this cold weather up there   it gets pretty chilly here   of course no snow but it is damp and rains lots.

Not much doing here on the 4th of July   a few lonesome but good looking "old glorys" waving over this <u>dago</u> land.

I have been having a great time   one of the "U.S. battleships." the "Atlanta" was here for a couple of weeks and I almost lived on board   learning them all the latest coon songs I knew   for it had been 2 years since they left   they had a minstrel troup among themselves and seemed to have a good time   wanted me to enlist and join them   they told me when I got "on the rocks" and wanted to go to Gods country that they would make up enough to send me back

two of the boys deserted them here   both officers   one of them a fullblood "Oneida" Indian from New York state   the only Full blood in the navy   he is here   just ate supper with me. he is going back home

There is a Texas Cow boy here that I think will go with me to South Africa

You ought to hear me singing in an English Speaking Concert hall where all the Sailors and men off of all the the boats go at night

I havent heard a line from home and I want you all to write me . . . .

Tell any of my friends that would like to hear from me that I would be pleased to hear from them and will reply personally (not through my secretary) at once on receipt of said Epistle.

If things are not exactly satisfactory to your "Royal Nibs" in those parts I may return to the U.S. Shores by a chartered "<u>shift</u>" thence overland on foot (as I can see the landscape better) <u>via</u> Catale and Whiteoak

What I think of the people of this portion of the globe wouldent look good in print and I can leave it without doing serious injury to my palpitator.

Well I must shove off. hope to hear from you soon and my parting sylables are "dont worry bout me   get along yourself"

Lots of love to all and I do hope you are all well.

from your loving Uncle E.

Care of   Capetown.
American Consul   South Africa.

"Coon songs" and ragtime evolved from Negro tunes and spirituals such as *Swanee River* and *Old Black Joe*. Will Rogers sang in blackface a few times in show business, but it was not his style. Amazingly free from prejudice for his time, he no doubt still suffered somewhat from discrimination toward Indians. He knew how it felt and he tried never to hurt anyone. His statement "I never met a man I dident like" was an honest expression of his feelings.

"Dont worry about me/get along yourself" is from a popular song.

Catale and Whiteoak were communities near Oologah.

"I JUST BEGIN TO SEE WHAT A LITTLE I DID KNOW. . . . "

"DONT WORRY BOUT ME GET ALONG YOURSELF"

1 Sep 1902

My Darling Brother:

. . . Oh! how beautiful those collars were   I never saw any thing half so lovely. Every one envies us such a liberal brother, but don't spend your money on us so freely   I am afraid it might give out over there in that "dago land" and then you might have to sing for a living. I think we must have received every single letter and postal that you have written. And as every body is always asking about you we have every one published   How they are enjoyed Not only by us but by all the host of friends you have all over the country. We are so glad you are well and to know that you are in splendid spirits is a source of great consolation to us all.

We are all very well and are preparing for the great Chelsea Fair . . . . Beside our little local attractions of needle work, fruit etc. races roping contests etc. We are to have an automobile race and a Mexican bull fight, which two things are very [good] drawing cards. . .

Really the "bull fight" is more to show how it is done, for they do not intend to kill the man or bull either.

The automobiles are hired from Joplin, I believe.

My! but I wish I could go some where   I am living on the hope of going to New Orleans next Spring. Papa has promised to take Maud and I and pay all our expenses.

Tom is bulding two more little three room houses to rent. . . . I got four new songs. they are

"I've grown so used to you"

"You're only a Volunteer"

"Down Where the Cotton Blossoms grow"

"Any old place I hang my hat is home sweet home to me"

The last one is an especially popular song and I am sure you would like it. The sentiment would suit you exactly but I hope and trust you may decide to soon and forever more hang your hat in the Beautiful Indian Territory. But I'd a thousand times rather have you traveling all over the world than married to some of these "rattie" old girls. We will anxiously await your next letter. With lots and lots of love and the prayer that the best of every thing may attend you and bring you safely home.

I am

　　　　　　Lovingly
　　　　　　　　Your Sister
　　　　　　　　　　Sallie, Chelsea, I.T.

Talala, I.T., USA

9-2-02

Mr. W. P. Rogers.

c/o American Consul

Cape Town South Africa

My Dear old Pal:

I didnt ever dream of lining one out to you away off down in South Africa   You will have to excuse me Will for not answering your letter. As I kept waiting to hear from you after you got there. I would give most any thing to see you. I am at Vinita now and have been here for three weeks. We had a roping here the 24th and 25th of last month. Sam Cobb got first in 35. George Franklin second in 45. The second day Jim Harmon 1st Booth Mc Second and Ott Cork and George Franklin tied on third. They roped cows and yearlings. Cain's rope bounced off both days just a little hard luck was all but I am getting used to little things like that.

They had a contest at Talala the 4th of July. John Cochran got first in 37 1/2 and Booth got second in 40 and the next morning we all went to that hell of a place you call Collinsville. We roped mules there and the rules was that you either had to get the neck or neck and one front foot. Clint Cochran caught his steer between the front legs and away deep back of his withers and they gave him first. Brit Don scratched us on the right front foot and got second

Fred Baker the crack from San Angelo was there and Lew Hooks wanted to bet $10.00 he hung beef the first throw and he went out and they only allowed us two throws   Baker scrached in on the right front foot the third throw and they gave him 3rd money   I think his time was about 3 minutes   I missed my steer the first throw and up set my loop around his big piss quasa neck the second throw and went all the way and never looked back   I was mounted on Robbin and we parted that little lean grass just like it was a twine string. I went back and picked up my rope and went on and tied him. I think it was the best work I ever done considering every thing and I was the only man out of about 18 that caught around the neck without any feet in my loop. I have quit kicking about missing and having hard luck but I would like to have what I win fair and square.

They are going to have a roping at Chelsea the 4 and 5th next Thursday and Friday. I would give any thing if you was here to take it in with us. It dont seem like there is any thing doing if you aint along. these boys get to bragging on some button prick being an awful fast tie   I tell all of them there aint no body can catch any quicker, quit his horse or tie half as quick as Rogers   They bellyache a little while and then own up to it. They cant do any thing else.

Tram is with Pawnee Bills Show   Hop is with Buck Skin Bod's Mid West and Tom Isibell is with Buffalo Bill's.

I sold my steers   got 25 and $30.—   I havent got a thing left but Montie and Bomp a little bay bronc I got from Jeff Tyner. I guess I will turn them over to Aud J O sold all of his cattle but about 400 head of 2's and they are for sale   he aint going to put any more in this country. I am thinking of going down where Ollie is in South Western Texas.

I dont know just where I will winde up at but it is a cinch I wont stop until I strike a place near suits me and where they get up and work them cow boy style   I want to go where they go up and line them every day   I dont care if I dont see a man but once a year. May and Frank [Stine]were well and in good spirits when I left over there. I saw C V as I came through Claremore   he was showing me that large knife you sent him. Every one that ever saw it says it is the finest thing they ever saw of the kind. That loud blanket you gave Jo is right by me where I am writing   I quit writing every now and then and look at it and think how it would look on that Montie Dun   he is sure a peacock   Aud offered me old Dick and a black LK horse that he sold for $50.00 for him I says you aint said nothing to me. he is a bitch on a rope.

There is lots of pretty gals over here at Vinita. they gave a swimming and lawn party here at J O's the other night and they had a big time Miss Ray is pretty as ever. they bought the Carter place on Caney just above Tyners where we had hell with that yearling of Auds that time. I guess they will move out there about the first of the year. Miss Ray can hang her clothes on my line just any time. Sog-gone-it was up here the other day and we fixed it with a couple of girls at the Cobb house and went & paid for a bed just after dinner. We layed up there for two hours with a big hard on & Cousin's train come & he had to tear out and the girls never did come. I went down & taken a bed the other night and had one to come to my room.

Aud is trying to get up a crowd of boys to take to San Antonio next month. he got a letter from the association and they wrote him that it would take $25.00 to enter. Send money in when names were sent in 60 ropers were the limit and 40 had already entered. They had a roping at Tahlequah the 4 of August Parris got first in 46 Cocuran second and Mc Ginty third. And went down but I couldnt go. Aud & Clint Cocuran were the only boys missed from Cooweescoowee. I think Baker and Clint Cocuran have got one matched for $75.00 tie three steers a piece They are going to try and get in to come off at Chelsea They are going to have an automobile race and Mexican bull fight and all sorts of things. Aud wants me to go to San Antonio but I dont think I will go

Well old boy as this is the last sheet of paper I will have to quit unless I go down in town and get more it dont seem like I have written any thing that you would like to hear. I saw Comanche and your bay colt along early in the summer And they were looking fine. Well, old pal I will have to quit but I sure hate to. hoping this will get to you and find you well and having a good time I will close.

Always remember me as your best friend.

Jas H Rider

Mooi River Station
Natal. South Africa
Sept 11. 1902
My Dear Father

I have not had any time to write, as I have been as busy as I could since I came we made it over alright and I am out in the country 150 miles from where we landed I am with the man that owned the stock on the boat working for him it is cold here we are up in the mountains so far I am working with all kinds of stock I will write you a long letter soon tell Kates I will write him a letter from here about this country soon.

I have only got a minute so I will close

love to all write to the Girls and tell them I am here and doing fine. Write to me in care of the American Consul at Capetown.

Lots of Love to all.

from your loving son
Willie

He really did have a keen sense of observation, didn't he?
~James Blake Rogers

Mooi River Station
Oct 5, 1902.
My Dear Folks.

Well after so long a time I have at last a few spare moments so I will detain you with a few scattering facts gathered from the various places it has been my misfortune to see.

Fact No. one I am feeling as fine as a racer   working pretty hard but sorry to say a little shy on food. for there is no place I have been that you get the good old Grub that you will get even in the poorest parts of America

I have been at this place about 5 weeks working for the Man [Piccione]that owned all the stock on the boat   he is about the richest old <u>bloak</u> there is in this country   he would be worth $35 million in America   he lives right here at the farm

In the time that I have been here I have done more different kinds of odd jobs than I thought there were on a big farm and racing stable   I will try and give you a few of the things that I have already done   the principal thing of course is to help feed and care for some of the Thoroughbreds and then to take a lot of them out for an exercise gallop every day which is a <u>cinch</u> for there horses are supposed to be the best in this country   not a one of them under $3 thousand dollars in our money Oh you should view me up on one of those little saddles for they wont let my saddle get in the same lot with them for all the riding Saddles are little padded English style.

Then other time I am at work with the vetinary in the hospital as they have lots of crippled and sick horses and mules dying and we have to throw down all the wild ones to preform on them. I get to use my saddle on a big old horse and I drag off all the dead ones which is about one or two a day. then I have been helping the blacksmith shoeing horses this week at my odd times. Then I have helped dock a lot of horses that is cut their tail off up short for driving in traps and carriages and then to roaching mules. Then helping seperate horses and mules. but here is where I get put through in the center of one of the big rock barns there is a big place like a show ring for horses. Well when any buyers come here comes his Nibs and sings out "Yank" (as that is all I am known by) bring out such a horse   Well I walk him out there   he will start me in a run with the scoundrel around and around   him a hollering at you all the time for he is the only man that I ever saw that could holler louder and more at a person than Papa. Then he will pump that man with more lies in a minute than you could think of in a year   then out with another and so on till I faged [fagged] out

I have only rode one wild horse Another boy here that worked in South America was going to ride one here one day and he threw him and I by some miracle or other rode him and whipped him and I think I ruined my future chances for they said that was too rough fashion for them   so I guess I will not get to ride any more soon on those kinds of ponies   for the way that they do things is altogeather different from our way.

Well today has been an unusually busy day   it is Sunday and there was a couple of big buyers come to see the thoroughbreds

Well we worked like a fool getting all cleaned up and horses rubbed down then

". . . OH YOU SHOULD VIEW ME UP ON ONE OF THOSE LITTLE SADDLES. . ."

I always thought my Dad hollered louder than anyone when we were out with the horses, and it looks as if he felt the same about his father.
~Will Rogers, Jr.

out they come   well there is only two of us that ever take the horses out to show well we had to present every one on the farm and a lot of them are not brought out often and you are only allowed to have a halter on them   well they will jerk and pull you from one end of the ring to the other

Well this eve after that you finished what did the Rube do to show them some excitement   He has what is called a Riding School

It is only a building about 100 feet long and 20 wide with a solid board jump in the middle about 4 ft   there is not another thing in it   ground as hard as rock

Well he puts a mare in there loose that had only been ridden a time or so   he turned her loose and all the visitors and Ladies and all were in there to see them make her jump the hurdles as this was the first one that he has had in it since we came

Well they get a lot at each end with long whips and get after her and make her jump this high thing which is as solid as rock   well they were having great sport when I hearing the Melee rushed in to see and no sooner had I turned up till he bawled out at me to jump up on her back and ride her over. We had all seen the jump there and had said we would not jump a horse over it but he took me by surprise and before all hands on this farm I got up   I told him I had never ridden over hurdles, but guess I could try   Now fancy being on a horse with not a thing on it   bridle or nothing   and a lot of <u>Dagoes</u> after it with whips and a solid 4 ft wall in front of you for the 1st time.

Well I had no more than got up and planted my Lunch Hooks with a death grip into the mane and they took after her. well she cleared it alright and they kept us at it till she give out and I got so I could do it pretty good   But what was the worst of it   he had a long Ox whip about 30 ft long and sometimes he hit me and sometimes the mare   Well I think now he is going to School several at it and I am to be the Steeplechase jockey.

He took about 12 of us of [off] the boat and said he would give us work for you cannot land in this country unless you have $500 or a job. We do not know what wages we are getting   no one has asked him   but I dont think he will have work for all of us as he is selling out pretty fast. he has about 20 Negroes work here too and about 30 Indians from India   they all sign to work for a man for 5 years   We are about 3 miles from this Station   it is only a small Station but there is lots of English Soldiers camped all around

Has there been a letter published in the progress that I wrote from here   I wrote it a couple of weeks ago. I have only got 2 letters since I left America   one from Papa and one from Uncle Jim and a batch of Chelsea and one of Claremore papers I have not got any mail since I arrived here   you see it gets so far behind and has so far to come and through so many different people that it is a miracle if I ever get a letter at all

I seen in some of the Papers some Epistles from yours Truly   I had no Idea that they would come into print   Now dont dab this thing or any of the rest of them for I cant say that I am proud of them and I am obliged to pen them under very severe difficulties.

Well this is some three days later than I started this document and I am still prospering only I pulled up a bit lame after todays routine. owing to the other Show

"I TOLD HIM I HAD NEVER RIDDEN OVER HURDLES, BUT GUESS I COULD TRY"

Instead of moaning and groaning about his situation, Will finds the humor in it. And he knows how to entertain his readers. The talent he shows here belies later statements made by editors, and others who claimed they had to teach him to write!

~RC

Man being absent I had an unusually steady whirl.

By the Way I received some Mail last Night   A Letter from Sister Sallie Written about July 1st to B.A. and one from Maud written about Aug 27 to Capetown. I certainly was pleased to get them for I had not heard from you for over three months and more to hear that you were all well

But here is what would drive you to the Beach   Every Night the Music strikes up over in "his Largeness" quarters. his daughter a damsel of some twenty winters (Which by the way must of been a bit hard) and ably assisted by whomever has the nerve to chime in will break forth on that "Gizard breaking" ballad entitled "After the Ball."   The Fatal wedding is After the Ball "Sweet Rosie Ogrady" is a close third and gaining favor Nightly. "Sweet Marie" only comes on special occasions as it calls for special talent. Oh but one Maggie certainly does an injury to The Girl I loved in Sunny Tenessee."

They have heard of the Lady that was bred in Kentucky and have written for particulars.

But when his Nibs Seceretary (A bloak with a face like a pickle and a voice that well it dident need to be brought out   it was out to far already) piped "All Coons looked alike to him." I was so enfatuated I lost my balance on the pailin fence and went down and out. But never mind the tip is out that the first time there is no company we shall have access to the front yard and the Parlor Windows shall be cast ajar and we shall have a treat fit for the Gods.

All hands were chirping some kind of an Irish Pady Song (When I sniggered out in the Night Air) a Mick on the Pailin next to me was going to swat me   he said you yanks dont appreciate good songs when you hear them.

The Doxology is that loving little ditty christened "God save the King" when all uncover [take off their hats] even to the Irish if they should have had the good fortune to be in the loft asleep. Complete words and music to any of the above can be had by examining the Music racks of any of the young ladies in these parts who are considered to be "up to snuff" in the latest. above statement made under my hand and seal this the longest day I ever seen "Amen"

Well as the Tom Cat Quartett have hushed it must be late   All hands join me in wishing you all a speedy Christmas and a Sunshiny Fourth.

dont be surprised if I beat this thing there   you may still write to me at Capetown care of the American Consul as he is seeing after my Mail matter in my absence.

From what I can hear all of those females will be married pretty soon

Tell any of them that if they think they could subside as [survive on] information that not to forget to deal me a hand but that is all I can offer.

9 P.M. Some one day later than the above and I have had another fresh deal today as I have got to ride in the pastures all day up on a locoed horse and a gentlemens Saddle and I was glad to stop for it dident feel right in that garb

Tell Papa when he is in Oolagah to ask Lil Ellis to tell me where Jim Shepard is that is the boy that used to work for me. I think a lot of him and would write to him if I knew where he was   I last heard from him in California. By the way how is Kate   I hope she has not married too   When you go to Nowata give my very best to all I know especially Jim Keys and the Phillips Girls

"YOU YANKS DON'T APPRECIATE GOOD SONGS WHEN YOU HEAR THEM."

Tell Jim [Rider] he can rope old Comanche next Fourth   Tell Jim, Kell, Booth and Hamp and all the old boys that I have as yet failed to see a place that has got a show with the old U.S. and to find a place there and stay there . . . .

I had a great time coming over on that cattle boat but I will not try to detain you with any of the facts as I will tell you that when I see you for I certainly had some curious times   I was Night Watchman   I could sleep all day and had to stay up all night   I will mail you a special edition of my Drama "25 days on a floating dung hill or where did he kick you."

Oh them mules did play Ping Pong with them dagoes   they fed and worked all day and then mend up fresh kicks and bites and hooks at night.

Well I must stop   write me soon and a long letter   Give all my friends my best tell them I will be there soon

Lots of love to all you

Your loving brother
Willie.

One of the boys here cut my hair off right short with a pair of horse clippers and when I got up on one of them long thoroughbreds with a little saddle and my stirrups up short I look like a monkey up a stick.

C. V. ROGERS

BANK BUILDING

Claremore, Ind. Ter., Oct. 21st, 1902

Dear Son

Your letter come me the other day & found me in good Health & Sallie Maude & May & Children are all well. the Town is sorter quiet now. plenty of cars coming in. . . Your 2 Poneys are doing real well. Your Buggy Horse have grown quite a good deal.

No one have used either of them. . . Tahlequah have now got a Rail Road.

Big Show here at the Opra Hall here tonight   The Town site questions & the Grade of the land is now going on   We only get 65 acres to each of us at the old Home place. I will have to sell the balance to some one for we cant hold it. I will take the best of the field. . . .

I have all of my Houses Rented here in Town. Im going up Home in the morning. 60 acres of corn on the old Home place   I get one third. Wheat did not amount to but very little. I will have your Poney looked after this winter. There is not a cow, hog, chicken or turkey on the old Home place. One Peafowell.

I give several boys & Girls your address & they said they would write to you. I will write again soon. Do write when you can.

Your Father.
C.V. Rogers

C.V. was explaining some of the complicated rules involving division of the Cherokee land among tribal members. The better the "grade" the fewer acres of land. From the thousands of acres of Cherokee land on which Clem ran cattle and raised wheat, he was reduced to owning only a small farm, but he had wisely invested in town lots and businesses that secured his future.

"I WILL MAIL YOU A SPECIAL EDITION OF MY DRAMA '25 DAYS ON A FLOATING DUNG HILL OR WHERE DID HE KICK YOU.' "

I am sure Clem tried to talk him out of going [to the Argentine] in the first place. He didn't want to come home broke. . . . Like the insurance payments, it was pride. He made his choice and would live with it.

~James Blake Rogers

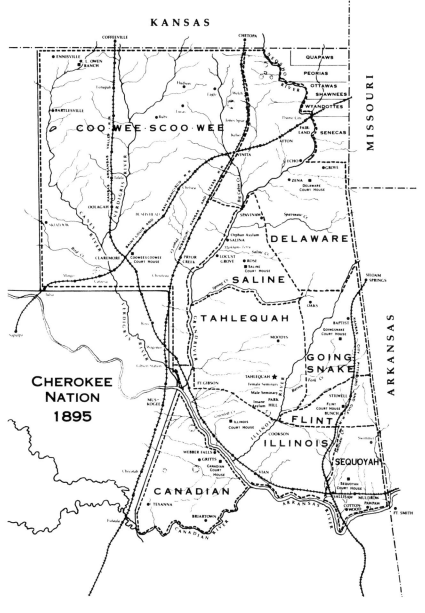

CHEROKEE
NATION
1895

The Cherokee Nation in 1895.
Courtesy of Nancy Hope Sober,
from THE INTRUDERS: THE ILLEGAL
RESIDENTS OF THE CHEROKEE
NATION 1866-1907. Map drawn
by Carl Brune.

*The days of open range were
coming to an end. Dad foresaw
what would happen when the
Cherokee land was divided into
small parcels. He had no inten-
tion of being a farmer, so he left
to look for bigger pastures.*
~James Blake Rogers

Chelsea, I.T.
Oct 30, 1902
My Dear Dear Brother

While every body is asleep I am going to write you a little letter. Do you have any idea how much we all want to see you? Jim and Vance were out here the other night and were asking all about you. They were on their way to their farm across the river to select allottments. Indeed that is the order of the day for every body now. Maud and Cap made a flying trip to Nowata yesterday returning today. . . .

Poor little Pauline . . . two weeks ago had a severe illness which Dr. Bagby called Infantile Paralysis and She can no more use her little feet than if she had none. We have great hopes of her getting over it, however. Dr. said it might be several months or a year, or two years, or she might never walk again, but I think she will recover after a while.

Tom [McSpadden] and Cap [Lane] you know never change. They are still the same henpecked husbands they have always been.

I realize I am not writing you a newsy letter, but since the baby first took sick I have been right with her and hardly know what is going on. I just felt as if I wanted to write and tell you how much we all love you, how badly we want you to come home and that we talk about you every day and wish we could see you.

May God bless and keep you, dear brother, and bring you safely home to us Is the prayer of

> Sister Sallie

Only a woman with Sallie's courage would think of the welfare of her brother at such a trying time in her own household. Pauline McSpadden, Sallie and Tom's baby, had the dreaded, often-fatal infantile paralysis now called polio. She survived the painful illness and the treatment which followed, including later operations paid for by her Uncle Will. As Mrs. Robert Love, she became the first curator of the Will Rogers Memorial when it opened in 1938 and remained in the position until her death in 1973.

November 17, 1902
Durban, Natal
My Dear Home Folks:

I will write you a short letter as you will get this about Christmas time and will know that I am "proceeding magnificently." I am back at the port where I landed. I shoved off from that big "stiff" I have been with. I have made a long trip up into the interior where the war was the hottest. I was in Ladysmith and passed several English grave yards that showed where there had been a battle and where probably one Boer horse was killed.

It is a very pathetic sight to see the Boer families returning to their former homes and finding some all torn down and others occupied by the English. The Boers are as fine lot of people as one would wish to see; peaceful, law abiding and friendly to all. They speak English as well as Dutch.

I am going up to Pretoria in the Transvaal with a lot of stock for a man here and when I return I'll be ready to go home, as I will have seen a large part of the country. You get good pay here but it costs more to live than at home, so you are none ahead. The weather is getting very hot here now and by Christmas will be at its hottest.

I am up against it good and hard now. Coming down the other day my "cargo of merchandise" was misplaced, consisting of clothes, saddle, and in fact my "whole works" except a small grip I had with me. They do not have a system of checking on the railways here; it is "catch as catch can" and I was caught for my roll. I have suspended operations till I hear from it but it has been ten days and no tidings so I began to prepare for the worst, which is to adopt the garb of my black neighbors.

I have just investigated the contents of the small bag and find that it contains thirteen collers, one shirt—all soiled—one unmarried sock and a clothes brush. The major part was occupied by a Spanish library of four volumes entitled, "How to learn Spanish in a Day," by Antonio Pedro Gonzalez; one little manual of 975 pages called, "Spanish Made Easy." By remembering these few hints and various others you will readily see I have not yet got next to their learning process. This grip also contained old letters and programs of every theatre from New York and London down to a magic lantern show in Zululand. I have gone to work brushing up the soiled linen, reading over the theatre bills and thinking what a discouraging scene I have just passed through.

Speaking of the song you wrote me about, here are some words I got up to the music of "Any Old Place I Can Hang My Hat is Home Sweet Home To Me":

I've traveled around this world a bit,
I've been from coast to coast,
Had every kind of food to eat
From beans to quail on toast.

There's not a land discovered yet
But's good enough for me;
So when I'm asked where I live
I answer on the QT—
CHORUS
I ain't got no regular place
That I can call my home;
I can't go back to America
She's far across the foam;
Walking, there's nothing doing
Passages ain't free
So any old place I can hang my panama
Is home, sweet home to me.

There's not a song I havent sung,
From the I.T. to the Zula
Twas one that left my happy home
For you-oo-oo-oo

But I ain't a going to weep no more
So good-bye Dolly Gray,
Just tell them that you saw me
And heard me sadly say—

I ain't got no regular place
that I can call my home
Etc., Etc.

Owing to the "inclemency of the weather and the failure of crops" it will be folly for me to send you even a part of the priceless presents that I should, but I am sure they would go down in mid-ocean. I will compromise, however by sending a "Good Morning Carrie," and wishing you a Happy Christmas and a cloudy Ground Hog Day.

As ever,
Will P. Rogers

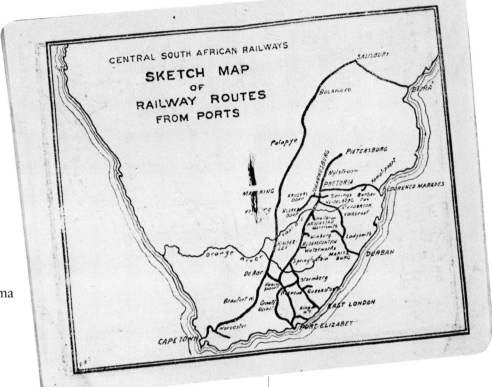

A shirt pocket-sized, stapled map book preserved at the Will Rogers Memorial was carried by Will Rogers on his trip through South Africa. He loved maps from the time he hid from his teachers behind a big geography book at school to the time he was an adult with a home office at the Santa Monica ranch where he kept a large globe and pull-down maps.

Letters tracked the fast-moving cowboy. This one went to the American Consul in Capetown, South Africa, then to Pietermaritzberg, O. R. C., thence to "Unknown" and the Dead Letter Office. But somehow, Will did get the letter from his friend Jim Rider, probably retrieving it from the "R" in the Dead Letter Office.

Durban. Natal.
South Africa.
Nov 26. 1902.
My Dear Father.

I will write you again and tell you how I am doing   I have only received one letter from you   that was when in Buenos Aires   but I know that they have gone astray for you are so prompt about writing all the time

I have been at work all the time but quit and come in here to get a pass to go another place (as you have to get a permit to go about in the country or on railway) and I lost all of my baggage   that is my saddle and outfit and in fact all but a little grip I had with me   it was lost or stolen off the train as they dont check things here and neither are they responsible for them   I have been hanging around here in hopes they would hear of them but I guess they were taken.

About the time you get this you should get a postal Money Order for 28 pounds in English Money   that is or should be in American $140.00 for my next insurance as I guess you had enough for the last out of what I was owed there   I only send this now because I have it and I dont need any money now for I go to work for a man in a day or so. I think I will be there before it is time to pay that again but by sending it now we know that it will be provided for.

I have the job taking a bunch of mules to Ladysmith   that is 250 miles from here   I will have some of the Native Nigger boys to help me. they drive a world of stock from here as this is where it is landed from other places as they are trying to restock the country after the war. it costs to much to ship them and they only have to hire one white man and a lot of Niggers so it is much cheaper   they often drive to Pretoria   that is close to 1000 miles   cattle and horses both   there little bit of South American Mules never sell under $125.00 to $200.00 apiece   Any kind of an old pony is worth that much too   A good young all around horse will bring three or four hundred dollars and so do the big fine mules from home

Oh cattle are up some there   little cattle with a big hump on ther shoulder that all come from an Island a few hundred miles off the coast   they sell never less than $75.00 apiece and good cows   as cows is what sells   will bring $150.00 and $200.00   I have seen common old milk cows sell at auction for $350.00 apiece everything is high. Wages are fairly good   you seldom do work for less than 2 dollars a day   that is for common   but for a man that has a trade bricklayers capenters and all them   get 6 and 7 and never less than 5 a day   but no one makes any money for you always board yourself out of that and they are falling for every ship brings from 5 hundred to a thousand [people] and it is the job that is hard to get not the pay   it is hard to get a job. oh it is a ruined country   you should know what it was before the war.

there is hundreds of men here without work.

Well I will close   hoping to hear from you soon

And if that [money] dont turn up pretty soon write and I will see about it as I have the receipt

from your loving son
             Willie

Address in care of Consul at Capetown

Dont look for me for a couple or three months as I could do nothing by getting there in the Winter but expect to turn up about <u>April.</u>

Lots of love to all

Write me all the news and send me some of the papers as I got those you sent to B.A.

Potchefstroon. Dec. 15.

[Posted December 31, 1902]

My Dear Father

I will write you and let you know how I am getting on and what I am doing.

Well since I last wrote you I left Durban with some horses that were shipped 6 hundred miles up this way and to the town where Texas Jacks Wild West Show was at and I went to him for work and as soon as I showed him what I could do with a rope he said he would take me so I am on the road with him now   he wants me to do roping in the ring but one of his riders that ride the pitching horses is laid off and I have rode a pitching horse every night since I have been with the show which is about 10 days   he also has a lot of Plays showing western life and I take the Indians part in some of them and some of them the Negro. I get $20 Twenty dollars a week and sleeping cars to sleep in but have to pay for my meals which are very dear at least 75 cents a meal   there is about 40 people with the show and about 30 horses.

We generally stay in a town two or three days and in the large ones longer   we have a crowded Tent every night.

I like it fine and Jack himself is the finest old boy I ever saw and he seems to think a great deal of me   he is a man about 40 years old and has traveled all over the world showing   he is a much finer shot than Buffalo Bill and a fine Rider and Roper   theres now about 7 or 8 Americans along

It isn't a wild mob like them at home for he dont drink a drop or smoke or gamble and likes for his men to be the same

I never did hear of all the things of mine   I lost my saddle and all and dont suppose I ever will   I use his saddles and things.

Did you ever get the Money I sent to you   if you did not write me and I will have it looked up for I have the receipt for it $140. in english Money for my next insurance

Send this to the girls as I havent time to write them now   I hope you all had a fine time Xmas   give my best to all the people and tell them I am doing fine   write as usual to American Consul at Capetown

Lots of love to all

    Your loving son

        Willie.

Will let himself be branded as a Texan in "Texas Jack's Wild West" show but he insisted on his own Indian tribe when he was dubbed "The Cherokee Kid, the Lasso King." He rode bucking horses (called "pitching" horses in South Africa), played himself in a drama, and did rope tricks the likes of which had never been seen by his audiences.

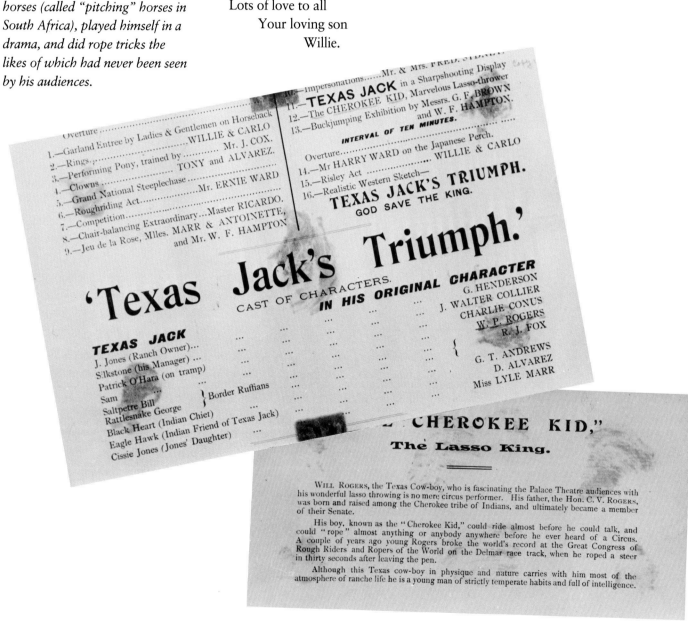

Standerton, Transvaal,
December 28th, 1902.
My dear sisters and home folks:

I will write and let you know how I am getting along. I am with the Texas Jack's Wild West Shows yet. I have been with him almost a month and like it fine. We just got in here today and as this is Sunday we won't open up until tomorrow night and will be here about two weeks, as there are about five thousand troops here. We have showed at seven different towns since I have been with them. We stay two and three nights in a place. We have the best show in South Africa; about 23 horses and 35 people and only eight Americans with it.

The play is partly a circus act and then they play blood curdling scenes of western life in America, showing encounters with Indians and robbers. I was an Indian but I screamed so loud that I like to scared all the people out of the tent. Then we have riders of bucking bronchos, roping and fancy shooting, and a little of every thing. I joined the show to do trick roping, but as our new tent without a center pole has not come yet, I have not commenced. I ride the bucking horses every night. I think I have a job as long as I want one. . . .

We had a real good time Christmas. They don't take on over Christmas and have trees and give presents here like they do at home. I went out to the Canadian soldiers camp and saw a base ball game. It is a sight out here, as America is the only country they play that game. I took supper and spent an enjoyable evening. I sung a lot of coon songs and they thought the kid (as that is what Jack and the show men call me) was allright. I know you all had a fine time Christmas. It is certain that I will be with you next year, for Jack said he may sail for America from here. We will finish up this country about the last of July. We are supposed to finish up in Capetown where he started from, but he don't know for sure as he has India and Australia in mind. I am going to learn things while I am with him that will enable me to make my living in the world without making it by day labor.

I have not got my mail from Capetown in three months. I will close with lots of love to all.

> Your loving brother,
> Will Rogers.

As the second year of the century drifted into the third Will was still with Texas Jack. Back in the Cherokee Nation that year, William Rogers (not related to Will) became the principal chief of the 40,000-member tribe. Maud and Cap Lane settled into their big new house in Chelsea, I.T., which had a place for roller skating on the third floor, a music room, a double parlor for dancing, a big dining room with sliding doors into the hall, a second floor office with a sleeping porch that could hold four beds for company, and four bedrooms, including "Will's room" which they kept ready for him all the time.

And the whole family hoped he wouldn't wait too long to fill it.

When he wrote home, he gave the family a geography lesson, and added some highlights especially for his nieces and nephews.

"I WAS AN INDIAN BUT I SCREAMED SO LOUD THAT I LIKE TO SCARED ALL THE PEOPLE OUT OF THE TENT."

Harrismith
Orange Free State
South Africa
January 28. 1903
My Dear Home Folks.

Well I will write you all again and let you know how I am getting on   I have not had any mail since the middle of October   dated from home in August   over three months ago but I guess I have a lot of mail at Capetown   I have written for it so hope to get it in the next town we stop in.

Well I am still with Texas Jacks Wild West and am getting on fine
I have been with them about two months now.

There is four of us that ride bucking horses and I do all the Roping now and it takes big   they all call me the <u>Kid</u> and that is what I am on the Programe   The first time I come on to do my Roping act I was called back twice and they made a big to do over me   you see they dont use Ropes here to catch things and it is all a mystery to them to see it   and I have learned to do quite a bit of fancy Roping that they think is wonderful

Then I play a nigger in a play that we put on some nights   do a cake walk and sing a coon song

I am going to Rope and tie down some steers in the next place in the ring.

Jack thinks I am all right   I dont have to do a thing all day only my work in the ring at night   I have had my wages raised to $25.00 a week   I can save a little but it takes a good deal to buy food and clothes in this country and you see I come to the show almost nacked [naked] after loosing all my things

I never did get a sign of a thing back   Saddle bridle clothes blankets boots hat and everything gone and after sending home that $140.00   When I went to the show I was broke to the world.

I will only stick to this till I get money to go home which wont be long for I want to get there in the Spring.

Still this is as easy a job as you ever seen   go to the stables and order out one of the ponies and ride around   only have to be there when it is your time to go in the ring   you horse is saddled and at the entrance ready to go in   When you have finished go sit in the audience and watch the rest.

We came here for two weeks and only have a couple of more nights then on to a big town where we will stop for probaly a month   you see we can put on so many different changes of programe that it makes a different show   but the Roping and Bucking horses are on every night.

I will tell you how I missed making $250.00   Jack [Texas Jack] does a trick with a rope (the big whirl where he lets out all his rope around him) and he has been offering 50 pounds that is $250.00 for any one that could do it and he has been offering it for 5 years outside of America   Well I went down to the show one morning on getting into the town where it was and I seen him in the tent and asked him for a job   he asked me what I could do and I told him I could rope a bit so he sent for his rope and I got into the ring and the first thing I done was this trick which is common at home now.

". . . THEY MADE A BIG TO DO OVER ME. . . . "

Well I dident know anything of this 50 pounds he was offering so he give me a job and now he wont offer that and as I belong to the show I cant get it so it was my misfortune that I did not hear of it and then go to the show some night when he offered it and step down and do it   then I would of got the $250.00   oh but I was mad

Well I started this letter just one month ago as this is the 1st day of march   I kept putting off writing thinking of hearing from home but I suppose the mail has been lost for I had it sent to me from Capetown to the last town and it never arrived   so I guess it is lost   the last letter I got from home was dated the latter part of August so you see that was about 7 months ago and I am getting in a hurry to hear   but no telling when I will.

When you dont hear from me dont worry for I am in good health and doing fine.

Jack is talking of sending some one home for some fullbloods and a few more cowboys and to get a lot of Saddles and costumes and things and if he does he will send me   I dont know just when it will be   if it is at all   but at any rate it wont be long till I will see you all

We are showing in Durban   now that is one of the biggest towns in South Africa   have been here one week and had packed houses every night   have just got a new and larger tent   we will be here two more weeks then we go to East London by boat   that is about 208 miles   then on down towards Capetown

which we will reach in about 4 months from now

Children I am sitting out under the shade of the tent writing and all of the Monkeys and baboons are playing around me so I dont know what I am doing   they are all bigger than you Kids   some of them are five feet high when they stand on their hind legs   I have seen lots of wild ones out here   they are very common   these here ride horses and have races and pull each other off when one is passing another   I wish all you kids were here this evening for Matinee   we have the whole tent full of Kids on Saturday at Matinee for the children. On next Saturday afternoon We give a Medal to the little boy who can throw a rope the best so I am the Kids Ideal for they see me rope in the show and they follow me around to get me to show them so they can get the medal   You should be here Herb to show them   but you see these little boys never seen a lasso before   neither did their fathers   I like to rope at Matinee for it takes big with the Kids   they applaud every throw till their hands are sore.

Oh I found my Saddle and bridle Leggins and spurs but could never hear of any of the other things   clothes and all that   it had been stolen and raffled off and I found it and have it now   oh but I was glad for it is so much better than any other one with the show

Well this is about a week later than the previous lines   it is now the 6th of March We are still in Durban   will be here till the 16th   We have Tremendous crowds every night   I will send you some of the Programes   the one is Where I am on to ride the Bucking horses or Buck-jumping as it is called in this country is our opening programme in a town then when they change I do the Roping instead of Jack as I do much more than him   you can see how I am billed up.

I havent time to write to all of you but send the letters and all to Papa and May for it is <u>to all</u> of you as I cant write to all as it would be the same   not a line of Mail and dont suppose I ever will get any

Well I will stop   lots of love to all   I know   tell them all I am flourishing   living the life of a millionare but will see you before the 4th of July.

Papa dont let old Comanche be touched till I come home but do as you think best with the bay colt   but dont let them take my buggy or harness   have him driven there in town but dont sell him

There isent much use to write for I will never get it

Yours lovingly   "The Kid"

Jack is crazy for Denny Lane and Booths brother [Forrest McSpadden] the one that rides and ropes.   I have told him so much of them these people would go crazy over them here   if I come home I will sho get them

C. V. ROGERS
BANK BUILDING

Claremore, Ind. Ter., Feb 9th 1903
Dear Willie
South Africa

Your letter of Dec 15th come to me a few days ago & found us all well   All of our people are well & have been since you left. Chelsea People are doing all right. Stine & May are now living at Oolagah. They quit the Hotel at Talala. Stine is runing Butcher Shop. John Lipe have got your Poneys at Talala . . . . He is sure taking care of them.

I have 2 Arkansaw Boys on my Home place. . . . I keep old Minie [a horse] here at Claremore. she dont look same. she is getting to old to eat corn. . . . Dick Parris is at Tahlequah & wrote to me to send him a Dimond stud pin that you had of his. I did not send it, but put his letter with your things & you & him settle it on your return. . . . Jim Rider have been sick & stayed a long time at Hot Springs

Little Charley McClellan died in Tennessee where he was going to school just before Christmas   They brought him home & buried him here at Claremore Cemetary.

People commence to take their allotments on the first of January. I havent taken mine yet. I got my & your No. They are about 3434 & 5   Willie if you dont come home this fall you will have to send me a Power of Attorney to take your Allotment for you.

Every person of age will have to take his own allotment, or give some one a Power of Attorney to take it for him. Me, you, & Spi will take the old Home place. I got the money you sent me   it was $135.82. I paid your insurance on your accident policy you taken out at Talala before you went off. It were $13.00 for this year. Your big policy is not due untill next September. Plenty money to pay it off here

I guess I have got every letter you wrote to me. & the Girls have got several. I publish yours in the Claremore Progress. Sallie & Maude wrote to you some time ago & sent you some money. They Banked it to Cape Town care of American Consul. This only makes the 3th letter that I have wrote to you. & only sent you Papers once. This winter havent been cold. but has been awful wet, Rained all winter.

Sallie Maude & me will go to New Orleans in May to the big Confederate Reunion. the Ellis Girls says you must write to them. Every body sends you love for them & write to me when you can

      Your Pa

          C.V. Rogers.Claremore, I.T.

This is one of the warmest letters Clem Rogers ever wrote to his son. It was clear he missed him. It also showed that he was interested in the goings and comings of the local young people as well as in business. He had taught Will well—money for his insurance was important! Any cowboy was exposed to more than his share of danger, especially one who traveled as Will did. He made sure his insurance was paid, even if he didn't have enough to eat on.

Charlie McClellan was one of Willie's earliest friends—the boy he wrote to when they were both in about the fourth grade. They both enjoyed a sense of humor. Charlie wore a long Indian braid, but when he went to school at Vanderbilt he was required to cut it off. When he did, he had it cut in a Mohawk. It was shaved up way above his ears, leaving just a strip of hair over the top of his head and down the back.

The cowboys Clem mentioned were all friends of Will's: Dick Parris, the one who went to South America with him; Clem Musgrove, C.V.'s namesake and grandson of his mother, Sallie Vann, by her second husband; Jim Rider, one of the best steer ropers in the Nation.

The allotment was not a good deal for C.V. Rogers or for any of the other big ranchers. But C. V. was a pragmatic man. " If you can't whip 'em, join 'em!" When he saw that division of the land was inevitable, he became one of the inside team that evaluated all the holdings for the Department of the Interior. Thus, they paid him, and he got a chance to check out the choice spots to be assigned. He decided his own land and home was the best deal for him and his family, so he planned to take his allotment there and to have Will and some of the other family members—including Will's cousin, Spi Trent—take allotments adjoining his. Some of the former slaves—now citizens—who were qualified to receive land also took their allotments adjoining Clem's.

He knew that not every Cherokee would want to become a farmer or rancher and that many of the allotments would be sold. If they were part of his big ranch and adjoined his allotment, he was willing to purchase them as soon as possible.

Even so, he knew he would never be able to return to the large, successful ranch operation he'd had. So he started buying property in Claremore—lots on which he could build rent houses for the new settlers, the livery stable, the bank, a hotel, a hardware store. He even bought land on the north side of Claremore and constructed a track for horse races. Out of season, it could be used for fairs and other activities.

Clem enjoyed the business acquisitions and operations for their own sake; he was no doubt a good businessman. As the only son, Will could look forward to owning them some day, and, Clem thought, he should be home learning how to operate them instead of running around all over the world.

C. V. Rogers, far left on the back row, was a member of the Dawes Commission that evaluated land holdings for the Department of the Interior in preparation for allotment.

Feb 21—1903
Mr W.P. Rogers. Esq.
My Dear Old Boy—

If you ever get this letter you will be surprised to hear from me.

I read a long letter in the Progress from you today. I saw Cousin Maud and Mrs. McSpadden just a few day ago.

Willie every body is getting married   Old Scrim got married to Miss Phillip's

All these girls are getting pert near grown. May Bullet and Alice Walkley and Byna Murphy. and the rest of them.

You had better come home and pick out and step off. Every body would be glad to see you. I wish I was with you to ride some of those bronks and hoop [whoop] right keen and tell them I was a wolf. . . .

You woudnt hardly know Claremore, it has grown so. You tell Jack that I am a wolf and dont care who knows it. Willie I wish you would come home   I would give any thing to see you.

I will close with lots of love.
                    Your Friend
                              Denny Lane
Answer soon.Talala. I.T.

2-26-03
Mr Wm. P Rogers
Capetown
South Africa
c/o American Consul
Friend Will:

I recieved your letter about the 20th of Dec. but you told me not to write until you wrote again.

I sho would like to see you. I saw your father some two weeks ago and he was showing me some pictures you had sent him also a picture of your self. You must be getting lots to eat   you are looking fine.

It is raining here now and has been all winter   Mud is ass deep to a camel in most places. We have had the worst spell of weather on cattle we have had for about four years.

Aud and Johnnie have both got the blues. And old Dug is wintering his cattle principally on scenery and the scenery isnt the best in the country.

I tried to die all fall. I taken down with the rheumatism at Chelsea while I was on a round up. and they took me from there to Vinita so I layed there in bed flat of my back five weeks with both my knees swelled up as big as your body.

I finally got so I could creep around so I went to the Springs and stayed six weeks. I am feeling about as good as usual at present. I havent done any work this winter only what little I have helped Johnnie and Tom

Your father wanted me to take Comanche and keep him for you until you come back. he said at that time he was looking for you home by April. I told him I dident like to take the horse as he might get crippled or get an eye put out and I

A whoop is a sound cowboys make at work—sort of a yip, yip, yip that communicates certain things to the animals. Being a "wolf" means having strength, fierceness—a wolf is a wild person, one to be feared. "Pick out and step off" meant to get married.

~Will Rogers, Jr.

never would feel right over it. So I came on up to Talala   I hardley been home for over two months. I seen Clem and Bill Musgrove and they said their woolies were chasing hell out of your horse and then would turn him out on the range with McClellans old mares. Johnnie and the rest of them told me the same so I told your father I would take him   not that I wanted to get any service out of him but taken him to keep them buttons off of him.

When I left for the Springs I left old Montie with Johnnie. So I told him when I came back he could keep either of the horses Comanche or Montie as I knew he would care for him as good as I could or better as he has lots of oats and he decided to keep Comanche and he has sho got him fat. he looked awful bad and his hair was dead but he is looking good and feels fine.

They had a big time at Oaklahoma City the 10, 11, and 12 of this month. Of course they had a contest with the cat gut. Hop got 1st in 58   Sharp Jun. 2nd in one minute and some thing and Clem got 3rd. The prizes were 200. 1st. 100 2nd. 50 3rd

They had it in the paper that Hop tied in 34 but Clem said he tied in 58.0

I dident get to go as I was at Vinita as a witness in a cattle case. None of the boys dident take any horses from here.

I guess you heard about Clem getting beat out of Robbin. They all went to St Louis last fall to a contest and the boys all came home but the man that was to come back with the horses. When the horses came in old Robbin dident come back   Clem claims Mullhall kept him out on him. but I think Mulhall must have bought the horse. As Clem wont talk much about him   There was seven rode him at Oklahoma City. Clem says he is poor and has got his mane and tail chewed off. Clem rode him second and he come in bleeding at the nose. Some one asked Clem why he dident make Mulhall pay for the horse at Oaklahoma City. Clem said Mulhall offered him a draft for $250.00 but he wouldent take it. That sounds funny.

I saw Keys here a while back   he is as big as a mule. I think he is killing lots of booze from what I can hear. Miss Ada [Foreman] is as sweet as ever. Miss Vick is going to school at the Seminary. Miss Ada is teaching school at Talala   I tried to get to go to school but they said I was moss [most] too large. Your girl Miss Ray is attending school at Mexico Mo   she will be living out here on Caney next summer so you had better come home and throw in with us. I havent saw your Ellis girl [Kate] but once and that was at Talala The 4th of July.

Inclosed you will find a progreamme of what they are to have at El Paso. Tex.

I havent got any cattle now. I dont know just what Ill do or where I will go yet. but when you write Mail my letter to Talala and if I am gone they will forward it to me

Well old pal I will close for this time

Hoping this will find you having a good time and enjoying good health

As ever

Your friend

James H Rider

"Adios"

The "buttons" Jim Rider hopes to keep off Will's horse are youngsters and immature cowboys. The contest with the "catgut" simply means the roping and tying.

Following is a letter about which we know little. No date or place is given. "Kiddie" refers to the Cherokee Kid: Will Rogers. And it came from his collection. (This same collection was perused by Betty Rogers when she wrote her book on Will, and she kept the letter intact, so we feel it did not disturb her so many years later.)

Dear Kiddie

I have come to the conclusion. Now I want to make a proposition to you   oh my darling   I can not let you leave me   dont you think that this would be a good idea if you have not given Jack notice yet then dont do it just stay with the show & work & I will go back to Syd [Sydney] & let both of us try & save as much money as we can & if you think it advisable send to your people and get some money & then we will also have saved a bit Then we could go away sweetheart I could live much better if you were in the show   we need not be intamate we could just make out as if everything is over between us   now dont you think it is a good plan. send me an answer by Harry & then I will know what to do oh darling dont say no to this   then I will realy begin to believe you dont love me now darling I love you so much that it seems to me I should die if you leave me so tata my darling   think it over well & let me know   oh I wish we had last night over

Yours lovingly
Mamie

No further identity for Mamie has been found. She begged him not to go home, which he must have been threatening to do, but to stay on with Jack. She offered to go on back to Sydney, Australia, if it would help the situation. Notice she did not mention going to the United States. None of Will's letters home mentioned Mamie or gave any clue to his having a girlfriend at all.

How serious their relationship was is unknown, but she had evidently caused Will some problems with his boss. Mamie told him he did not need to give Jack notice if they restrained their romance, indicating Jack did not like the situation in which Will was involved, whatever the reason. He may have thought Mamie was not suitable for Will and tried to force them apart.

We have no proof that Mamie was the reason Will went to Australia when he left Jack's show later in the year, but it would appear that his attraction for the woman had something to do with his delay in starting home. And when he wrote home, he failed to mention the name or gender of the friend he was spending time with in Australia. Clearly, his love life was disturbing, to say the least.

KINGS HOTEL
EAST LONDON, SOUTH AFRICA

March 17, 1903
Dear Sister and Folks:
    I will write you a short letter and tell you how I am getting on. . .

"THE CHAMPION LASSO THROWER OF THE WORLD"

We came from Durban to East London by boat, were 24 hours on the road and then had to wait out in the bay 24 hours longer before we could land. It was the same old story—sick from start to finish. We came off last evening and I guess we will open here tonight. We will be here perhaps ten days, then go back inland. There are lots of towns in South Africa. East London has a population of thirty or forty thousand.

I have not received any mail for a long time, the last letter from home being dated in August of last year.

I am getting on fine with the show. Texas Jack is making lots of money and is enlarging his show all the time. We carry a fine band with us now. I will only remain with the show until we reach Cape Town, which will be in three or four months, then I'm off for home. I surely do want to see all of you good and plenty about now.

I would like for you to send me some new coon songs, for I can't get them here. Also put in a few sentimental songs. They take well here. I sing in the concert, after appearing in the big show as "the champion lasso thrower of the world," and riding bucking horses.

Send the songs to me at Cape Town, in care of our consul, and I'll be on the lookout for them. They will be worth a whole lot to me here if I get them in time.

Give my friends my best regards and tell them how I'm getting along. Hope you are all doing fine. Love to all.

Will Rogers.

East London.
March 22, 1903.
My Dear Papa

I will write you this short letter   I just wrote to you all a few days ago and will write you a longer letter in a day or so   this is to ask you to send me some Rope   I want about 100 feet of the best kind of hard twist rope   you can get it there   any of the boys will show you what I used to use   pretty small but hard twist   I cant get a thing here that we use. some nights I rope with old tie ropes or any old things

Please send this at once   send it so it will come the quickest and safest and surest way. no matter the cost.

I'm getting blooded aint I. . . .

I am getting along fine and will be home as soon as I make money enough which will be in a few months

Now papa please send this at once.

I wrote to Sallie for some Coon songs   if she dident get the letter tell her to send me a whole lot please   to me in care of the American Consul in Capetown we will be there about the time that will get there for there is a big exhibition on there then and I will have the rope to work with there   then I think I will go home and maby the show to.

Lots of Love to all the folks and best regards to the friends.

Your loving son
Willie

They used a hard twist manilla rope—not used today.
~James Blake Rogers

The Claremore MESSENGER and the Vinita CHIEFTAIN papers reported that C.V. Rogers bought the rope from Mr. Barrett, a saddler at Vinita, paying $1.50 for it. But the postage to mail it cost $6.15. These newspapers as well as the PROGRESS published every scrap of information about Clem Rogers' wandering boy.

~RC

Chelsea, Indian Ter. U.S.A.
April 25, 1903.
My Dear, Dear Brother:

I'll begin my letter by telling you we are all well and I think we get every letter or card that you ever write. We are so sorry that no home mail ever reaches you. Papa has been sick occasionally this winter and Tom was in bed for three weeks but Papa is well again and so is Tom. I am getting along splendidly so are Maud and May and their little folks. May and Frank [Stine] have a little girl at their house about 3 mos. old named Mattie Lane Stine. They call her Lanie after Cap. We are all always so anxious for your letters and every body is always asking about you. You can certainly have your pick of any of these girls when you come home. There will be sixteen girls to graduate at the Female Seminary the 2nd of June. Among them are Vic Foreman, Scrap Lane, and Maud and Lizzie McSpadden. They are all making great preparations "to dress" Kate Ellis seemed delighted over your letter. She is teaching in Oolagah. Maud and I went over to see May about 5 or 6 weeks ago and seen the Ellis girls. May's husband runs a butcher shop in Oolagah. Papa has your fine trotting horse in Claremore and is having old Comanche taken care of. . . . Papa is going to take Maud and I to New Orleans to the Confederate Veteran Reunion, next month. Cap is going also. only he pays his own way. Tom is going to keep house for me, with the assistance of a negro woman, and sister May is coming over to keep house for Maud. We are anticipating a fine time.

The [St. Louis] Fair was postponed and will not open till May 1904 but the Dedication Ceremonies take place next Thursday, Friday and Sat. Quite a lot of Cow-boys are going from here. . . . Maud and I sent you a little Christmas greeting in the form of a draft or exchange, for $10.00 each but it never reached you and was returned to us. . . .

I am mailing your songs this morning and will send you some newer ones next week, as I'll order some from Kansas City tomorrow. So you may look out for them. All the boys want to join the show now, since you have. Every body is just wild to hear you tell of your travels. So hurry and come home. Where we all love you so well and are anxiously awaiting you.

>   Your loving Sister
>   Sallie McSpadden

Port Elizabeth, S. Africa
May 21, 1903
C.V. Rogers, Claremore, I.T.
My Dear Father:

I will put this short letter in with the power of attorney that I am sending you in case I do not get back to the Cherokee Nation in time to take my allotment. I hope this will be all right, for a good lawyer over here said it would.

I sent you some money a few days ago, amounting to about $310 in American money. It was some I saved while with the show and don't need it here. I never got any letters, let alone money, from the girls. I don't think I ever got half my mail, so

Married in 1885, Sallie and Tom McSpadden became pillars of the community of Chelsea and helped hold the family together after Mary Rogers died. Will loved to eat Sallie's biscuits and gravy with fried ham (from the hogs Tom had raised) when he came to visit.

Sounds as if Sallie is doing a little matchmaking between Will and Kate Ellis. Maybe Sallie thought Kate could keep him at home.

>   *~Will Rogers, Jr.*

don't send any more money for it would get lost. Did they register it?

Well, I am getting along better all the time with Jack's show, and have promised to make another trip which will take four or five months, and then I will be ready to go home. I am getting homesick, but don't know what I would do there more than make a living.

As it is, I am off here bothering and worrying no one, and getting along first rate.

Of course the show business is not the best business but so long as there is good money in it and it is honest, there is no objection to it. I still keep sober and don't gamble, and Jack thinks a lot of me. I am taking his part in lots of things in the show, and he says as he is getting old I can take the show before long and do his work. He will furnish the capital and I think I would do well to try it a bit anyway.

Write when you can. Love to all.

Your Loving Son,
Will Rogers.

It is not clear why Will was sending $310 home at this time. The sum was far more than enough to pay his passage home. Possibly he had good luck at a card game? Or, perhaps the money was his savings for the trip home, which he would not need now that he was signing up for more time with Jack. There is no indication in the letter that he planned to go on a trip in Australia with no job. Perhaps he was "putting temptation behind him"—sending the money home so that he would not spend it on Mamie.

Just sixteen days after the heated letter from Mamie, another South African girl wrote to Will. He must have been a real heartbreaker!

Graaff Reinct
June 6th 1903
My Dearest loveing boy
    only these few words to let you know that I do love you so much I realy dont know what to do when you are going to leave me   my heart will break all over, you my Dear this is what I must tell you   plese dont follow me to night because the child father is coming to fatch me to night after the play   I will come and see you tomorrow afternoon and take you out for a walk for the last must kindly give me your adress this is mine

Annie Greenslade
River Street
Graaff Reinct

Annie too begged Will not to leave her. His relationship with her must have been even more clandestine than the one with Mamie. We can guess that Annie was a local girl because she indicated she would be seeing Will for the last time. He kept the letter and it survived all the years of his marriage. Betty also kept it with the collection when she did the research for her book, *Will Rogers: The Story of His Life Told by His Wife.*

"I AM OFF HERE BOTHERING AND WORRYING NO ONE. . . . "

Orange Free State
June 20. 1903
My Dear Sisters and home folks

I have just received the songs and also your letter and of course it is useless to say how glad I was to get the music also to hear from you for it had been about 5 months since I had a letter   so glad to hear you all were well.

Well I am as usual doing all right   am still with the show We are on a second tour of the country now but these places are all new to me as they showed there before I joined them   We are going into Portugese East Africa on this trip as all the country we have been in is British Territory that formerly belonged to the Boers   This town we are in was the capitol of the Free State that the English took from the Boers   then we go to Pretoria   that is the Transvaals Capitol they are large towns   we will be here 10 days. The country is getting settled down now and it is as great a place as you could find   only you see lots of Soldiers are still in the country.

The frequency of English Graveyards remind one that there has been something doing around these parts.

There is a great boom on in these towns to give you an Idea of things   in a town no larger than Vinita with only on [one] Rail Road one lot with 150 foot front   no improvements sold for 200.000 pounds that is equivalent to one million dollars at home   Well we consider that a dollar at home is worth as much as a pound here even though it is 5 of our dollars   carpenters Brick layers and all kinds of skilled labor get a pound and a half and two pounds a day   that is $7.50 to 10.00 but then when you go to buy anything   away it goes   you have no Idea how little regard money that one would think a lot at home is thought of here and most all of it is carried on your person   that is by the working class   it is in belts worn around your waist or small ones on your arms above the elbow or below the knee   you will often see an old fellow pull out his old belt and count out a hundred pounds that is 5 hundred dollars and ofttimes as much as two thousand and still no one is robbed at all. but still you see just as many poor men for while it is easy made   it is just as easy spent

Well here it is the 27 and I havent posted this letter yet.

Oh it is cold here now   of course not like it is there but it seems cold   for it is disagreeable   there is sometimes a sheet of ice over the water.

Well I will send you some pictures that a friend of mine took   they are not very good but will answer   send two to papa and also one to May

Will also send you a couple of clippings telling you of the fire and also of our opening night in this place

Well I will close   write soon and a long letter for I am always so anxious to hear from home

My best to all my friends and will see you all in a very few months.

> Your loving brother
> > Willie
> c/o American Consul
> > Capetown

[P.S.] Tell Papa I got the Rope and I also got 3 bundles of songs   only one letter

Maud Rogers had a sense of humor nearly as acute as her little brother Willie's. The Lane home welcomed house guests, partygoers, and family anytime. Maud's husband was a successful druggist in Chelsea.

July 12, 1903.

My Own Dear Brother,

What an age it has been since we have had a letter from you, but I fear it has been eaven longer since you have heard from us. We keep hopeing you will soon be home, but as long as you are well and doing well I guess we hadent aught to expect you soon.

Sallie papa Cap and I went to New Orleans the 17 of May   stayed a week and just had the finest kind of a time, went down to the gulf and about five miles out on a little tug boat   that little trip gave me a great longing for a sea voige and if you stay over there very much longer I fear I will attempt a trip across the deep to see you.

Papa was up here the other day. he is so full of buisness since he was anominated for the senit   [Cherokee Senate] he and Joe LeHay with Bill Rogers for Chief, papa had not been feeling at all well this spring but now he never has an ache or pain   and to let him tell it Bill is the very best man on earth.

Sallies baby has had quite a sick spell   she looks so bad and is so cross. Gunter is getting to be quite a large boy and thinks he is the greatest man going.

Papa said you had written to John Lipe and were mad at Sallie and I because we have parts of all your letters published. Yes we have been, because if you could know how all your friends love to hear from you and how they all look for a letter from you, still if you dont like it we will not put any more in the papers. just anything so you write to us often.

I have no cook this summer and you should see me mooning around these hot days I tell you everything has to come up all O.K. or they hear from me.

Papa has your young horse down at Claremore. I tell you he is just fine   what would you take for him?

Papa bought a place there in Oolagah for May to live in   it is the place the Ellis bought and then found they did not want to live there always.   Miss Kate has been teaching the Oolagah school and I think makes a fine teacher. We will start Ethel and Irene to school this fall   they are not any larger than when you left but they are old enough to go.

Write when you can   all join me in a world of love to our own dear boy.

> Loveingly
> Maud.

Pretoria. South Africa.

Aug 2, 1903

My Dear Father.

After so long a time I will again write to you but there is nothing of importance to write of   I am still at work and doing very well and enjoying the best of health.

I have not had any mail from home for some time   I got the rope alright that you sent and was glad to get it

This place Pretoria is the capitol of the Transvaal and the home of Paul Kruger it was before the war the principal Dutch town and a very pretty little city too We have just left Johannesburg   that is the great gold fields and the largest of all the African towns   We next go into Portugese Territory that is over in the east part on the coast. Jack himself is leaving the show for a trip to America to bring out some new people   he wants me to stay till he gets back as I take his parts in the show while he is away   he says he may get down that way and if so he will come around and see you.

I will come as soon as he gets back for I am getting in a hurry to get home. Did you get the Money I sent you about three months ago it was 65 Pounds.

I will drop you in a newspaper notice or two that I have got out of the last paper so and you can see how I am getting on

Give all the Sisters and folks my best love and regards to all my old friends. and most of all to my Dear Father who has always done all in his power for me and for which I am certily thankful.

I will close   write when you can   to your <u>contented</u> son

Willie

Capetown S.A.

c/o American Consul
Dont any one write untill you hear from me again as I wont be here that long.

Instead of the usual "Papa" Will used the address "Father." The tone almost sounded like that of a final goodbye. Yet he seemed contented and secure in his position with the show. Then on September 5, he wrote from Wellington, New Zealand, that he had been on the ship twenty-five days from South Africa.

He must have made a sudden change in his plans and left Texas Jack not long after he wrote about taking over the manager's job. The only explanation we have for his fast move was that he "had seen South Africa."

17 Aug 1903
From Maud Lane
My Dear Old Boy.

I keep thinking of you more and more, the nearer fall comes the worse I want to see you. Well things are moveing on here very much as they always do   just as fast as any of our girls and boys grow up a bit they have to get married and the most of them could not buy a pound of soap. Papa was elected to the senate   he and Joe LeHay from Cooweescoowee with Will Rogers a Chief and Mr Dave Faulkner assistant. they say this was the hottest ellection we have had for a long time. All the U.S.C. people were Nationals and wanted Cookson, they called the Dowan [Downing] party Democrats and the Nat. [Nationals] Republicans. so everyone took a hand in it Mr W.E. Halsell worked so hard for Cookston and they say he spent about $10000.00 but it has done him no good   he and papa have fallen out over it.

Papa is now at Tahlequah   went down to file   he took Ethel and Irene with him   they thought they were going most around the world when they started.

Sometime ago papa saw a man in Claremore who just came from S. Africa and he had been to Texas Jack's show, said he remembered the Cher [Cherokee] Kid. I wanted to send for him and have him come up but I knew he could tell me nothing about you for he only saw you while you were preforming. But I would give anything in the world to see some one who could tell me all about you.

It cost fourteen cents for Maud Lane to send the letter posted August 19, 1903, New York to Capetown, South Africa. From there it went to Sydney, Australia, and to Wirth's Circus, Murchison, Victoria. It arrived in Sydney at noon, November 12, 1903 and at Murchison, Victoria on November 25.

~RC

We are going to have another little country fair this fall   2-3-4 of Sept. how I do wish you could be here just to be with all the Blue Creek folks   I had them all last year, Lanes Formans and McLellans just twenty two in all for three nights. this year all of us old widdows are going to give a play. say dont you wish you could see me before the foot lights   well I know I will make a great hit   this will be our seccond attempt as we gave one last Jan   did so well I think we will start out on the road.

Scrap Lane got this little school down here by Busheyhead and she will stay up here most of time   it is only about 4 1/2 miles from here   she can sure ride that far.

We are all expecting Lizzie McS. and Bartley Milam to get off [marry] very soon. Lyle (that is Mrs. Joe's baby boy) got his leg boken about three weeks ago and Bartley has just most stayed out there   he and a Mr Philips who is very much in love with Maud.

Dear Brother please do write to us just as often as you can. I heard you did not like it because we have been publishing your letters   well we did not mean to offend you but if you could know how all your friends love to hear from you and how they all watch for your letters and one paper coppies it from another till it has gon all around so you see you are a great boy at home, but if you dont want us to print any more we wont   only do please write to us often

Loveingly

Maud.

Maud rambled along, relating to her brother all the little newsy items she thought would keep him in touch with home. But many of the persons mentioned were important to the history of the area. Sallie's husband, Tom McSpadden, was first president of the Bank of Chelsea in 1896; he was the first Sunday school superintendent of the Methodist Church of Chelsea, and he was a successful rancher-cattleman. His father, Reverend Thomas Kingsberry McSpadden, a Methodist missionary, was sent to Tahlequah in 1869 to serve the Cherokees. He founded the church at Chelsea, among others. He had seven sons, many of whose descendants have made history. One son, Joel, was the father of Elizabeth Peach (Lizzie) McSpadden who was mentioned by Maud as about to "get off"—to marry—J. Bartley Milam. Milam became Principal Chief of the Cherokees (as well as founding an oil company) and sired children who became prominent. Another son of Joel was Theodore (Theo) or Ted who as a roper in St. Louis in 1904 worked closely with Will Rogers.

Tom and Sallie McSpadden's grandson, Clem Rogers McSpadden, was an Oklahoma senator for several years and was Senate Pro Tem, then was elected to the U.S. House of Representatives. Following his father, Herb McSpadden, in ranching, Clem is also one of the top rodeo announcers in the world and hosts the World's Richest Roping contest each year at his ranch at Bushyhead in Rogers County.

Wellington, New Zealand
Sept. 4. 1903
My Dear Papa

Dont get excited when you look on the map and see where I am now. left Africa and the show for I had seen it all and I was afraid you all would think I had permanently located there as I was there for a year but I must see a bit more and get back home   consequently must be on the move. I went east from Africa to here across the Indian Ocean   went to the south of Australia   we touched the island of Tasmania then on here   landed yesterday Sep 3 after 25 days rough weather and a distance of over 7 thousand miles   Tomorrow I leave for Auchland about 400 miles north of here   Will be over here a week or so then drop over to Australia. Will be there a couple of months   then as you see I am heading around this old Globe to America on the west coast then on home which will not be later than Dec 1st. In regard to this country it is as prosperous and good a little country as I ever seen   sheep raising and farming are the principal industry.

This is the capitol   a nice little city of 60 thousand. Of course all New Zealand belongs and is governed by the english and English is spoken. it is supposed to be the best of . . . . [he drew a square and through it wrote space]
P.S. [at top of page] Please tell me if you got the money I sent you about 4 months ago. about $300

Will was on the move again, with little or no explanation. His promise to be home by December 1903 was not to be fulfilled.

"A specially clever turn is provided by an American cowboy, styled the Cherokee Kid. He keeps clear of the beaten paths of other cowboy performers, and gives a healthy original exhibition with lasso and on horseback.

The Cherokee Kid's work with the lasso fairly dazzled the crowd. He seems to be able to lasso anything from the asset of a professional bankrupt or a wildly galloping steed to the business end of a flash of lightning.

It was certainly the best performance of the sort ever seen here. The Cherokee Kid is a gentleman with a large American accent and a splendid skill with lassoos. He demonstrated what could be done with the whirling loop by bringing up a horse and its rider from impossible positions, once throwing together two lassos [sic] encircling man and horse separately.

He also showed the spectators how to throw half hitches on to objects at a distance, and did other clever work with the ropes. It was a very interesting performance."

From The Auckland, New Zealand HERALD, reprinted in the Claremore PROGRESS March 5, 1904

Wellington
New Zealand Sept. 5. [1903]
My Dear Sister and all
Please (Notice)
Procure one of the childrens geographies and acquaint yourself with the where abouts of this particular place.

I just yesterday completed another jump in my Roving trip by crossing the Indian Ocean from Capetown off to the east and south of Australia calling in at The island of Tasmania then to this prosperous little city of 60 thousand souls the capitol of New Zealand. After 25 days of pitching and tossing intermingled with Sea Sickness as usual and also Toothache all togeather formed a hard combination

The Show in Africa wanted me for another tour over the same country but I wouldent go and as I had had enough Africa I thought I had better be going if I was ever going to get any where for I will be with you before long.

This may seem at first to be a long way from home and every where else but the fact is it is really closer and much more easily reached to and from America than Africa was as there is a direct line of steamers from here and Australia to Frisco which go the six thousand miles to frisco in 17 days from New Zealand or 20 from Australia so you see I am really nearer so write to me at once and I will get the letters before I leave for I missed all of my mail from Africa that music was the last thing I got or will get out of that mail for it could not reach us here I would be gone. I am in the best of health and feel fine but getting quite homesick

Write to me at once and tell me all the news
Your loving Brother Willie
c/o American Consul, Sydney. Australia.
[From a pictoral Post Card addressed to Mrs. J.T. McSpadden. Chelsea. Indian Territory. United States of America via Frisco]

As Will traveled toward New Zealand the allotments for part of the Cherokee land were made. The record shows: William P. Rogers, homestead allotment number 23839, Cherokee land Office, Tahlequah: NE 10 acres of Lot 3 of Section 19 twsp 23, Range 16. West 20.04 acres of Lot 3, Sec 19, to NN 23, Range 16.

Chelsea, Ind. Ty.
14 Sept 1903
Dear, Dear Brother:
We were all so glad to get news of you through the letter papa received last Tuesday. All your friends are so anxious to hear from you. . . . . Oh, we want to see you so badly. We all enjoyed the pictures you sent home. Of course we show them to every body. You say in your letter that "Jack" is coming to America. Well that means that you won't be home for several months then. But if he does come here we will certainly "feed him on the fat of the land," for being so nice to "our boy" over there. I cant understand why you don't get more mail from home. for we write often. and send papers also. And I don't think we have ever missed a single thing, either letter or paper, pictures or money that you have sent to us.

Maud's folks are all very well. so is papa. You know papa and Mr. LaHay were elected Senators on the Downing ticket from Cooweescoowee. Will Rogers is our next and last chief. He takes his seat in Nov. The election was a very exciting one. Cookson was the National Nominee.

Our third Chelsea Fair has passed into history. It was quite a success. Maud and I took our dinners the 2nd day and fed just 46. among whom were John Lipe & family, Alf and family & Jim Rider.

I know Maud told you all about Gordon Lanes hurt while out practising for the contest at fair so I'll only add that he is improving all the time. . . .

Tom and Papa are through filing, but Cap has to file for Stell, Ethel and Gunter yet, and I don't think May and Frank have been down yet at all. Did you get the last two songs I sent you? They were "In the Good Old Summer Time" and "Under the Bamboo Tree" . . . .

Well, I am not going to write such long letters but will write oftener than before and you will stand a better show of getting more in quantity at least, if not quality.

We are all very, very well and want you to be home in time to go to the World's Fair with us which opens next May. Every one sends you bushels of love, and hopes to have you with us soon again.

> Lovingly Yr. sister
> Sallie C. McSpadden.

Both Sallie and Will write positive letters. Sallie made no mention of the fact that little Pauline was crippled from polio and would be all her life. Will did not tell the home folks what caused him to leave Texas Jack's show or about his "girl problems."

Sydney. Australia.
Sept 28. 1903.
My Dear Father and home folks.

I suppose you received my cards from New Zealand so you will not be surprised to hear of me out here. I went from Wellington to Auckland by boat was there a short time then over to Sydney which is $1500 miles from New Zealand was four and a half days on that boat. New Zealand is the most prosperous little country I have ever seen since I left. very good stock and farming and nice cities and towns. Australia though much larger is not so good they have had a drouth here for the last 5 or 6 years and most all the stock are dead. It was the greatest sheep country in the world and lots of cattle but in the last year it has just began to rain and it will take years for it to be what it was. The tracts of land here held by the ranches I think are the largest in the world for it takes so much to keep a sheep or cow on and the ranches here hold hundreds of miles. it is a great timbered country most all the land is covered by thick timber it is an enormously big country and very few people only in the cities and away back in the interior is nothing but Negroes and they are still a bit skittish. The Natives of New Zealand is a kind of Indian called the Mouive [Maoris] but the Natives of Australia are Niggers and the way they can toss that Boomerang aint slow. it will shave your hat of [off] agoing and your head of [off] a coming back. Kangaroos are as common as Rabbits at home. They dont handle stock here like at home the [they] ride just little flat padded saddles and dont know what a Rope is they use long

In August, 1935—shortly after Will Rogers' death—THE ARGUS, a Melbourne, Australia, newspaper, reported the following: "Not long ago Rogers recalled that when he was in Warrnambool he was arrested for having led an elephant through the streets at midnight. The elephant's keeper, he said, had become intoxicated, and fearing that the animal might wander about and do some damage Rogers took it for a walk until he was stopped by a horrified police constable." We have no further evidence to verify this, but it has the ring of truth. Being with a circus, he would have become familiar with the animals, and likely was concerned about the elephant as well as his friend.

~RC

stock whips to drive them with. they are not near so good stock men as even the Gouchos of the Argentine are but the most conceited set of people on the face of the globe in regard to what they can do and what they know.

Sydney and Melbourne are the principal cities of about $500.000 five hundred thousand each. And are greatly like American cities more up to date than any I have seen since I left home much more so than England It is very amusing in all these countries any thing new or what they havent had before will be called American. You hear electric street cars called American Tram cars. All the refreshment places are advertised in box car letters "American cold Drinks American Soda fountain the bars will have up drinks mixed on the American plan. the barber will advertise "American barber chair." You see if it is one of their kind it will be just a strait old stool chair where you set up as straight as if you were in church and they will shave you and that shave is something chronic. I was always proud in America to own that I was a Cherokee and I find on leaving there that I am equally as proud to own that I am an American for if there is any nation earning of a rep abroad it is America.

I have had arguments with every nationality of man under the sun in regard to the merits of our people and country. from prize fights to the greatest internation questions of which I <u>knew</u> <u>all</u> about for you are not an American if you dont know. no matter what it concerns you must know whether you know right or not. for all these big fish stories are traced to the Americans so you have got to uphold the <u>rep</u>.

I was out to the races the other day this is the greatest racing country under the sun everybody man woman and child bets on the races the very poorest must have their small bet on the races. oh but the race courses are pretty ones all their tracks where the horses run are left with pretty grass are not cleaned out like ours and there is no dust. I seen the great Australian Derby worth 40 thousand $. run and there were 44 starten a mile and a half and at the finish the last horse was not 15 feet behind the first they were all locked togeather around the track think of 44 horses running like that Ive seen two and three race around a track togeather but not 44 the horse that finished 10th head was at the winners hips it was the greatest sight I ever saw.

In the hurdle or steeplechase races the horses had to run up and down a steep hill and the jumps were 5 ft solid rock 8 horses fell over different jumps 1 horse and one rider killed

Well it is just Spring time here and things look very pretty. I am going out into the country in a few days then down to Melbourne.

If you have already written in reply to my last from N.Z. you had better not write again for I dont think I will be here over two months yet My last letter from home was dated the middle of April. I am in the best of health feel fine and hope you all are same. I hope I will be able to see you all before many more months I am as ever your loving son

Willie.

My best to all

(Tell Kates I dont know any more to write him but he can publish this one if he likes.)

"I WAS ALWAYS PROUD IN AMERICA TO OWN THAT I WAS A CHEROKEE AND I FIND ON LEAVING THERE THAT I AM EQUALLY AS PROUD TO OWN THAT I AM AN AMERICAN "

". . . ANY THING NEW OR WHAT THEY HAVENT HAD BEFORE WILL BE CALLED AMERICAN."

In this letter, Will had started using periods to end his sentences and was more careful of his spelling. Perhaps he had someone helping him proof his letters, or he was writing better because he knew his correspondence might be published. A. L. Kates was the publisher of the Claremore *Progress*.

BANK OF CHELSEA

Chelsea Indian Territory Oct 3 1903

My Dear Willie:

We just received your card a few minutes ago and we are all so glad you are coming home. I have just written the fact to papa who is not very well, but I think when he really knows you are on your way home, he will be like a boy again. All the family are well. Clem is a Sophmore at the Rolla School of Mines. Rolla, Mo. and likes it splendidly. May, Herbie, Irene Stell and Ethel are all pupils in the Chelsea Academy. Gunter is a younger edition of you, and Helen takes care of Pauline for me.

Johnnie [Yocum] goes to school to Miss Kate Ellis at Oolagah and is doing splendidly and Jake and Lanie are helping their mama keep house. . . .

We want you home by Thanksgiving, if possible. We all spend that time with me, and if you are only with us, it will be a real and true Thanksgiving.

Christmas we all go over to Mauds and we are sure you will be home by then. I am just writing to tell you how anxious we are to see you, and will tell you the news when you come.

All send bushels of love and echo the cry "Hurry Hurry Home."

    Lovingly Yr. sister
    Sallie C. McSpadden

Oolagah, I.T.

Oct 4 1903.

My dear Brother.

Well we recieved your dear letter yestaday. And was so glad to here from you again, but we hope and pray we will see you soon. Well it has been so long sence you left and I have written and I have so much to tell you I hardly no where to begin. We quit the Hotel and moved to Oolagah. Frank runs a butcher shop in the winter and a Ice Cream parlor in Summer. Johnnie goes to school to Miss Kate Ellis. Jake runs over town. and our daughter Laney is the sweetest thing   every body says she looks like you. she is seven months old. You no where John Kimbroughs house was here. Why Mr. Ellis bought it. [Then] Papa bought it from them. And so he give it to me, so I have a home.

The Street Fair at Claremore wasent very good   the baby and I went one day. Collinsville Fair closed yestaday   we dident go. Miss Vic Foreman teaches school at Talala.

Kate teaches here   she has sixtey inroll. she gets $45 a month. then she has about 15 whites, Miss Lulu Bennett also teaches here.

You just much be at home by Christmas   are [or] it wont seem like Christmas. Papa hasent be [been] up in quite awhile   he was real sick the last time he was up. he had Irean and Ethel with him. I havent been to Chelsea since May. I tell you Oolagah is building. And they is folks wanting houses here every day and cant get them. They is lots at the coal banks. They are sure at work.

When ever we here from you why Frank just takes it up to the Shop for every body wants to no what you had to say and when you are comeing home. Well I will close for I don't no nothing to write of Intrest for I never do leave Oolagah. All I hope is the next news you give us will be in person. May God bless and pretect, and return you safe to the ones that love you so.

They all join me in love.

May

Will must have been very glad to hear from May, who seldom wrote. May Stine had many burdens to bear. C. V. kept in close contact with her and was very helpful in setting up business situations for her husband. He also helped support the children. Whenever May or the children were seriously ill, Maud or Sallie, or both, went to the Stine home to stay as long as they were needed, so the girls remanined close. But she didn't get to be with them at regular Sunday dinners and other gatherings.

Wild West shows continued in the Cherokee Nation, but not everyone approved. The Vinita newspaper blasted the "wild, reckless, gambling crowd" that attended the shows. The editor particularly wanted the Sunday shows stopped, and they were stopped in that town by injunction.

Chelsea papers advertised that Colonel Mulhall and his company of cowboys would give an exhibition of riding and roping at Chelsea on October seventeeth and eighteenth. Lucille would rope and tie a steer, the report said. The next week they would go to Vinita. Clem Rogers no doubt attended one or both of these.

Papers reported that Mr. and Mrs. C. L. Lane had returned from Kansas City where they saw *Ben Hur*. C. V. Rogers said he was expecting his son home soon.

On November fourth Will turned twenty-four years old. Only twenty-one when he left the I.T., he had experienced more than some of his friends would in a lifetime. The same month, Betty Blake was working in the office of the Rogers, Arkansas, *Democrat* while the editor was on his honeymoon. Will sent a postcard home announcing he would not make it by Christmas.

Postcard From Barrella. Victoria. Australia.
Nov. 22, 03.
"A. A. A."
(All About Australians)
"A Native Australian"
My Dear Father And all the folks

I will drop you this card and tell you how I am getting on and tell you how sorry I am to not be able to be at home Xmas but it will be impossible and cant be helped   I know you people dont want to see me any worse than I want to see you I leave here about the 1st of Feb   I am getting on O.K. in this country and away back in the Interior. Am going down to Melbourne soon. I am out on one of the big ranches here but they are different from those at home.

Best to all and a happy Xmas   Willie

May Rogers Yocum Stine was the youngest Rogers daughter.

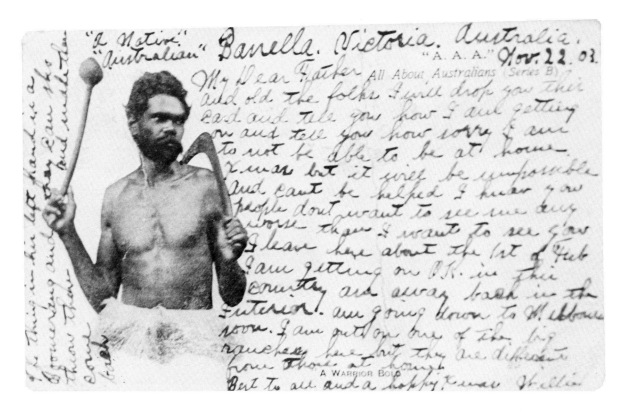

When Will sent the card of November 22, 1903, he was out on one of the big ranches, but he made no mention of why he was there or with whom or of what he was using for money. He might well have been the houseguest of a friend, possibly a girlfriend and her family. For some reason, he does not say who is with him or with whom he is staying.

[Received in Claremore December 29, 1903.
Posted New York July 11, 1903; arrived Melbourne November 24, 1903.]
Fair View
My boy:
  Do you with-hold your self from me longer, and will you refuse to write to me after I have made you this confession: Forgive me Will this one time for the last. for as I forgive you now—you shouldnt deny me this plea of my heart forgiveness.
  Are you ever coming home? Write me in your letter when you are coming. I hope it will be before another letter can get to you. though it will be a pleasure for me to write you; but a far great pleasure to see you.
  Will if you can understand in these few words all they is ment you will never have a right to believe again as you wrote John.
  Will when you come home I shall be the happiest person the world holds—if I am forgiven and if not then I shall be very unhappy.
  I will not give you your choice of these statements, but if it is the latter, then you will never know how miserable I am. and if I never receive an answer to this I'll know you have accepted the latter. . . Though I am still your most affectionate.
      Ada Gray. . .

This postcard pictured an Australian native and Will Rogers wrote: "The thing in his left hand is a Boomerang and they can sho throw them and make them come back"

Ada Gray's letter went full circle—to New York, South America and Australia, where it arrived November 24, then was sent back to Claremore where it arrived December 29, 1903.

      ~RC

[From the *Claremore Progress,* January 23, 1904]
Murchison, Victoria, Australia
November 27, 1903
My Dear Sister and all the Troop:
At last I have received a few of the letters you have written to me, four of them that has followed me from Africa, and one each from you and sister May, directed to me to Sydney, Australia, written on October 4. Some of these were six months old, but it had been eight since I had last heard. Oh, no! It was only a rumor that I wasn't glad to get them, and more than glad to know you were all well and getting on nicely. Well, as for me, I am as usual in the best of health and doing very well out here in Kangaroo land, I don't like this country very much except for farming. It is not as good a stock country as the Argentine Republic. Nothing but trees, no open country. All just like a grove, with very little underbrush. All big trees. There is about as rotten a government here as one would wish to see. I am now out here with a friend of mine on one of the big ranches or stations as they call them. I am going down to Melbourne soon, will be there about Christmas.
I think I will depart from here about the last of January or the first of February.

There is a native camp of black fellows here, and I was trying to throw the boomerang. About the best way I could get it to come back was to send one of the little black fellows after it. I have been out chasing kangaroos on some of the fastest horses I ever rode. Out here all of the horses are jumpers. The fences are all rail fences, and you are no horseman at all if you go to the gate! You just top the fences, which are five feet high, and which is considered no jump at all. The horses are part thoroughbred, as all the ranches have their horses bred up like that, but they ride only one or two horses each. The saddles are little plain padded ones, only it has big pads in front of your knees, like wings, so you can grip it good. They have no horn or back. They don't use a rope at all; but, say, they use a cattle whip, not like our old big ones, but they are small and long, about twenty or twenty-five feet. Oh, but they did paralyze me when I saw them use them.
I did not know what a whip was made for until I saw these fellows use them. I tried one, but only succeeded in tying knots around my own neck. But that wasn't so bad as the Bolos that I tried in South America. I knocked knots on my head so that I could not get my hat on for a week.

I still have my saddle and outfit with me; these fellows call it a rocking chair.

Well, I have seen the horsemanship of all these countries and it is all on somewhat different principles, but they all accomplish the same thing, and in the end get their cattle work done, and that is all that is required. I think the cowboys are the kings of the lot.

I see by your letter that papa still has my young horse, but you don't mention old Comanche. You don't mean to say there is no Comanche, or that he is dead. If so, I will never come home, for it would not be home if he was not there.

You were both saying in your letters that I was mad at you for publishing my letters or parts of them. You are mistaken. I don't care, if you like to have them published, or the parts of them that might interest any of my friends. I was only ashamed of them, is why I didn't like them published.

I got a nice letter from May, which told me all the news. You all only write about two pages, then stop. You used to write long letters. I have received only two from papa since I left home.

I know you people are planning to attend the World's Fair. Don't be alarmed but what I will be there. I will be by your side. I did not get the last songs you mentioned. I only got two packages at the same time. As for papers, I never received any since those first ones I got in South America.

I can't tell you where to write, for I may not be here to receive it, so wait until you hear from me again.

> Your loving brother.
> Will.

[As published in the Claremore *Progress* January 30, 1904]
Manachusin, Australia
December 4 [1903]
Mr. S. E. Trent:

My Dear Old Friend: It has been quite awhile since I heard from or about you. I answered your letter which I received a year or so ago, but did not get a reply. Well, I should think that by this time you are one of the firm, if you are still at your same job. I know it is useless to ask you if you are doing well, for I always predicted that you would. As for me, I am the same old Will, doing very well and seeing the biggest part of the world. I am away back in the interior on one of the big ranches with a friend of mine, having quite a time.

It is all English-speaking white people in Australia, but a few blacks who are still a bit cranky. There is a camp of them close here. They are not kinky headed like Negroes, but have straight hair, more like an Indian. Say, but they can throw a boomerang. It sails all about the place, then back and they catch it in their hands. There are lots of stock in this country. I have seen a lot of it since I landed, and will see a lot more before I leave, which will be about the first of February, l904. So I will have traveled 34,000 miles since I left home, and seen quite a bit of the world. Still I look forward, longing to see the old home country again, for there is no country like home.

Well, I hope this will find you married and settled down. How is old Paris and R.O.? I hope they are not starving some good girl to death. When you write home tell them I will try and write to them before long. Also to Paris. I guess he is still taking in roping contests. They don't know what a rope is in this country. Well, I will stop. Hoping to see you soon, I am, as ever your old friend and cousin.

> Will.

P.S. Give my very best love to cousins Mollie, Georgia, Tom, R.O, and all the rest. Tell them old Will is enjoying himself as usual.

In the last two letters, Will made no mention of having further employment, nor of the Wirth Brothers Circus. He may have had no plans at that time. He spent Christmas in Melbourne and after that became involved with the Wirth show.

"I AM THE SAME OLD WILL. . . HAVE TRAVELED 34,000 MILES SINCE I LEFT HOME. . . ."

[Published in the Claremore *Progress*, February 13, 1904]
Melbourne, Australia,
Jan. 3, 1904

My Dear Father and all the Home Folks:

Christmas has come and gone, and I hear you all had a good old time up to Chelsea. I would have given anything to have been there but I could not; still I had a right good time away off down here. I was in Melbourne, the largest city of Australia, and a very pretty place to put in Christmas. [Christmases] out in these countries are as nothing compared with at home. No Christmas trees, scarcely any presents given, only cards sent to your friends, and to cap the climax it is as hot as the 4th of July.

This is the last old Christmas away from home for me. I received some letters from May and Sallie dated Oct. 3, a few weeks ago; have been looking for more; but they haven't come yet. I have been writing to you all regular, and I hope you have gotten the letters.

I am in the best of health and feeling fine; have got a good job here but will leave soon I can't tell you just when I will land up there, but I can tell you that I will be there in plenty of time for the opening—not closing—of that "St. Louis Street Fair."

I will drop in on you all some of these days when you are not looking for me or thinking anything about me. Well I will close. Give My best love to all my folks and freinds.

Ever your affectionate son,

Will.
P.S.—You need not write for I would not get it

Will's "good job" was with Wirth Brothers Circus. A review of the opening of the show at Freeman's Bay, New Zealand, was published in the Auckland *Star* January 20, 1904. The review said the show was in Auckland "last winter;" New Zealand's winter is June through August.

Whangarhei,
New Zealand
February, 4, 1904
My Dear Sisters and all the Home Folks:

I will write you all and let you hear how I am doing and to tell you that I am coming home very soon now, sure. I will be there certain before the opening of the St. Louis Fair, honest.

Well, since I last wrote I am back over in New Zealand, where I was when I first came from Africa. Have been here about two weeks. You see that is on my way home, as it is five days nearer Frisco than Australia. They want me for twelve months, but I have seen enough for me and want to come home.

We played the first place over here at Auckland. I am doing a roping and trick riding act and have been a big success, for it was never done here before. I will send you a sheet with some of the newspaper clippings, also lithograph photos of myself with some fancy roping and a program of the show, which will show you and all my friends what I am doing.

This little New Zealand is the prettiest place I ever saw. Oh, such beautiful scenery! We are away up a river tonight; just came in by a little steamboat about an hour ago. We are not showing till tomorrow. There are high mountains all around us. This is just a small town. I am up in my hotel all alone writing this. I want it to catch the Frisco boat that leaves Auckland, which is fifty miles from here, on the 5th of February. I have not had mail but once since I left Africa; that was a letter from Mae, dated Oct. 3rd. I won't get any now, I don't suppose. I hope you are all as well as I am. I will see you all for sure this time not later than May 1st.

Well, I will close but will write again soon. You needn't write, for you won't have time. Lots of love to all of you and my friends.

Brother Willie.

The red velvet, gold-trimmed Mexican roping suit made by Mrs. Wirth for Will to wear in the circus in New Zealand and Australia lends excitement and draws kids to watch in wonder as he does a few rope tricks outside the tent. But when he wore it later at the St. Louis Fair in 1904, Betty Blake was embarrassed by the flashy costume and said so. Will never wore it again.

Chapter Three

1904-1906

"It Is Either Stage and Make a Good Living Or No Show Business At All"

By the time Will returned to the Indian Territory in 1904, he was twenty-four years old, an experienced entertainer, a casual world traveler, and a homesick American.

Things had happened in the two years he'd been away.

Henry Ford raced a mile a minute in his seventy-horsepower car. The first auto was purchased in Indian Territory. The Pacific cable was completed and President Theodore Roosevelt sent a message to William Howard Taft in the Philippines. Carrie Nation stormed into Senate chambers waving her hatchet and was arrested for her efforts; 588 people burned to death at a theater fire in Chicago. The Wright brothers made their historic flight, Charles Lindbergh was born, and Clay McGonnigle roped and tied a steer in the Cherokee Nation in twenty seconds flat.

Intruders flooded into Indian Territory, towns became cities, and some people looked forward to statehood for Oklahoma. Others did not.

Will Rogers showed up out of nowhere at Oologah on April 11, 1904.

The prodigal son was home, and the Honorable C. V. Rogers set up a big dinner for his daughters and their families along with Will at a hotel dining room in Claremore the next day. The children clung to Will, asking questions, wanting to hear him speak some "foreign" words and to tell them more tales. His sisters did their share of questioning at the happy occasion and made him promise to stay awhile and spend some good old days at their homes. His old friends—the cowboys—all wanted to hear his stories of "what it was really like."

But he didn't tarry long.

Excitement was brewing over the big Louisiana Purchase Centennial—the "World's Fair" they called it—set to open in St. Louis on April 30. Millions of dollars had been spent on the Exposition to celebrate 100 years of progress.

Will knew that Colonel Mulhall and his troupe planned to be part of the big show.

Colonel Mulhall (just above the post on the second step), his daughter Lucille (beside him) and officials (on the bottom step) are backed up by the cowboys from Mulhall's Wild West Show. Will always managed to stand out in a crowd somehow. Here he is directly above Mulhall, near the top, with his hat slanted to one side, just left of the man wearing a bowler. Will won a Blue Ribbon at the 1904 World's Fair for entertainment; he wrote Betty that he "sorta valued it, somehow."

Dressed as a real Dapper Dan from the big city, Will (right) visits Betty and a friend in Jenny Lind, Arkansas, where she worked as bookkeeper when her brother Sandy Blake was manager at the railroad station there. The short stopover with his "dear old pal" was a disappointment to Will.

Facing page: A rare photo of Will (far right) with the Mulhalls. From left to right are Agnes ("Bossie") Mulhall, Lucille and Charlie Mulhall. Lucille, born October 21, 1885, was twenty the year of the St. Louis show. Will never mentioned in writing that Charlie Mulhall was born to Georgia, a young girl brought home and "adopted" by the Colonel who took her as his mistress and by her had two children who were to be raised by Mrs. Mary Agnes Mulhall. The youngest, Mildred, a noted equestrian from the age of seven, was the second child of Georgia and Colonel Mulhall. The family's relationships were a closely guarded secret until released in a pamphlet by the Territorial Museum in Guthrie and in 1985 privately published by Kathryn Stansbury of Mullhall, Oklahoma, in a book called Lucille Mulhall, Her Family, Her Life and Her Times. *The information was also related to this writer by Martha Fisch, granddaughter of Colonel Mulhall, at her home in Guthrie, Oklahoma, in 1985.*

~RC

They had sent word for him to join them. He took the train to the Mulhall ranch north of Guthrie in Oklahoma Territory, worked out details for the show, taught Lucille some rope tricks, ate lots of Mrs. Mulhall's good cooking, and then went back home to put his famous roping horse Comanche on the train with the Mulhall stock being shipped to St. Louis.

Will had made it home with the red velvet suit he had worn with the Wirth Brothers Circus where he was billed as a Mexican Rope Artist. He packed it, along with some boots and chaps and more practical garb and climbed aboard the train for yet another adventure.

It was in St. Louis that he would cross paths with Betty Blake again.

A working girl, still unmarried and not worried about it, Betty spent most of the year at Jenny Lind, Arkansas—a little town near Fort Smith—helping her brother, Sandy Blake, take care of the railroad station there.

Will ventured to Arkansas once to see her—from a distance, at a party—but caught the next train out again. He was still smitten with her but was afraid of another turn-down.

Betty always had zest for life. She enjoyed her job, but went home to Rogers and to the nearby utopian town of Monte Ne as often as possible. At the resort, her old boyfriend Tom Harvey was putting up a new rock hotel. With or without a date, Betty could join her sisters and friends as they attended dances on weekends. The "jolliest parties" at Monte Ne lasted until two o'clock A.M., the Rogers *Democrat* reported.

Benton County was famous for its fruit. Thousands of apple and peach trees lit up the countryside on sunny spring days. Maiden Blush apples were advertised. A local distiller made apple cider, peach brandy and wine from strawberries, blackberries and raspberries. Intoxicants made in Arkansas that year counted for 350,000 gallons of the total consumed in the state, the paper boasted. Just across the state line, Indians were not permitted to buy alcohol. Missionaries and tribal officers had long preached against the dangers to the red men from demon rum. It was a "known fact" that Indians "could not hold their liquor." Adventurous tribesmen went to Arkansas to slake their thirst, sometimes causing a ruckus in the "white" state before going home. Such incidents increased prejudice against Indians, including the "civilized tribes."

Unfair, of course, but such attitudes lessened Will Rogers' chances with Betty. She was independent enough to make up her own mind, but he just didn't seem to fit in with her world. Besides, she was in no hurry to be tied down to one man.

It seemed all anyone talked about in Arkansas was going to the Fair. Betty had stayed in Jenny Lind while her brother took a vacation. Now it was her turn. With a railroad pass and a sister who lived in St. Louis, she was on her way.

Will was quite a catch. He was the son of a very well-to-do father, he liked to party, sing, go to social functions, and travel the world. He was attractive to Mother and it's obvious he was to the girls in South Africa. But he knew he wasn't established enough to get married yet.

~James Blake Rogers

Still a teenager, Lucille Mulhall shows maturity in this studio portrait which Will Rogers kept in his personal collection through the years.

In her book about Will Rogers written years later, Betty said she had no idea that he would be at the Fair.

As Betty was planning her trip, Will was already in St. Louis where he wrote to his father that it was raining every day and the grounds were "a sight." It was a slow start, but the Fair would soon pick up steam.

Will lived with the Mulhall family most of the time, something not many of the other cowboys got to do.

The "big house" (the Mulhall house in St. Louis) was operated by Georgia Smith, the Colonel's mistress who traveled with the show for several years and was listed on programs as one of his daughters. (Actually, Georgia was the mother of the Colonel's son Charley and his youngest daughter Mildred; he claimed Georgia was his adopted daughter.) "Mother Mulhall," whom Will adored, never reconciled to the fast life of her husband and the "un-ladylike" conduct of her daughters, and she remained at home on the Mulhall Ranch although her Catholic faith and her innate goodness caused her to take in the son and daughter of her husband and his mistress and to raise them as her own.

If Will Rogers knew about this, he never mentioned it to anyone in his letters home. Nor did he mention any romance of his own—not even his love for Betty.

Colonel Mulhall kept a tight rein on his "girls"—all of them. Will, Tom Mix, Jim Minnick and a few other riders and ropers with him in St. Louis went with the Colonel to the bars and "took in" all the sights, probably including women at the Fair.

But the Mulhall home was a "proper" one, and the girls were treated like ladies. Lucille Mulhall and Will were stars of the troupe, and they spent lots of time together. He and the Mulhalls had always seemed to appear at the same events, even before he went to South America, and Colonel Mulhall no doubt appreciated the young cowboy's talents. The fact that Will was part Indian made no difference to the colonel, apparently. He needed the Cherokee Kid in his show. It was just that Lucille was too young to be getting serious. And she was always the real star of Mulhall's show.

Shortly after the exposition opened officially, Colonel Mulhall got into a scrape that made papers all across the country. On June 19, 1904, the *New York Times* carried a front-page story on the altercation, noting that Ernest Morgan "who was shot in the abdomen" died. Frank Reed, "boss of the Wild West show," and John Murray, a cowboy, were recovering in the Fair Grounds Hospital.

Mulhall was banished from the Fair Grounds until after the trial.

Actually, Morgan did not die and the Colonel was sentenced only to three years in prison. He appealed and eventually was freed of any serious charges, even though he later had to pay through the nose to settle with Morgan.

Later, Will wrote home to his father about it.

Will shows off his big crinoline rope trick at the Mulhall ranch as the troupe prepares for the trip to Madison Square Garden in 1905.

LINDEL HOTEL

Claremore, I.T. Tuesday Night 1904
[April 20, 1904]
My Dear Sister

Will write you to let you hear where I am   have been up to Talala, Mays, Halls Ranch, the Farm, Lanes, Lipes, and all and will leave for Tahlequah in the a.m. will only be there a bout two or three nights.   then back around by Chelsea for a day or so then on to the Fair   I heard from Mulhall and he wants me   they will send old Comanche in a day or so with a shipment that he is bringing from Sapulpa   but I wont go for a few days   Papa says it is all right with him and he seems well pleased.

   I will close

      Love to all

         Willie.

April.2. 04.

Dear Papa.

   I got your letter a few days ago but as we have started to work now I havent so much time.   We commenced to show last Saturday   we are only showing in the day time yet for our lights are not very good up yet but will be in a few days.   It is raining here every day and our grounds are a sight   I dont see any people from down there   I guess they havent started to come yet.

Things are finishing up pretty fast but it will be a good month before they are all finished.

When are you coming up   let me know before you come but I guess you will come with Maud and Sallie. . . .

I will sell you the <u>bay</u> <u>horse</u> and Buggy for $350.00 <u>Cash</u>   I kinder want to buy me a horse or two up here   now if you want him this is your chance for he is cheap at that   I give $300.00 for him when he was a colt. . . .

Well I will close   write soon and say if you want that horse   Lots of love to all

Your loving son

Willie.

Greeting From the World's Fair

[St.Louis, Mo. June 3, 1904]

Sunday morn

Dear Papa.

I got your letter yesterday and was certainly sorry to hear about the granary burning down but it was lucky that the house did not go too. Did you have any insurance.

Well I guess you will read in the paper about the big shooting scrape we had at our show.

Mulhall and the boss stable man got into the scrape and after the night show last night they met out at the front when all the people were coming out and got to shooting. A Town boy that was standing near was shot in the stomach and it is doubtful if he will get well   Johny Murray from San Angelo Texas a cowboy was trying to stop them and he was shot through the side but he will get well and Reed the fellow Mulhall was shooting at was grazed twice   Mulhall done most of the shooting and if he had only hit the fellow and killed him it would have been all right the other fellow was no good. I think the show will go on just the same   Cummins is the whitest man I ever saw and will keep all of us on just the same   I dont know how Mulhall will come out of it he is still in jail   he was offul good to us boys   They can all say what they please about Mulhall but he has done more for us boys than any man on earth   last night we were paid up in full all that they owed us   I got my expenses up there and all we will get our pay every week. The show will go on tomorrow just the same none of the Cowboys were mixed up in it   only the one that tried to stop it.

I got the boots all O.K. they were tight but if I cant wear them I will sell them to one of the boys and have him make me another pair. I dont think he made them to the measure I sent him   they are too little in the instep

All right I will sell you the horse I dont want all the money now   I will write to you in a day or so   I only want part of it when my saddle comes and you can keep the rest there with my other money   take out what those boots cost out of my money. By the way   how much does that leave beside the money for the horse. I drew $50.00 when I come up here and $12.00 for boots   how much did I have there when I come home.

I will write to you in a day or so.

Lots of love to all

Willie.

St. Louis, Mo.
June. 11. [1904]
Dear Papa

I got your letter a couple of days ago. . . . Yes I think it would be a good thing to get that other land. you can buy it if you like   you know I cant do it and I am not going to borrow the money to do it for I am out of debt and going to stay as long as I can. I kneed the money or I wouldent have asked you to buy my horse. I dont want him at all. I am going to buy me a saddle horse here and a <u>fine</u> new saddle and outfit   now you take that horse papa at just what you are willing to pay. I wont sell him to any one else at any price for you like him and I wont take him away from you.

Now if he is worth only $250.00 or $300.00 to you why only give me that and if you wont buy him why I will give him too [to] you. I wont sell him away from you. But I need this money for this other stuff worse than I need him and I wont want to use what I have in the Bank for that is for Insurance this fall. so set your price and it will suit me   or you can have him for nothing.

Say Papa give that old Bootmaker this other paper and make him make me the best and lightest Boots he can make   make him hurry up too. pay him and take it out of my money and send them to me here at the Indian Congress on the Pike. By express.

Write to me at once
Lots of love to all

Your son
Willie

[Undated. Addressed to Miss Betty Blake, 3435 Vista Ave., St. Louis, Missouri.]
Dear Old Pal

I sho was glad to hear from you, and it is only a Rumor that I dont want to see [you] right now.

Come to Delmar Track this eve if you can for it is all the combined shows of the fair in one I am working there send for me when you get to the front and I will come out and take you in

If you cant come meet me in front of the other wild west show at Delmar Garden at 8 oclock tonight

I just got your letter 5 minutes ago this is about 12:30 oclock Sunday
Come this eve sho and we will have a time tonight

Your Cowboy friend.
Will Rogers
4643 Washington Ave.
St. Louis, Mo.

Betty and her sister and friend took in the Fair sometime that summer. In the book about her famous husband, Betty related that she had happened to hear his name mentioned and asked where he was performing. She sent him a note, and the above is his immediate reply—probably hand-delivered by a messenger.

Ranchers prided themselves on being good horse traders. Dad always thought he knew how to get a good horse for the best price. He and his Dad were just playing the trading game.
~Will Rogers, Jr.

It's easy to see she had made an impression on him. Just one note, and he can't wait to see her again.
~James Blake Rogers

"There have been lassoists before, but never perhaps, such a master of the art as Will Rogers, who seems capable of doing everything with a rope except of hanging himself."
DAILY CHRONICLE

This was his first letter to Betty in three years, yet he was ready to take up where they left off as if nothing had happened!

Betty and party did go to the show that evening and watched Will perform his fantastic rope tricks dressed in his red velvet finery. Betty was more shocked at his outfit than pleased by his performance. The other girls had teased her about having a date with a Mexican rope thrower, and an Indian to boot!

As soon as Will finished he rushed to find the girls. He persuaded Betty to go to dinner with him, and the other girls left them. They later went to hear John McCormack in concert. It was late when he took her home.

During the evening Betty had told him how embarrassed she was to see him performing as a Mexican in his gaudy outfit. Shocked and hurt, he never wore it again. Still undaunted, however, he tried to persuade her to be more than just "an old pal."

Betty, in turn, tried to explain how unacceptable he was to her family and friends—an Indian-cowboy, following the Wild West shows all over the world. So irresponsible. What would her people say!

[Undated letter. Probably hand delivered.]
Dear Betty

Say do you know that it is going to be impossible for me to be with you this morning but it cant be helped and I am certainly <u>some</u> of the sorry.

But the old man told me this a.m. he had my fare home for me and I will have to go I think at 2:30 today. Also my horse I think I will get away today also.

I do hate so much to disapoint you and I would of enjoyed it immensely myself or I never would of asked you to go.

But say will you drop me a line to Claremore in the next few days and tell me where your address is please for I want to write to you <u>see</u>.

I am sorry I wont get to see you but will have to go out for my pony. My best to all the folks

Yours

Will

No evidence exists to explain the meaning of Will's sudden decision to go home. The note sounds as if he has to go home at once because his pass is ready. But the fare home by train was less than ten dollars one way, about the same for his horse. He had that much money or could have borrowed it.

We know he was staying with the Mulhalls because of the address on his first note to Betty. Lucille was on the same playbill and Will in his joy at seeing Betty again probably told Lucille about his "old girlfriend" in the audience. Or possibly Colonel Mulhall saw him with them; perhaps he had to sign the pass to get them in as Will's guests.

If Will had been "courting" Lucille—or if she had a crush on him which he encouraged—she would have been furious when he returned home so late. She and her doting father could have waited up for him and tried to "lay down the law" about other girls. Colonel Mulhall had a hot temper, as he had shown, and was paternalistic with Will.

Something serious must have happened after he arrived home late that Sunday night to make him suddenly decide to take Comanche and go home!

The Mulhall shooting was June 18. Mulhall was jailed by June 20. Papers carried the story June 23.

On the Pike
June 24. 04.
Dear Papa.

I will write you again to tell you the news. . . .

Well some of us boys that were working for Mulhall are not with the Cummins Show now. the show still goes on but Mulhall is out of it. I could of staid with them but they found out I was for Mulhall and so some of us left. Hopkins and Me are working for another smaller Wild West on the Pike and are doing just the same. It cut a big hole in the show when Mulhalls crowd left   he had all the best horses and furnished most of the show

I dont know how he will come out   he says he wants to start a show of his own and if he does he will want me. I got all even with the show every thing they owed me. I will write to you for some of that money in a few days when my saddle comes and I may get one of the Mulhall horses now. Love to all

write often

Willie .

Address me in care of. Old St. Louis Arena, On the Pike.

Colonel Zack Mulhall (center), with white hat and bow tie, surrounded by his cowboy and cowgirl cast in 1904 at the World's Fair. Far left is Bill Pickett, the famous black performer who invented the act of "bulldogging" steers by leaning over their necks, biting into their upper lips, and hanging on "like a bulldog" until the animal flipped over. The colonel was born 22 September 1847 Zachariah P. Vandeveer. Orphaned, he was raised in St. Louis by his aunt and her husband, Mr. and Mrs. Joseph Mulhall, and he took their name. Another orphan, Mary Agnes, a relative of Joseph Mulhall, was also taken in by the household. In 1875 she and Zack married.

Colorful red, white and blue mail helped advertise the big event which started out to be a celebration of the anniversary of the Louisiana Purchase and wound up being called the St. Louis World's Fair.

CUMMINS' WILD WEST SHOW

St. Louis, June 27. 1904
Dear Papa

I arrived here all.O.K.   havent done any thing yet only laying around untill the Saturday. Our Show is in connection with the Cummins Indians. there is 4. or 5. hundred of them and quite a lot of Cowboys. Mulhall is the head of the Cowboy outfit. but its all the same show. it is the biggest one at the Fair as there is 6 or 7 hundred people. We are just outside the ground but the opening is in on the pike so you see it is just the same thing as being on the pike   you go in off the pike then you are put back on the pike. I dont know how I will like it but will work till I see it all.

I will write you again soon. Pony is doing fine. I wont trade you that horse of mine but you keep him on. Love to all

Willie (dont Publish this)

St. Louis, June 27 1904

Dear Sister and all

 got here all O.K. it was cold but is warm now   only staying out at Mulhalls house   living fine   till Saturday

 Our Show is the biggest one at the fair   600 people   we are in connections with Cummins Indian Congress. Mulhall only has the Cowboy part of it. part of it is on the pike and part off of the Fair ground   but it is all the same   you see it all and are put back onto the pike. Tell Theo [McSpadden] I promised to write to him but Mulhall said tonight he would   so tell him I am the only Territory boy here. There is lots of good Cowboys from Buffalo Bill's and other wild west shows here so a man will do good to hold a job   I will write you soon. Write soon. Willie.

St. Louis, Mo.

On the Pike.

Indian Congress

July 2. 1904

My Dear Papa

 I got your letter yesterday and the check   thanks for answering so soon. I am at the Cummins Show now. Mulhall and his folks are not doing anything.

 I see Jess B - [Dr. Jesse Bushyhead] and all the girls from home   they have all been to the show

 When are you coming up   You better hurry up for I may go home any time   I have seen about all the fair.

 I hope Mays Baby is better by now for I certainly feel sorry for her   she works so hard.

 I may sell my Pony when I get ready to leave but I need him now.

 I will show you all around when you come up.

 Well I will stop   write soon.

your loving son,

Willie

 Dr. Jesse Bushyhead, son of Principal Chief Dennis Bushyhead and Elizabeth Alabama Schrimsher, was first cousin to Will Rogers. Elizabeth and Will's mother were sisters. Dr. Bushyhead was a highly respected physician. Will claimed him as his favorite cousin and later helped pay for his specialized training in New York City.

 "Old Scrap," in the next letter, is good-natured Gazelle Lane, sister to Cap Lane and a part of Will's social group at home. The other girls lived not far from the old Rogers Ranch.

Saturday
on the Pike
[Before July 4, 1904]
My Dear Sisters

I got Mauds letter yesterday   was sho glad to hear from her   but say Sis you spoke of a Hdhq. [Handkerchief] I sent you. You are mistaken I dident send you any thing   it was some one else   if I did I was asleep   I havent seen any thing worth sending   it was some of your numerous friends.

Well I see the Girls from home   old Scrap dont get to have much fun   she has to stay all the time with Ida [Collins, half sister to "Scrap" Lane] and they dont come around very often   but Rosan Harange and Anna Sevier are the fast set   I see them often. they were all in the show the other night and I had them Ride in the Stage Coach when the Indians held it up. they seemed to of had a time

Jess B___ was in last night   I see lots of people here now that is from home

When are you coming up   you better hurry for I may go home in a month or so but when you all come bring Papa and I will show you around.

I am back with the Cummins Show now

Mulhalls are not doing anything yet

The 4th will be a big day here   I guess we will show all day.

Business is picking up now   more people are coming and it is all open now.

I hope Mays Baby is better by now

Well I will stop   write soon   Love to all
                    Willie.

Will trained his horses carefully to work with him while he roped. Although Teddy, the horse here, is not a "trick" horse, his reactions had to be right on the dime to keep him out of the orchestra pit.

St. Louis, Mo.
July 4. 1904.
My Dear Papa

I got your letter a few days ago but have been taring around with Maud and Sallie so that I havent had time to write. Sallie and Tom suddenly went home I think little May had been writing to her how Clem had been going on and that she had to do all the work and it worried Sallie and they went home but they seen a lot while here for they went all the time

Maud and Cap are just going from early till late I tell you they sure do see it all they are going home Sunday. I am with them most of the time for I dont have much to do during the week.

When are you coming up I never have had that check cashed yet I told them to let that Saddle go that I ordered as I dont need it I may need some of this money but not much as I think I will be there before long. I will stop write soon love to all

your son   Willie .
4643 Washington Av.

Chicago
Wednesday
[Posted October 29, 1904]
My Dear old Pal

Say I just got your little letter that had come up from home after I left I went back to St. Louis for a day or so then up here I don't like it much up here I am doing all O.K. I dont know how long I will be here I think I will be back in St. Louis soon at the Columbia . . . .

. . . then I will get my horse and take him along and make a big act out of it.

Say Betty I was offuly sorry I could not keep my promise that day But papa wired me to come on some business and I went that day at 2:30. We would of had some fun that day "and not got Loaded either."

Oh but things are on the Bum down home I dident do a thing down there this trip only see the folks I will be there Christmas and I would like to see you some old time there.

But say I am Goatinskying here just as though I knew all about you. And had things all fixed. And I only seen you a minute and then only found out you were not married that is about all Lord knows how near it you may be for I know about how you would stand with all those Rail Road Gisables and you know according to form we both should have matrimonied long ago It wouldent do for this young gang to look at our teeth you know

Now what I want to shake to you is this if you are contracted for or have a steady fellow why please put me down and out in the 1st round. But if not then please file my application.

Out of paper kindly take a back track.

Do you know I havent had a girl since I left on that trip as Kate was my last. on the tour I had all I could do to live much less sport a damsel and when I come back I felt so out of place and behind the times I was ashamed and they will tell

Will Rogers went home in mid-August, spending a week with his family. When he left, he went through Tahlequah to visit kinfolks and returned by way of Arkansas. He still had not mended his fences with Betty after their encounter at the Fair. But the trip was a failure, as far as his courtship of Betty was concerned.

~RC

". . . IF YOU ARE CONTRACTED FOR. . . PLEASE PUT ME DOWN AND OUT IN THE 1ST ROUND."

They both knew they were meant for each other, but they were too stubborn to admit it.
~James Blake Rogers

you at home now that I am a girl hater. shows what they know about it. I could just love—a girl about your caliber see you know I was always kinder headstrong about you anyway. But I always thought that a cowboy dident quite come up to your Ideal. But I am plum Blue up here and kneed consolation and havent a soul that I can confide in. now for Good luck, hard luck and no luck at all Experiences I am the limit.

And then I am about froze Is it warmer down at Jenny Wren than it is here If so I am only awaiting transportation. and at odd times when you are not <u>Kidding</u>, Conductors, brakemen and such, I will teacheth thou the manly art of Lasso Manipulating then you are <u>doomed.</u>

Now I must reluctantly draw this Long distance interview to a close hoping some of these broad minded views of mine (especially the one pretaining to said application) have met with your kind approbation
I am yours
  Any old time
  Bill, thats all.
 By the way
 Subject this penmanship to rigid treatment of <u>guessing</u>, then serve.
 I cant give you an address
But this will reach me

Please write soon and a long letter.
c/o Pike Hotel
 St. Louis
 Mo.
 Pike Entrance

Betty (in the front row, with gloves) was puzzled by the cool way Will treated her when she attended a house party given by Maud Lane for her brother. He is as far as he can get from the girl he'd courted by mail from all over the world, being hugged by pretty sometime-girlfriend Ada Foreman. Others in the wagon in which they'd driven that day to visit Clem Rogers in Claremore were Ida Collins, step-daughter of Dr. Lane and half-sister of "Scrap," beside Betty; standing in the wagon with a cigar in his mouth, Dick Parris; Tom Lane; Taylor Foreman; and Denny Lane. Seated are Bess Schrimsher, Will's cousin; Shasta Lane; her sister Gazelle "Scrap" Lane; Miss Foreman; and Will.

A major turning point in Will's young life occurred during late summer and early fall. He moved up from Wild West shows to vaudeville. Because he had free time between weekend performances with Mulhall, and because he was attending shows in St. Louis and talking to entertainers and showmen, Will was hired for a week's performance in a St. Louis burlesque house, the Columbia Theater. The owner of the Columbia also owned a house in Chicago and he sent Will there for a week to do rope tricks and make funny comments on stage. That month he had his first experience entertaining in a vaudeville show and with just the ropes alone. He must have made a hit, or he wouldn't have been invited to Chicago.

Even though he knew he made folks laugh—and feel good after seeing him on the stage or in person—he still believed his real opportunities for fame and fortune lay in his skill with the ropes. And his most newsworthy tricks involved roping a running horse and rider as well as roping from horseback. In the advertisement for "Col. Zack Mulhall's Congress of Rough Riders and Ropers" at the Delmar Race Track, October 1, 1904, Will was listed as "Cherokee Indian—Most expert fancy roper in America."

If he could get on stage and become a "real" entertainer instead of just a cowboy in the Wild West shows, maybe Betty would look at him differently. He would go see her again and try to let her know what he had planned. It was only for a few minutes, but at least he got nerve enough to begin their correspondence again.

He continued to practice every day, hour after hour. Every trick he saw performed by another roper he kept trying until he could do it, too. And usually better!

Will's reference to checking their teeth would have been understood by Betty. It was one way to judge the age of a horse. She had turned twenty-five on September 9, but she never admitted her age to Will. Even her marriage license is incorrect as is her death certificate. Women simply didn't tell their ages in her era—especially if they were older than their husbands—and she may have forgotten it herself over the years. But the 1880 census recorded her as eleven months old and the Blake family Bible lists her birth as September 9, 1879. Betty didn't think Will's comment was one bit funny.

Jenny Lind, where Betty still worked for the railroad was transformed to "Jenny Wren" for comic effect. A "jenny" is a female wren, as Will would have known.

Back to the Pike
Saturday Night
[Posted November 6, 1904]

Well Bravo Betty.

I knew you wouldent shake an old pal when he was down and out of mail for yours is the only news since I left home. and I am deeply grieved to think that I was so unthoughtful as to refer to something that you could in the least get offended at but it was all a joke meaning we both should of married <u>each other</u> or somebody by now <u>sabe</u>.

Say that old Spending a day down home strikes me just fine and dandy and it makes me want to go home all the more for Xmas.

I could of went East from Chicago but dident care to till after Xmas. I made good in C—— and may return to play two other Theatres there   dont know for sure yet about using the horse

He's going to go whole hog into show business.
~James Blake Rogers

"WELL BRAVO BETTY. I KNEW YOU WOULDENT SHAKE AN OLD PAL WHEN HE WAS DOWN AND OUT. . . ."

But as usual I never know anything one day in advance. I am here for a big combined show to be held inside the Worlds fair grounds one day next week Range Day

My Pony is still here   all the Mulhalls people and stock went to Oklahoma but I hear will be back to show here a week from Sunday and want me here then. I will be here for the Fairs show but dont think I will be for the Mulhall show.

I know my letters are of great interest with nothing but work and shows and all that stuff that is of no interest to no one   I am getting homesick and want to go home and stay   not for a day or so but a month or two. I am tired of all this Hurrah for awhile.

Now write to me soon Kid. (Excuse my familarity) but that is my star expression. I always enjoyed your letters so much for I know you have a head of your own. Well I know a few more than when I last knew you if my actions dont show it   but Betty Honestly how can I change and do different   I havent been a bad fellow and never did anything bad only just foolish and a spendthrift and blew in a little fortune all my own   not a cent of my Fathers as people might think only mine

But at that I have done some good   I spent it on other people   I have done lots for other boys there and given my people lots   now I am making my own way and dont feel like staying at home for people would say I was living off my Father who of course is pretty well fixed and would do anything for me.

I still own the old home place and farm and am even with the world and am as happy as can be but thats why I dont stay at home

Now Dear I will expect to hear from you soon and a nice long letter

Your dearest friend,
Will

Best to Sandy and the Folks
Pike Hotel
Pike Entrance   St. Louis.

C. V. ROGERS
BANK BUILDING

Claremore, Ind. Ter., Nov 20th. 1904.
My dearest Pal

Well Betsy I put off writing you for a day or so till I knew where I was going well I am back at home and think I will be here till after Xmas anyway   I just lobbed in from the Pike today   We had a great show there in the Worlds Fair Live stock Pavalian for the benefit of the visiting cattlemen and oh, there was a crowd there   President Francis of the fair and a bunch of officials and he presented me with a First Prize Blue Ribbon of the worlds fair when I finished my act and I am kinder foolish about my little Ribbon.

Then on sunday they had another one of those combined shows (I guess you have heard of those) at Delmar   well we done our part and the finish was to of been a head on collision   well they set one old enjine at one end and then they tried to run the other into it   well there was a little up hill to start and the old

He wants her to know he is not just that shiftless Rogers boy who lives a few miles out of town.

~James Blake Rogers

"I JUST TURNED MYSELF LOOSE AND OH I SHO DID ENJOY MYSELF."

Overleaf: Will's postcard to Betty from New York was printed on leather, but it went through the mail. Will says he was a hit in Madison Square Garden "and I am letting my head return to its natural size before going home."

enjine couldent get up and the Cow boys all hooked on and pulled the enjine up the <u>grade</u> and me <u>four flushing</u> as usual I roped the head light and jerked it off and run all over the place dragging it and caused the biggest laugh of all   "it was a shame to take their money".

You railway people should of seen it   it was a gorgeous Spectacle.

Say how about that Navata [Nowata, I.T.] trip   I am here and will sho you a time any old time.

My Pony went through here and was not unloaded and went on to Mulhall Oklahoma with their horses now I will have to go out and ride him back.

There is a big Ball Masque on tap here for Thanksgiving   I dont know if I will attend   cant you come up and I will guarantee you a good time   I will sho go then

Well Kid I was a bit creepy when I wrote you before but then even the gayest of us have our serious spells and then I kinder wanted to tell you anyway for I dont like to "sail under false colors" in any over estimation and not for the world would I do so with you for you are my style through and through.

See here Betty Blake   a longer letter from you next time and take care it is not one that I will have to take to my overcoat to read for the other was on the chilly order

Write me right away will you please

> Yours
>> Bill .
> Claremore
>> Ind. Ter.

Bank Building

Claremore, Ind. Ter., Nov 30. 04.

Miss Betsy

My Dearest friend

Well I sho did get your letter and with all that big envelope Mo. P. paper I thought the Railway was notifying me of a law suit. not that I was expecting one but you never know   Well Thanksgiving is a dead one and oh that Ball   it was the kind we used to make long ago   Oh there was a lot of the old gang there and on the square I had more old fun than I have had for some distance.

I was masked as a kind of a Simple Simon or a Hobo or something and had them all fooled to death   some got next [to my identity] when I had acted a fool so long and said yes that Bill for he is acting so natural. I just turned myself loose and oh I sho did enjoy myself.

We will have some kind of a Ball Xmas and New Years and I am plotting very deeply for your presence.

Well Kid I am here I guess for the winter as my Father is in very bad health and I am the only one who can stay with him all the time and he dont want me to go east after Xmas so I am having a time as usual   so will remain

Now you come up here and stay a long time and I will show you a time. My best old Boy Pal lives in Navata [Nowata] and I will see him when you are up there, <u>see</u>

I know you had some fun at home   I saw some one you know here the other day, Joe Reavis, from Van Buren   he lives here   do you know him?

I am keeping up my Rope practice pretty good and I have a nice little rope for you to start in with when you come up so beware

Now look here Betty Blake you had better write me a fine long letter at once or—

Now you come on up here see. I want to see you bad.

your admirer
Bill
Claremore. I.T.

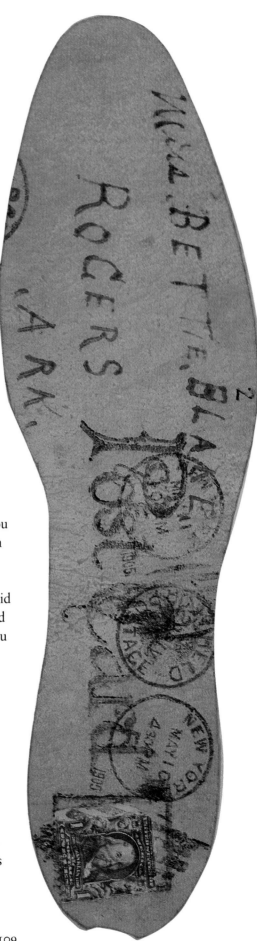

The Missouri-Pacific Railroad is often called *Mo Pac.*

Theodore McSpadden—a nephew of Tom McSpadden's and one of Will's roping buddies—lived in Nowata.

Will spent Thanksgiving and December at home—most of the time with his sisters in Chelsea. The *Progress* of December 10 reported he'd gone to Mulhall after his horse Comanche "which had been cared for by Lucille since Will left St. Louis."

C. V. ROGERS
BANK BUILDING

Claremore, Ind. Ter. Dec 16. 1904

My Dearest Friend,

Well Betty I just got in here from up to the farm and around last night and found your letter here   of course its only a rumor that I am glad to hear from you for the way you "jolly me along" is mearily kidding me about what a jollier I am why Lady you have on the dead thieving square got me beat a thousand ways from the centre as a laugh distributer.

Say <u>podner</u> that extensive trip you are contemplating Xmas   are you not afraid you will get homesick staying away so long   come and stay a month anyway and we might scare up something but I will try my best and get a birdseye view of you somewhere on the trip   but you see I have to spend Xmas with my folks at Chelsea   that is not on this road and I am plotting densly to try and strike a plan.

I am thinking of going to the city in a day or so   either K. C. or St. L.   I dont know which.

Now when you write tell me once more just when you will be up here and go back and I sho do want to see you. Well it is train time so Goodbye

All the time
Bill .

As far back as he could remember, Will loved to do three things—peck around on the piano and sing, twirl a rope, and eat good home cooking. At the Mulhalls he got his fill of all three, and, besides, they appreciated his talents in the arena.

Will twirls a small "wedding ring" around Lucille Mulhall, whom he taught to twirl the big "crinoline" with a 90-foot rope. Both are in stage clothes. The picture was likely made near the frontier town of Mulhall, named for Lucille's colorful father, an agent for the Santa Fe and later for the Frisco railroad. The portrait of Lucille below shows her to be feminine enough for the tabloids, although she won plenty of column inches in the legitimate newspapers along with her pins and ribbons, and was highly praised by President Theodore Roosevelt. When he was vice-president to McKinley, Roosevelt visited the Mulhalls for a wolf hunt; Lucille, then fourteen, caught a wolf and had it stuffed and presented to the vice-president. For skill and courage, she took a back seat to none of the cowboys. Her mother and father both had attended Notre Dame and her mother was distressed that her young ladies spent their time in such activities.

Maybe he was more cowboy than Indian, Will decided. And when he was in front of an audience, he could be either or both with no problem.

He also enjoyed the good-natured rivalry in the roping ring and the horseplay that went on in the bunkhouse at night. Here he got better acquainted with Tom Mix—establishing a friendship that stretched into Hollywood and Beverly Hills. And with Jim Minnick, the horseman who was handy with a rope and who also bred horses for Wild West shows and even for the polo games becoming so popular in the East.

In late January, Will became a member of the Claremore Masonic Lodge #53. He signed his petition "William Penn Rogers, farmer, Claremore, I.T." Then it was back to Mulhall on the train, home again for a few days, and back to Mulhall. Surely it was a romantic interest that pulled him there as well as the Wild West shows.

He returned to Claremore to receive his degree in Masonry on February 18, 1905—the coldest day in recorded history there. It was below zero in double digits.

Will made a short trip to St. Louis, perhaps to attend court for Colonel Mulhall. Clem was better and up to enlarging his livery stable and running the bank.

On Sunday, March 12, Will and his father were in Chelsea having dinner with Sallie when a telegram came inviting Will to go with the Tulsa Commercial Club on a special train traveling east. It was a booster trip with sixty business promoters who would travel through Missouri, Iowa and Illinois, stopping at over a dozen towns to have a parade, furnish entertainment and talk with folks about the opportunities in Tulsa. His reputation as an entertainer was spreading. Will was the hit of the show. He played in the band, marched down the streets and then did his rope tricks and talked to the crowds. Local papers all had something to say about him. One newspaper said, "Chief Bill Rogers gave an excellent exhibition of rope throwing that won him the admiration and plaudits of the crowd."

To Muncie and Marion and Terra Haute and Springfield he went, and back through St. Louis. He was no more than home when he left again for Fort Worth, Texas, and the International Stockman's Association to "represent Claremore."

On April Fool's Day, he wrote a letter to his father from Mulhall. He was helping to get things ready for New York where the cowboys and Indians would present a Wild West show in Madison Square Garden during the prestigious New York Horse Show.

He shipped his fancy new saddle and Comanche with the other Mulhall stock, but he turned down a chance to perform for the president in Washington, D.C., in order to wait for the birth of his new nephew, Sallie and Tom McSpadden's son Maurice. Then he headed out to catch up to the group. But he made a stopover in Rogers, Arkansas.

The show at Madison Square Garden on Friday, April 28 made the *New York Herald* with a colorful story titled "Wild Steer Stampedes Audience at Madison Square Garden—Escapes from the Arena and Scrambles Up Passageway and Dashes Behind the Boxes, Chased by Cowboys—Women and Children in Panic—Band Flees in Terror." The red steer that Lucille Mulhall was to rope lunged up the aisle into the boxes, leaping "with the agility of a cat" all the way up to the second tier, scattering members of the audience and orchestra musicians in its wake. Will lassoed the animal. However, the steer broke loose, after dragging Will over seats and down the aisle, and

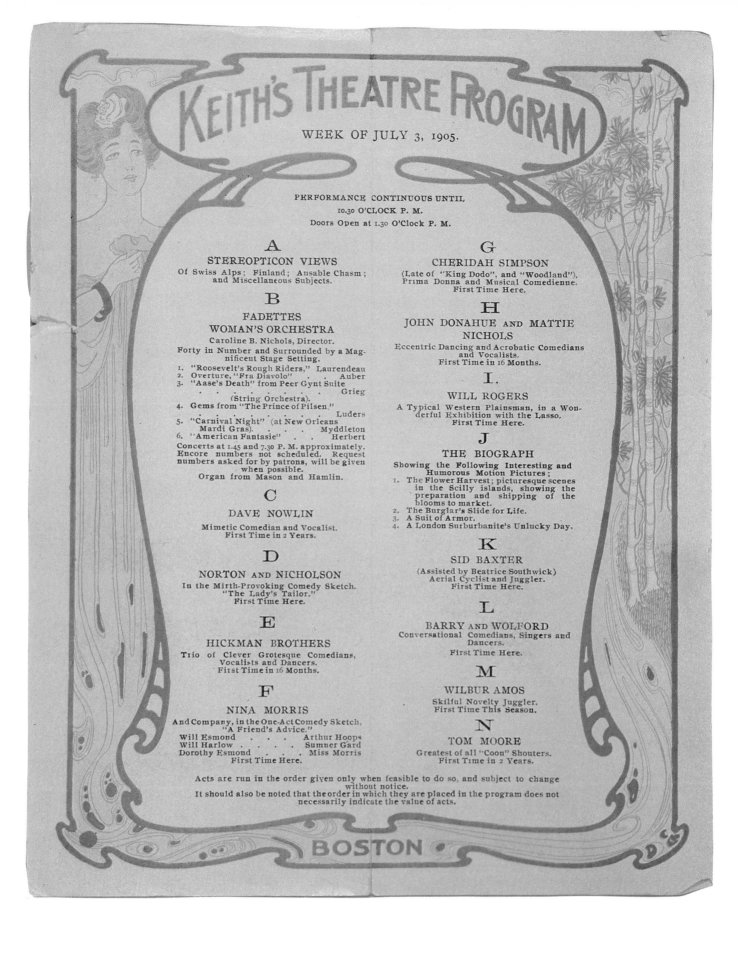

KEITH'S THEATRE PROGRAM

WEEK OF JULY 3, 1905.

PERFORMANCE CONTINUOUS UNTIL
10.30 O'CLOCK P. M.
Doors Open at 1.30 O'Clock P. M.

A
STEREOPTICON VIEWS
Of Swiss Alps; Finland; Ausable Chasm;
and Miscellaneous Subjects.

B
FADETTES
WOMAN'S ORCHESTRA
Caroline B. Nichols, Director.
Forty in Number and Surrounded by a Mag-
nificent Stage Setting.
1. "Roosevelt's Rough Riders," Laurendeau
2. Overture, "Fra Diavolo" . . . Auber
3. "Aase's Death" from Peer Gynt Suite
. . . . Grieg
(String Orchestra).
4. Gems from "The Prince of Pilsen"
. . . . Luders
5. "Carnival Night" (at New Orleans
Mardi Gras). . . . Myddleton
6. "American Fantasie" . . Herbert
Concerts at 1.45 and 7.30 P. M. approximately.
Encore numbers not scheduled. Request
numbers asked for by patrons, will be given
when possible.
Organ from Mason and Hamlin.

C
DAVE NOWLIN
Mimetic Comedian and Vocalist.
First Time in 2 Years.

D
NORTON AND NICHOLSON
In the Mirth-Provoking Comedy Sketch.
"The Lady's Tailor."
First Time Here.

E
HICKMAN BROTHERS
Trio of Clever Grotesque Comedians,
Vocalists and Dancers.
First Time in 16 Months.

F
NINA MORRIS
And Company, in the One-Act Comedy Sketch,
"A Friend's Advice."
Will Esmond . . . Arthur Hoops
Will Harlow . . . . Sumner Gard
Dorothy Esmond . . . Miss Morris
First Time Here.

G
CHERIDAH SIMPSON
(Late of "King Dodo", and "Woodland"),
Prima Donna and Musical Comedienne.
First Time Here.

H
**JOHN DONAHUE AND MATTIE
NICHOLS**
Eccentric Dancing and Acrobatic Comedians
and Vocalists.
First Time in 16 Months.

I.
WILL ROGERS
A Typical Western Plainsman, in a Won-
derful Exhibition with the Lasso.
First Time Here.

J
THE BIOGRAPH
Showing the Following Interesting and
Humorous Motion Pictures;
1. The Flower Harvest; picturesque scenes
in the Scilly islands, showing the
preparation and shipping of the
blooms to market.
2. The Burglar's Slide for Life.
3. A Suit of Armor.
4. A London Surburbanite's Unlucky Day.

K
SID BAXTER
(Assisted by Beatrice Southwick)
Aerial Cyclist and Juggler.
First Time Here.

L
BARRY AND WOLFORD
Conversational Comedians, Singers and
Dancers.
First Time Here.

M
WILBUR AMOS
Skilful Novelty Juggler.
First Time This Season.

N
TOM MOORE
Greatest of all "Coon" Shouters.
First Time in 2 Years.

Acts are run in the order given only when feasible to do so, and subject to change
without notice.
It should also be noted that the order in which they are placed in the program does not
necessarily indicate the value of acts.

BOSTON

stamped back to the arena, where half a dozen cowboys confined him. Lucille calmly went on with her act, roping the steer as planned "with apparent ease."

To the homefolks it was just another trip for the wandering Cherokee, but this one was to take a new turn that would establish his identity as no other had.

Putnam House
May 8, 1905
My Dear Papa

Well I guess you think that I am not going to write but I will at last . . . had a great week here . . . I will stay a week or so yet and do some work on the stage as I made a great success the week I worked here but I might be there any time

your loving son

Willie

[reverse] To Kates

[Editor of the Claremore *Progress*]

I never did get to write you but here is a clipping or two I made the biggest hit here I ever dreamed of in my roping act and finished my good luck by catching the wild steer that went clear up into the circles of the garden among the people I will stay here to do some theatre work for a while.

Yours   Will Rogers

PUTNAM HOUSE

June 3, 1905
My Dear old Pal [Betty]

Say you are the extremity, you are one Kid that puts me in the guess list for fair. its me to the dopey gang when I unfold one of your packages   you can make me feel better and worse than any one I know.

Look here Bettie dont think I am Kidding you   on the level you are my best old pal and I like you for it and again I hate you for not allowing me to be more.

You always kept me at a distance all right   you know Bettie thats why I dident write to you after the Nowata affair.

I just sized you up that night and I thought No she dont give a d—— only to be a good old pal and honest it hurt me and I said I wont even write to her for your letters are no encouragement to me   I wish to G——that I could look at it as you do but I cant. I know you might laugh and say old Bill is just handing out this line as he always does but it aint so I swear   You know I have had some experience and have been some to the flirt talk with lots of them but this has been maturing for years. I got to love someone and it dont take me many guesses to tell who it is.

What would be my object in telling you all this and you there and me here if it wasent so and so whatever you do believe me even if you wont do anything else

I know you will say this is a foolish letter and that you dont like me in this new role but thats why I am taking chances on losing a friend simply because you got to know some time

Here is a couple of clippings from a swell horse show I worked at in the swell suburb of N.Y. I have worked on the stage using my horse and I open June 12 at the swellest vaudeville house in N.Y. I think I can make good I am on a fair road

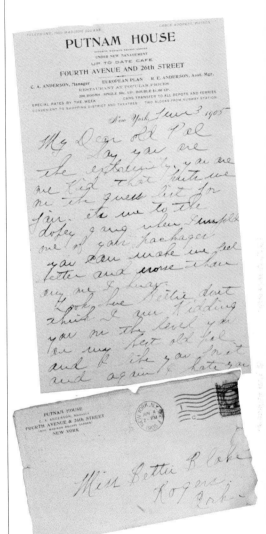

Facing page: Finally Will was in a real printed program in a real vaudeville show. He kept the program.

to success in my line . . . I am acquainted with some pretty big men here and stand pat with them. But there a little lacking some old place. See if you cant offer some remedy for it in the way of honestly good encouragement   only truthfully tell me that you could some time learn to love me just a little and I bet there will be a cowboy doing 100% better act and feeling fine.

Now Sister Bettie I am as honest in this and if you dont like me a little bit Bettie dont even write to me for it would make me all the worse.

But I hope to — you will be able to write to this <u>Nutty</u> <u>foolish</u> <u>cowboy</u> you will then get pictures in bunches.

Yours
Bill.

PUTNAM HOUSE

June 3 1905
My Dear Sister

Well I know you all have forgotten how to write   it is generally me but not this time   here I am writing to hear from you.

Well I am still in our big city and will be for some time yet. I am getting my act in good shape to do some good and make some money. I have had it on the stage using a horse and all. Here is a little Clipping from a paper at a swell horse show I worked at in the Swell Suburs where seats the cheapest were $20.00   I got $25 a show   worked three shows.   only engaged just for a little novelty for the big bugs.

All the Mulhall outfit have gone back but one boy [Jim Minnick] and I   he is selling his pony here.

It takes time to get my act started but I start the 12 of June over the Keith Vaudeville Circuit the swellest in the east.   I will take a spin down home as soon as I get a little money and time which wont be later than August 1st sure

I sold old Comanche to a man in N.Y. and Mulhall sneakingly bought him from him and he owns him now for little Mildred   he bought him when he found out I was going to stay east   he thought I would follow him as he was mad because I quit them.

But here is good news for you all it is either stage and make a good living or no show business <u>at all</u> for me never to the Wild West show any more.

I have the finest little pony that is really better than old Comanche for he is some younger and he works fine on the stage. he suits me better for my present work than Comanche   I bought him from Mulhall. I will send you some pictures in a few days as I have to have some made to use in my act

Well I will close   write when you can
Lots of Love to all

yours
Willie

send this down to Papa
None of this is for publication only to let my <u>own</u> folks know how I am doing see

Will knew he was a hit when he told things in his funny way, but he refused to believe he could succeed without his horse and rider and his trusty rope.

~RC

June 18, 1905

My Dear Sis and gang

   I got your letter and was glad to hear from you   Well I am doing all O.K.   got started last Monday at Keiths Theatre and finished last night my first actual week using the pony and all. the act was a hit from the start   I am being offered lots of work   I go this week tomorrow night to Hammersteins Roof Garden for a week that is the swelest Vaudeville place in America and it is a great thing to be able to work there   they sent for me too   I dident ask them for the work   if I go good there I am alright and every one says I will be a hit there.   Oh it is a grand place on top of one of the big buildings just like a garden covered over with a sliding glass roof   Keiths was a fine indoor theatre but this has them all beat for the summer. My pony is a peach. send this to papa   tell him I got the letter and papers and I see he is quite a big thing down there making so much money   I will be down to help him spend some of it.

   I go to Philadelphia week after next to play Keiths place there
   Write all letters to the Putnam House   N.Y. City.

   Here is a Programme of last week and Bill from this mornings paper of the people that will play at Hammersteins Next week. I take my pony up on the Roof on the elevator about 10 or 15 stories. hope I dont fall off.

   did you and papa get the photos.
                    Your loving brother
                        Willie

Boston, Mass.

July 5th. 05

My Dear Sisters

   Well here I am in Boston and doing all O.K.   Will play here till Saturday night then back to N.Y. and play there for 4 weeks   1 week at Proctors Theatre then back to Hammersteins Roof Garden for 3 straight weeks I like to work in N.Y.   I have my pony here shipped him up on the boat   the act went fine every place so far.

I want to get home for a few weeks in August or September   here is clipping from the Boston papers   you see it is the way I do my work is what takes with them and a few funny things I say.

   Write to me at the Putnam House write often
   I will close did you get last weeks clipping from Philadelphia I sent you
        Love to all
            Willie

July 16, 1905

My Dear Papa

   I have been waiting to write to you till after pay day so I could send you the money that I borrowed from Godbey $100   I dont know when it is due and I had $30 in the bank to my credit   so you can pay the interest and it should leave me

"Will Rogers made his debut at this house, being billed as 'The World's Champion Lasso Manipulator.' To even the layman it was apparent that he had some right to his claim, and the audience marveled at his skill."
From a review of a performance at Keith's in New York 12 June 1905.

"Another of the topliners at Keith's this week is the lasso thrower, Will Rogers, and his bronco. They are typical of the plains and both do some clever stunts. The man part of the show does some exceedingly clever lassoing with a rope of marvelous length. Dressed in chaps, red shirt and sombrero, not forgetting the spurs, he tosses the lariat as if to the manner born. And the bronco, you expect him every monent to butt through the scenery or jump out into the orchestra circle, but he is really a well-behaved little horse."
The BOSTON HERALD 4 July 1905.

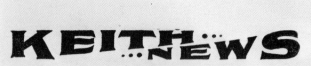

THE ONLY DRAMATIC PAPER PUBLISHED IN RHODE ISLAND

Vol. 2.   PROVIDENCE, R. I., NOVEMBER 20, 1905.   No. 13.

The Keith News
VOL. 2. No. 13.

One drop of ink makes the world think. Sweet are the uses of advertisements.

PUBLISHED WEEKLY

By mail, one cent a copy, Thirty cents per volume, payable in advance.

The Keith Theatres and Vaudeville Performances may be Seen in Eighteen of the Principal Cities, as follows:

PHILADELPHIA
NEW YORK
BOSTON
BALTIMORE
PITTSBURG
BUFFALO
DETROIT
ROCHESTER
CLEVELAND
PROVIDENCE
PAWTUCKET
WASHINGTON
SYRACUSE
YOUNGSTOWN
PORTLAND
SALEM
TORONTO, CANADA
LONDON, ENGLAND

Next week will be truly a week for thanksgiving. Mr. Albee is endeavoring to give both his patrons and his employes cause for giving thanks—the former by an exceptionally entertaining program as can be seen from the list of acts announced on another page, and the latter by a big Thanksgiving dinner, for the theatre attaches and the members of the Pawtucket Albee Company.

WILL ROGERS, "THE LARIAT KING."

Perhaps the most interesting entertainer we anticipate presenting this season is Will Rogers, known as "The Lariat King." Rogers is at once a character compelling admiration by his skill with the lasso and mirth by his quaint humor. A year ago had any one foretold that a demonstration of rope throwing could be made sufficiently interesting and entertaining to attract big crowds, the prediction would have been greeted with smiles of derision. Today it is an established fact and Will Rogers who is now drawing a big salary at the leading vaudeville houses and is admittedly the most popular novelty of the vaudeville season is the man who has done it. Like young Lochinvar, Rogers comes "out of the West." His home is in Indian Territory, and he is part-blooded Cherokee Indian, his father, a judge, bank president and a senator, being one of the leadnig members of the Cherokee Nation. He is only about twenty-five years old, slender, square-shouldered, alert, keen-eyed, clear complexioned and with an unmistakable, inimitable Western accent. From the time he was two years old, Rogers says he used to "rope" his mother's turkeys out on the ranch, and prairie dogs and other things not meant to be lassoed. "When," said Rogers, with a far-away look in his steel-grey eyes, "father sent me to school to try to make a preacher of me, I couldn't curb my fondness for the lariat, and as there was nothing else to lasso except the professors—by accident, of course—I wasn't popular and was sent back *(Continued on Page 4.)*

A WORTHY CHARITY.

A big benefit concert will be given at this theatre on Sunday evening next, November 26th, in aid of the suffering Russian Jews, whose awful fate in far-off Russia has horrified the entire civilized world. Coming as it does at this time, just after the exhaustive war, the calamity which has befallen Russian Jews is a double one and people all over the country are uniting in an endeavor to alleviate the awful condition of the unfortunate people. The Keith Theatres are rarely opened on Sunday (the last time was when the benefit for the Galveston Flood Sufferers, when something like $1,000 were made) because of the fact that our employes with continuous performances work pretty hard during the week. Mr. Keith and Mr. Albee, however, are ever anxious to aid those in need and with the hearty co-operation being given the concert promises to be a pronounced financial success. Several prominent professionnal people, of the legitimate and the vaude- *(Continued on Page 2)*

With only slight exaggeration, the Keith News boosted the "Lariat King" in several states.

about $25 there   I am working in N.Y. and will be here till August 14th   I play 4 weeks in one theatre.   I want to come home perhaps after that

It is sure hot here
I sent Gordon Lane $20 for wintering my old pony
Write me all the news when you can
I will close   Love to all
Willie

New York, July 24 1905
My Dear Papa

I just got your letter this morning and was glad to hear from you

Well I am still working in N.Y. City will be here 3 weeks yet at one theatre . . .

Here is $50 you can keep for me as I am going to save up a little money . . . .

Thousands of people died here from the heat during the hot spell

Well I will close write often
Love to all
Willie
Maud is going to pay my insurance when its due for the ring.

New York
July 26, 1905
My Dear Sis and gang

Just got Sallies letter and one from Papa telling of Mays baby dying which was too bad, but it was never strong was it. How is Mays health and how are they getting on   I dont hear from her.

I want to get down there in September . . . if I can. . . will be at work for the next 6 weeks steady havent lost a day since I started in but I am homesick now . . . . I am still a Hammersteins Roof Garden on my 3rd week and have two more yet as they gave me another the other day   then I go for a week to Rockaway Beach on Long Island a swell summer resort. I will get plenty of baths (which I need)   the theatre is out over the water, then the week of Aug 21 I go a short piece from there to Manhattan Beach another resort for a week   then Aug. 28 to Newark N.J. for a week that is right near here   then I will try and come home.

Well I will close
write often
Lots of love to all
Willie

New York, Aug 10 1905

My Dearest Bettie

Well I landed your letter a day or so ago. Why dont you write often for if you knew how anxious I always am to get a letter from you

Well its the same old thing   out twice a day and do a little bum Roping   hear them holler and applaud   smile   bow and then do it again the next day   I am still on the Roof. Finish Sunday Night then to the beach and I will take a few <u>long needed</u> baths

But here's what breaks my heart   I wont get to see you in September   I had planned to, and a manager wanted me for 5 weeks about then   I told him I was going home but of course if he would pay me so much (I wont tell you) I would take it and I dident think he'd kinder do it but yesterday he sent me the contract and I had to take it   I will finish Oct. 9, and then Willie for Rogers and the old I.T. for a few weeks   and say I can get engaged for Europe so go to piling up your doll rags and prepare to see the world as the <u>wife</u> of Rogers the Lariet Expert. this might sound like a joke but its certainly so   I go to about Nov 1st if I take it   play several weeks in Paris then London and Berlin   back to the Ark. and I.T. hills for the Summer of 1906.   Now, what better than that, can you beat that.   get to thinking and we will pull it off if you are willing

Now you know what I think of you or should by now and when I make up my mind I at least want to do all I can to accomplish   now I suppose if I cryed and begged and acted nutty then youd believe me.   Now you better give me an outline of my prospects in the next letter and it must come pretty soon.

With all my love I am yours
Bill.

New York, Sept. 11 1905

My Dear Papa

I got your letter a few days ago and was glad to hear all the news   I would like to see Claremore now.

I will send you this $166.00   did you get the last $60.00 I sent   this will make $450 wont it

When is Sallie going west [the McSpaddens moved to California "for their health" but did not stay]   I am playing in Brooklyn this week and was to have gone to Pittsburg, Pa. next week but they changed it to a Theatre in N.Y. City so I will be here till Sept 23rd.   then go to Buffalo N.Y.

I will close   write soon   send me some news of the Coffeyville Roping Contest.

Love to all
Willie
Putnam House

"GO TO PILING UP YOUR DOLL RAGS. . . TO SEE THE WORLD AS THE WIFE OF ROGERS THE LARIAT EXPERT."

Aha! Now he has an agent and look what a difference it makes.
~Will Rogers, Jr.

Look at that. . . . He's just decided to stay away for another two or three months without seeing her, then 'Boom!' here comes the proposal. No wonder she kept refusing him.
~Will Rogers, Jr.

New York, Sept 18 1905

My Dear Papa

just got your letter   will write and send you some money as I know you are in need of some   Here's $110.00 One hundred and ten . . . This is my last week in N.Y.   I go to the Empire Theatre, Cleveland Ohio   next week they have changed me from my original route   Write me there and I will get it.   I am there from Sept 25, to Oct 1st. then to the Garden Theatre Buffalo N.Y. from Oct 1st to 7th

Lots of love to all from your son

Willie

He knows his father has plenty of money. Sounds as if he wants his father to brag on him for sending home so much. Clem might tell others how well Willie was doing, but he was not likely to compliment him in person.

Cleveland,O.

Sept 27, 05

My Dear Papa,

I arrived here from N.Y. all O.K. and am at the Empire Theatre and have been quite a success   finish here Saturday night and go to Buffalo next week then out to Toledo, O.

I will send you $115.00 which will make me $675 there wont it   did you get the $110 I sent last week

I am going to put in a part of the winter and save up my money and when I come home I am going to get me a little bunch of cows and back up on the farm I am going

Did you get the pictures I sent you by express from New York.

Papa send me about 35 ft of small light hard twisted rope like the boys use there to rope with   any of them would know   get one from one of them that they have used if you can as it will be better. Light hard twist. to throw not to twirl. also two good red or big check flannel shirts size 15 1/2. and one of those pretty stripped Osage Blankets that you buy at Ruckers for a saddle blanket   Gordon or Clem or Bright or some of those boys will have the kind of rope   send them so I will get them Sunday Week Oct 8th in Toledo. By express and I will pay you what it is

% Arcade Theatre
Toledo, Ohio

Love to all

Willie

Toledo, Ohio

Oct. 11th, 05

My Dear Sisters and All.

Well I am about as far out your way as I will get this trip for after next week in Detroit all my work up to Xmas is in the East   I am the headliner or the main squeeze here this week   I finish Saturday night and my man and pony will go up

". . . I AM THE HEADLINER OR THE MAIN SQUEEZE HERE THIS WEEK"

by boat Sunday to Detroit, but not any boat for me if I can go on land

We open there Monday afternoon. <u>Heres</u> a lot of newspaper stuff that has appeared this week the picture was in Sundays. It is getting a bit cold up around these lakes. Say I wrote to papa for some things did he ever send them? he dont even write and I dont know if he gets all the money I send him   did Maud get the package of summer clothes I sent and did you all get the 4 large pictures   please tell me when you write.

Now here is my route if you will just notice when you write you cant miss it   I am in each town from the beginning of a week till the end   just allow two or three days for it to come and it will get me.

week of Oct. 16th. Temple Theatre Detroit, Mich.

week of Oct. 23rd   Cooks Opera House Rochester, N.Y.

week of Oct. 30th   Chasses Opera House Washington

from Nov 6th for the next two weeks I will be in N.Y.   address Putnam House untill Nov. 20. I play one week at Hammersteins and once in Brooklyn   then Nov 20 I go to Boston, Mass. for a week.

Nov 27 Providence, R.I. a week.

Week of Dec 3rd. Philadelphia

Week of Dec 11th New York City

Heres some paper clippings for you or Sallie

She wanted some.

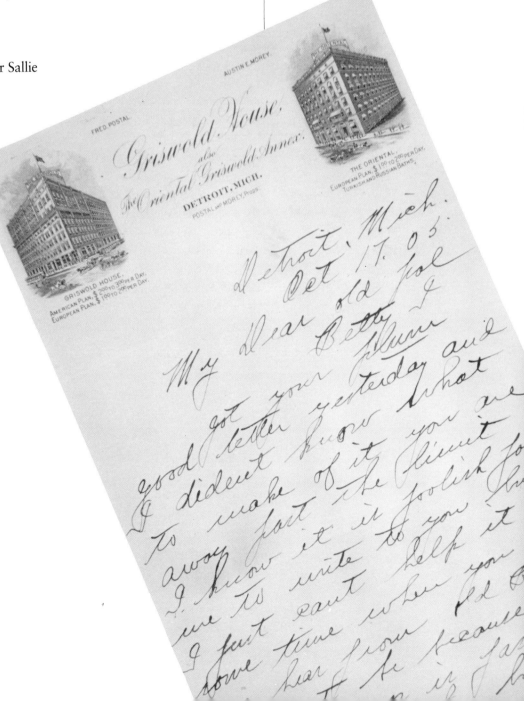

So he did wear the flashy colors on stage. Judging from the way he dressed later, it's hard to imagine.
~Will Rogers, Jr.

Toledo, O.
Oct 13 05
Dear Papa
I got the Blanket and shirts all O.K. yesterday
Say havent I got two red shirts in your trunk or some place there.
I finish here tomorrow night and then go to Detroit.
See about that rope
Address Temple Theatre Detroit Mich

Promises, promises!
~Will Rogers, Jr.

Betty's reply to his proposal must have been a blow! This is his first letter in two months. She must have written to him twice—the most recent one to ask what was wrong.
~RC

GRISWOLD HOUSE
Detroit, Mich.
Oct 17, 05
My Dear old pal

Betty I got your plum good letter yesterday and I dident know what to make of it you are away past the limit I know it is foolish for me to write to you but I just cant help it and some time when you dont ever hear from old Bill it wont be because he is mad or is fascinated with some other but only because he is at last able to abide by his own judgement

you know Betty old pal I have always had about what I wanted and it breaks my heart when I think I'll never get it. I am ordinarily a good loser but I guess my nerve is fooling me this trip

I dont know how long I will stay at this

I might leave it any day and go back to the ranch I have made a success and thats all I wanted to do.

I want home afful bad and I am going to stay there too.

Here's another bunch of stuff you can glanse over if you care too

I am going big here a swell stage high class people and lots of them this is a beautiful city almost as good as Washington. Say give Jim Hinton my best regards he's a good fellow.

Well Goodbye
just Bill

Oct 17, 1905
Detroit Mich
Tuesday
Dear Papa

I got two letters from you yesterday you said you got the $110 and $115? Why dident you get $175.00 and $125 last from Toledo the cards came in all signed up and you have had plenty of time to get them now I should have since the insuranse and the $10 you took out I should have about $825 is there that much there

I dident send any money this week havent got the rope yet
next week at Cooks Opera House
Rochester, N.Y.

Rochester, N.Y.
Oct 26, 05
My Dear Sis

Well I am back in N.Y. State . . . finish Saturday night and jump to Washington Sunday   open Monday   It is pretty cold up around these lakes.

I go from Washington back to N.Y. at Hammersteins again. I certainly would like to see you all but cant for a couple or three months I guess. Will Sallies folks be gone Xmas   if she is not there I think I will put off my trip till spring for I can get steady engagements all winter I think and then I can stay when I come home. I want to put back a little money and then go back and restock the farm and stay there. This is nice work but I am not in love with it only for the money   ask Papa if he is going to give me the rent off the farm this fall as I am trying to get a hold of a little money and he might help it along.

Say you all are dandies   I dident want that old cheap thing of a shawl I wanted the Mexican one I got in San Antonio like I give you all one and if it is not nice and pretty dont send it for I want to give it to a married couple I know for a cozy corner. If its nice send it to me at Washington next week please. And tell me for the Lords sake did you get my clothes I sent you 5 weeks ago I cant find out   I will wire and ask you

   Well goodby Lots of love to all
         Willie

Nov 5th to 12th Putnam House
I will be playing N.Y. City at Hammersteins
Nov 13 to 20 Keiths Theatre Worcester, Mass.

Will must have been at odds with his father at the time of these letters. He asks Maud to find out from him if he will get rent money from the farm in the fall. Will's promise to come home must have been for his father's benefit.

Washington D.C.
Oct. 30, 1905
My Dear Sis

I just got Cap's letter telling me you were not so well. Say sis I ought to be whipped for not writing you oftener and paying more attention to how you was But say I just today realized how sick you had been and how little I had thought of it for you know none of us are ever sick much and when I would get letters I would think it was just sick for a day or so and I dident take it seriously at all. Now I see how heartless I was and I feel ashamed of myself. But I am certainly uneasy for you now and just for a little I would come home and see you, if you dont get better soon I will certainly be there. It might not do you much good but I know it would do me a lot of good to see <u>you</u> and I could make you forget you were so sick.

I hope May is still there   tell her I said <u>to stay there till you are all well for I know</u> how lonesome it will be without Sallie.

I dont think they will stay long out there   I give them to Xmas at the longest.

Well I am going to send you a lot of clippings and things to lay there and read. I got in here [Washington] last night at 8 o'clock from Rochester N.Y. was all Sunday on train it was through Pennsylvania and the poorest country I ever saw. It is nice and warm here.

I opened up at matinee today I was anxious to make good in Washington and from the way I was received this evening and tonight I have certainly made a hit. I think I went bigger than any place yet and thats saying some Oh it is a swell theatre all high class people come here a big stage and I like it they have me billed and advertised like a circus. I finish Saturday night and go to Newark N.J. right across the river from N.Y. City Monday You see I had this open Sunday as they dont show in Washington Sunday so I contracted or booked as we call it to play Newark I get $50.00 Fifty for that day alone you see outside of my weeks salary which is the same even if you dont play Sunday. Still I have quite a bit of transportation to pay sometimes two people and a horse I ship the pony by excess baggage and it dont cost much generally just about what it would be for one person making it, cost me three peoples fares in all.

You see in vaudeville you are working for different people almost every week some you might have to work for cheaper than others and you are with different acts as you are not in a company you are by yourself and book your act wherever you can see.

I am booked up till after Xmas my route is.

Worcester, Mass	Nov. 13 to 20
Boston, Mass	Nov 20 to 27
Providence R.I.	Nov 27 to Dec 2
Philadelphia	Dec 3 to Dec 10
New York, Keiths	Dec 11 to Dec 16
Syracuse, NY	Dec 17 to Dec 23
Pittsburg Penn.	Dec 23 to Dec 30
Baltimore	Jan 1 to Jan 7
New York	Jan 8 to Jan 15
New York	Jan 15 to Jan 22

Thats all.

You see the good part about it is that I havent lost a single week since I started Now some acts think they do well to work one week and lay off one for you know you cant always find people to play you at there houses but that will make me 32 straight even if I shouldent get any more. All other performers think I have the greatest act in the business and I stand well with all of them I play for a week with.

Dont know if I will make the White House this trip as old Teddy aint here and young Teddy is away at school I dont much care to as I did it once and they might think I wanted to use it for advertising purposes but I dont know what will show up before the week is over.

Say did you get my clothes a long time ago I am going to

send you some more summer clothes from N.Y.   Where is my friend Ada [Fore-
man]   She wont write any more   Is she married.   I met a boy in Rochester who
has a brother   a lawyer in Chelsea   dont remember his name.   Well sis, I will close
for now   I sho hope you are better by now for you dont deserve to be sick.
Maude if Papa says anything to you   about that money you dont pay any attention
for we know how he is and I dont want it for a long time and dont need it.

    Well goodby all   lots of love to Cap and kids and all I have got for you.
Your brother
Willie

    Evidently Clem was putting Will's money in savings for him—without telling him.
The rift between them must have distressed Maud greatly.

Washington D.C.
November 4, 1905
[To Maud]
My birthday
(say how old am I)
    I got your letter sure enough on my birthday and it was the most acceptable
thing you could of sent for it makes me feel good to hear you are able to write.
And I got a letter from Sallie at the same time too.   I am feeling fine   It is the
prettiest warm day here.   I go to N.Y. tonight at 12, it is 7 hours run.   Mrs. Dick
Adams was at the theatre the other day and afterwards envited me out and I took
dinner with them and I go out there for dinner tonight.
Also Judge Thomas was in last night and sent his card back and I was out to a
feed with him last night and he was pleased great with the show.
    I kinder fell like going home to get back to N.Y.   I know it so well
    Write next week to   Putnam House   N.Y. City

    He was probably serious about not knowing his age. When he enrolled at Kemper
he got the year of his birth wrong.

[Postcard Nov. 1, 1905, picture of Washington Monument]
Dear Papa.   I am certainly a big hit in Washington   It is nice and warm here.   I
walked clear to the top and down again of this monument.
I got your letter here alright.   I go to N.Y. Saturday night for one week only.
    Address the Putnam House
    Love to all
Willie

My route
New York, Worcester Mass., Boston, Providence, Philadelphia, New York,
Syracuse, Pittsburg Penn., Baltimore

He's breaking the ice with his father.

~Will Rogers, Jr.

". . . THEY ASK YOU A FEW QUESTIONS AND THEN PUT IT DOWN TO SUIT THEMSELVES"

"This is one of the few acts to play a return date at this theater. But last season the act created more talk than any feature of the season. . . "

Syracuse HERALD

". . . OPENED THIS AFTERNOON AT MATINEE AND WENT BIG. . . "

"The number by Will Rogers, king of the lariat, was no less interesting. He gave a clever exhibition with the lassoo and was assisted by 'Buck' McKee, ex-sheriff of Pawnee county, Oklahoma, and Rogers favorite broncho 'Arcade.'
With the horse and rider travelling across the stage Rogers caught the animal about the neck by throwing the lassoo with his foot. One of the most interesting feats was shown when the horse and rider were on one end of the stage, and Rogers, standing at the other twirled the rope in such a way that he put a double noose about the man's wrists . . . . Then he bound the wrists to the saddle and put nooses about the horse's neck and nose without approaching it. Then he tried catching the man and horse with a lassoo in either hand. His last feat was letting out a lassoo 82 feet long and swinging it about his head while on horseback."
The Worchester [Massachusetts]
EVENING GAZETTE,
14 November 1905.

New York, Nov 6th 1905
Dear Papa
     Well I am back in N.Y. for this week only at Hammersteins Theatre   thats where I made my success last summer and stayed so long.
It is warm here   they are sho having a hot time over the Mayor election which will be tomorrow   there is lots of excitement. I got your letters in Washington   No I dont want anything from home just yet. . . .
     Here is $150.00 one hundred and fifty   this will make me $1250.00 in all wont it   I heard from Sallie and Maud   Write to me to
          Keiths Theatre
               Worcester, Mass.
     Lots of love to all   Willie

Boston, Mass.
Nov 20, 05
Dear Papa
     got here this morning from Worcester . . . and will be here this week . . .
     Now here is $200.00 for you to put in the bank   that will be $1450.00 in all it is cold here. I think I will be home <u>sure</u> about Feb 1st but am engaged for Xmas Write when you can   what rent will we get from the farm this fall . . .
               your son   Willie

Boston, Mass.
Nov 20, 05
My Dear Dear Sis.
     I looked for a letter from some of you when I come to Boston today but nothing has showed up yet. I finished a very nice week in Worcester, Mass. Also was the same hit week before at old N.Y. This is a return engagement here as I was in Boston last 4th July   opened this afternoon at matinee and went big   am in my dressing room waiting to go on now, have only got one letter from <u>Sallie</u> two weeks ago   dont hear from <u>May.</u>
     I think now I will get home for a visit about Feb 1st but cant make it Xmas as I am booked till about Jan 22nd. I am powerful homesick   seems like ages since I saw you all.
     Heres another clipping from yesterdays Rochester paper   they ask you a few questions and then put it down to suit themselves
     Well goodby   ans soon
     Love to all
          Willie
I got the [saddle] blanket and my friends went wild over it.

Providence,R.I.
Nov 27, 05.
Dear Papa
     Just got here and got your letter in regard to the money   use it if you want it for I dont now

Here is $100.00 more for use   I am feeling fine   I may get home by Feb 1st
Write when you can
      with love
        from Willie.

When Clem complained about the cost of keeping up the ranch that was now supposed to belong to Will, Will offered money for maintenance of the property. Clem was prosperous and would not have needed the money for his own affairs.

OLD WASHINGTON TAVERN

Lowell, Mass.
Nov [December] 8, 1905
My Dear Folks

Well I will drop you a few   I was changed from Philadelphia up here to Lowell, Mass. this week and I go to Philadephia Jan 22.

Here another of those fishy writeups from here. Is May and all of them there I guess they are and if you dont hear from me for a month or so dont wonder for I will be hiding from Christmas.

I play in N. Y. again next week at Keiths   thats the house where I first opened at and then to the next week Dec 18 to 23 Grand Opera House, Syracuse N.Y. week Dec 25 to 30 Grand Opera House Pittsburg, Pa
Week Jan 1st to 6 Maryland Theatre Baltimore, Md.

Putnam House
New York, Dec 11 1905
My Dear Papa

I just got back in N.Y. yesterday and play here this week in the same theatre I first started in 27 weeks ago. had a snow where I was yesterday.

Here is $100   that makes $1750 in all as I sent $100 last week. I think I will get home in Feb.

Write when you can. . .

HOTEL ST. CLOUD

Syracuse, N.Y.
Dec 20, 1905
Dear Maud, May, Papa and all the others

I will write you all this letter togeather as I guess you few straglers that are left in the Nation will surely spend Xmas togeather at your house, sorry the health seekers and actors cant be present but will sho see you soon.

Well I just this eve forwarded you all a little satchel of stuff by United States Express   did you land it   it aint much but Lord I dident know what to get, sent Sallies a few days ago. Papa did you get the overcoat I sent and will you wear it   I dident send you any money last week and Lord knows when I can send any more.

It is as hot as summer up here. I will be traveling most of Xmas, so Xmas eve (Sunday night) you can think of me boarding a train after the show and leaving for Pittsburg, Pa. I get there Xmas day at 11:30 and show that day so it will be a moving Xmas with me.

"The whoop of the show is that of Will Rogers, the lasso thrower. Every time he makes a hoop out of his rope he whoops. So clever is his lasso throwing you can almost taste the. . . dust that would be kicked up if he was on the plains."
Syracuse [New York] JOURNAL,
December 18, 1905.

". . . I WILL BE
HIDING FROM
CHRISTMAS."

". . . IT WILL BE
A MOVING XMAS
WITH ME."

My route. Next <u>two</u> weeks, Jan 8 to 22

    Putnam House N.Y. As I will be playing in Brooklyn

Week of Jan 22 to 28   Keiths Theatre Philadelphia, Pa.

A great Xmas to all of you with lots of love

    From Bro Willie

    Will is lonely. No doubt he has other girlfriends, but they are not homefolks. The "Nation" is Cherokee Nation. "Health seekers" are the McSpadden family.

["Hotel St. Cloud" marked out on letterhead.]

Dec 22nd 1905

Dearest Betty

    As it is Xmas and you are "one best fellow" I want to send you a little token that I have carried with me and which I prize very highly (although not of much financial value) for I do believe you will receive it and apreciate it accordingly.

    Now Betty I got this Hdkf. in South America   it is supposed to be very fine work done by the <u>Paraguay</u> Indians who are noted for their needlework. I landed there quite flush and I bought my sisters some two hundred dollars worth of this and sent them by my partner [Dick Parris] who was coming home and he smuggled them in this country as there is a large duty.

The old Indian Lady I bought from then gave me <u>this</u> asking me if I was married   I said No. she said then give it to the wife when you do marry. I have kept it carried it all through Africa at times when I dident have a cent and was actually hungry. then to Australia most of the time in an envelope in my pocket   then back home and on all all my travels   I did intend always to do as the old woman said but I guess theres nothing doing for me   I will just give it to you as I kinder prize it and you might do the same.

Hoping you a grand Xmas and a Happy year

    <u>I am always the same</u>

      to you Betty

        Yours Will.

    Paula Love remembered "beautiful lace collars" sent by Will Rogers. Each of the four McSpadden girls wore her mother's (Sallie's) lace collar for high school graduation, and all except Paula wore the same lace collar for their weddings. (The house burned and the lace along with many other sentimental possessions was lost).

    Paula remembered the collar for its beauty—"much like drawn work but made with fine silk thread." She said it showed how sentimental Will Rogers was.

Hotel Boyer

Pittsburg, Pa. Dec 27 1905

Dear Papa,

    I got your letter Christmas Day when I got to Pittsburg   about the coat   now I tell you I think those fellows just switched that coat on me in sending it away for I know the one I bought was alright and I got me one also and it was a good one   I will see them when I get to N.Y. week after next   you can send it back to me if

you like and I will get you another one   I am afful sorry it is no good.
This is a pretty poor Xmas   I wish I was at home   it snowed a little here Xmas
day but is hot here now. . .   Love to all and a happy New year
Willie

A lonely Christmas was bad enough, but "Papa's" attitude about the coat must
have made it worse.

Clem may have been trying to prove (again) that Willie could never amount to
anything. He refused to send receipts for the money Will sent home. Now he refused
the gift as if it were dirty money that bought it.

It appears he wanted to "put Willie in his place."

Will was hurt and upset when his
father refused to accept an
overcoat he sent as a Christmas
gift. When his father sent it back
because it didn't suit him—wasn't
fine enough—Will told his father
he would keep it himself. This
picture, made in St. Paul, was
probably sent to his family. In it
he wears the overcoat.

Courtship and Correspondence 1900 ~ 1915   127

throwing two ropes at once.

David E. Coday Cleveland, O.

An unusual picture was used for a publicity poster, showing the typical "3-D" backdrop with Buck McKee and Will holding the ropes in frozen positions. The horse, obviously not Teddy, may have been a stuffed animal used by the photographer for the large indoor picture which required flashes of fire to illuminate it. Note that Buck's eyes are closed.

Will Rogers opened the new year at the Maryland Theater in Baltimore, hundreds of miles from those he loved. With his heart in Arkansas with Betty, he started saving his money, sending it home to Papa to bank for him. He would need a nest egg to get married. In January alone he sent $450, making a total of $2,400 in savings in a short time.

PUTNAM HOUSE

New York, Jan 13 1906
Dear Papa

I got the coat allright and cant imagine why it did not suit you   I am keeping it to wear myself and I gave mine to a friend   it was not as fine as some   for lots of them cost 3 and 4 hundred dollars and I could not afford a fine one but I thought it would do.

   Write when you can
   Love to all
    Willie

If Clem Rogers had been a less practical man, he would have kept the coat whether he liked it or not—so as not to hurt his son's feelings. But this would have been a senseless waste of money, he reasoned. The boy could just return the coat and get his money back. He could have. But he didn't.

Will still practiced early and late to perfect his act, to add new twists to it. His droll remarks kept the audience laughing, but he felt the main show had to be based on his roping. The big crinoline—the trick he'd used to get into Texas Jack's show—brought each act to a dramatic close. Using a rope about ninety feet long that was threaded through a loop fitted with a honda—a metal eyelet—Rogers would sit astride his pony and gradually begin to pay out the rope. Larger and faster the circle spun from his steady hands, growing until it swelled out around him and the horse and over the heads of the spellbound audience in a singing whirl.

When the rope dropped, the breathless audience released its tension in a burst of applause.

Will didn't talk much about his act when he wrote his sister. He was thinking more about home.

Philadelphia, Pa.
Jan. 26. 06
My Dear Sis

I just got your letter yesterday and mighty glad to hear from you   you are about the only one that writes often. And Mary [Gulager] is there   I wish I was there now   we would have a great time   she must stay till spring.

Well I am working as usual and I cant tell just where I will go or when I will get home but it will either be in March or April I kinder want to wait till it is warm

I am mighty homesick for I have been doing the same old <u>stunt</u> for 35 weeks   I am a bigger hit here than I was last summer. I go up toward new England for 3 weeks now then back to Brooklyn

It is as warm as summer here all the time

Say I got a letter from Theo. Mc [Spadden] and wrote him but have not got an answer

Say Cap [Lane] can you invest 5 or 6 hundred dollars in a little piece of land there on lots or anything so it will make me anything   or more if it takes more I havent any use for it in the Bank for I don't think they pay anything on it   only what Papa uses   I want to get a few cattle when I come home and back up home for me.

Write soon and often and tell old Mary to write me all the Tahlequah news

My Route Next Week Jan 29-Feb 4. Hartford Opera House. Hartford, Con. Week Feb 5-11 Al. Haynes Theatre   Fall Rivers. Mass

Lots of love to all
Willie

Lawrence Mass.
Feb. 13, 06
Dear Papa.

Did you get that $250.00 I sent you from Hartford, Conn. 2 weeks ago. I have never heard from you   write at once

address Putnam House   N.Y.   as I will be playing in N.Y. next week.

Love to all
Willie

Will is clearly somewhat disgusted that he can't get a receipt from his father or recognition that the bank balance is building up. He promised Betty that he would settle down and become a rancher, build a stake for them, if she would take him seriously.

"Another new act which will attract all the boys of the town will be the exhibition of lariat throwing by Will Rogers, an expert. He is part-blooded Cherokee Indian and gained his experience on the Western plains. He uses a genuine cow pony, sent him from his father's ranch, and performs some feats of wonderful dexterity with the rope. He was one of the features last season of the New York Hippodrome."
Clipping from WR's scrapbook.

And he must have meant it. He tried to make himself believe that show business was monotonous and no good for him. He even wrote to Maud in that mood. Then suddenly he changed his mind. He had an opportunity to go to Europe with his show and he would take it. A whole new adventure. How could he pass it up? Again the ranch was forgotten. He sent a postcard to Maud Lane, Chelsea, I.T.:

Feb 20, 1906
New York
Dear Sis. Will be home about Mar 2. or 3rd. for 2 weeks go to Germany to work a Month. Sail Mar 21 will see you all   Sallie is coming too. Sho am <u>glad</u>
Love
   <u>Willie</u>

Sister Sallie and her family had been in California for more than a year. Now they were coming home and Will would get a chance to see them before he sailed the ocean blue once more. Notice that correspondence with C.V. has stopped, perhaps because Will was a little peeved with him. Or maybe just because Clem was so busy in Guthrie helping write the constitution for Oklahoma.

MARQUITO APARTMENTS

Philadelphia, Thursday Night [March 2, 1906 to Betty]

Well I just come back from the show shop and found your letter there and am offul sorry you are not feeling so well   hope it wont last long

Well I am kicking in my last week in this country for a while   have only 4 more shows to do but I am very uneasy about my foreign <u>opening</u> as you never know how things will go any place   while they all predict a great big hit   <u>I dont</u>   and I do so hate the voyage although it is a little jump to some I have taken.

Well I finish here Sat night and do you know I cant get a train west untill 1 oclock Sunday   that will take me clear to St Louis but it is a fast one and I will get there at 1:30 Monday eve   then out of there and as you predicted (How did you know) should get to your place about 7 Tuesday A.M.   it does seem that trains and boats go <u>backwards</u>   There is none going near the

time I want them   Now I have to sail from N.Y. Mar 17.   now if I could get a
boat it might as well be Mar 20. or 21 see   and to go then I go to England and
tranship.   now that will only give me 6 days at home and I wont be able to stay in
your town only for a short time   I did intend to be there Tuesday and then up to
Monett [Missouri] Wednesday A.M.   but that train wont get me there in time to
catch the West bound and I really must be home Chelsea at my sisters Wednesday
on the Noon train   so all I see is get that 9.20 to Monett Tuesday Night   But I
think you will get an ample sufficiency of me in that time   Oh I have studied time
tables and steam ship sheets till I am black in the face

Now if I can catch a freight, Local, or something later so I can get to Monett by
9.35 Wednesday A.M. it will be the Candy Kid

My Horse and Man [Buck McKee] go back to N.Y. and sail on Mar 10. direct
to Hamburg then by train to Berlin   he will land in time to give the pony a rest as
it is hard on a horse   they have to stand up all the way over.

I should get there about 3 or 4 days before I open

And say   oh my there is more rough weather than you ever heard of   just
now   ships all late having rough passages (Now I am not saying this to scare
anyone) for I believe a rough sea voyage is considered the thing for coughs, colds,
noises in the head and overwork

Say never mind meeting that early train for if I do make it why at that hour
when I emerge I dont think I should be very presentable   for they wont get me out
of bed till the train stops and then me off with about half of the old rags on and

the other half in course of construction, but I will be raisin a disturbance at your door as soon as I displace a portion of soil gathered from many states, pull of [off] a small feed interview a barber (and say that town aint prohibition is it) Well I should arrive somewhere around the 9 hour   That is if I have a whole lot of good luck.

Now that big <u>9</u> might be a little <u>premature</u> for your convenience for thats a milk mans date   but look out about then and you'll see a dark Man coming with a bundle [of Music] Nothing worse I hope (or have you all got that song there   if not this requires a dictionary

Now I have you several pieces of music here   some late others not so late   still they may be there   but they are ones I have heard and like and think you would too   Anyway I will bring you a <u>supply</u>. if I knew just what you all had there I would know better what to bring

Now see here Betty   Nothing doing on the old entertaining thing. I am just coming down to spend <u>a good old day with you</u> and require no entertaining and meeting folks and all that. Pull through in your same way and dont you <u>dare</u> put yourself out one bit.

Well I must stop   hope all plans turn out O.K. and I see you as expected
My best regards
Will.

For months, Betty had waited for "Billy" to get away from the big cities long enough to come home. He kept insisting he wanted to be someone special in her life, to have a future with her. Now here he was surprising her with the news of another ocean trip, and only allowing her one day out of the week he would have at home! It was enough to exasperate any girl.

Will spent Tuesday, March 6, with Betty—talking, singing songs, and "courting." At least Will was courting her. He wanted her to drop everything and go to Europe with him! But she turned him down—again. He took the night train back to Monett, then down into the Indian Territory where he would have a big get-together with his father, three sisters, nieces, nephews and friends.

GRAND HOTEL

12 Boulevard del Capucines
PARIS
Le Mar 26 1906
Polly vue Francaise.
<u>Wee Wee</u> yah, yah. I dont know a <u>damn</u> word anybodys saying. But <u>Pal of Mine</u> I sho do know that I am in <u>Paree</u>   and old hand   <u>she</u> is certainly the Goods All I regret is you are not here if we wouldent go the pace <u>that kills</u>

from present indications I dont think the old Hamlet has been at all <u>overated</u> as to her speed for they do sho travel on 2 nothing.

Its got N.Y. whipped to a whisper for continuous performances and never stopping and all the other joints I ever saw <u>skun</u> 40 ways from the jack and take in the lookout.

I did when last I saw you intend going by London but on the boat I got up

"<u>WEE WEE</u> YAH, YAH. I DONT KNOW A <u>DAMN</u> WORD ANYBODYS SAYING."

against a good bunch and decided to come by France instead and up to now havent had <u>time</u> to regret

Well now to start in where I left you last which do seem a long time ago <u>Kid</u> (and thats no Paris booze you hear speaking either)

Say that was a lovely two hours I did put in walking up and fro on that <u>lousy</u> Rogers platform that night   and you knew all about railroading   why you are the Kandy Kid <u>strawler</u> to put me on a dead one or else you are the rottenest railroad guide in all the Ozarks. I hated you like a bull dog does a tramp.

Well I got to Chelsea the next day at 10. and all the folks were at one of my sisters and we did the big reunion act for 6 days   only went down to Claremore once and that was to lodge to get inisiated [initiated] into the Masons   Oh I am one of the hands now   Well we did have a good old time   just the family for the whole week and I kinder hated to put forth on this ramble   but then back to old N.Y. town and bid all the gang so long   (and found a <u>mighty</u> nice little letter there from a Pal) which kinder done my old heart good   but I just thought I wouldent <u>ans</u> till I got over here and I might have a bit of more news

That little letter was mighty consoling for you know <u>dear</u> its kinder lonesome when you shove out on the old blue and leave all behind and not with a soul you know and it made me feel good to know that I at least had one good old Pal that wished me a safe return and I am more thankful for it than you will ever imagine

Well we put out and sick   oh <u>louie louie</u> I thought die I should   but I stuck it out   but it lasted till Wednesday afternoon (sailed Saturday) then I got a bite to eat down that by some miracle that couldent find its way up again   and I done pretty fair the rest of the way   and oh that Ocean was certainly having a revolution most all the way   Well we got to Cherburg France Sunday Morning early and went ashore and took a special train for Paris   about 7 hours and   oh the pretty sights en route would pay on [one] for the trip   oh it was grand   got to Paris Sunday afternoon and Sunday is the day of days   oh I never seen such a mass of people as are out on the Boulevards on a Sunday. I have been about some but you got to hand it to Paris for a wide open place   there seems to be no laws and especially of morality   when the [they] kinder jar me they are going some but I must admit they kinder did   but then its all to be expected here   thats Paris. Stage Women aint one two ll. with these for paint and make up   oh how they do <u>strut</u> you see some very well groomed women and offul pretty dresses but the Men they just seem to be a disgrace to appear in their get ups with the women   why they havent the 1st idea of dress   there is absolutely no fashions   they just curl their mustache and put on all they have got   why any Mut in America has them skinned a mile.

And how they do sit and drink at Cafe's with the tables right out on the sidewalk   they seem to have nothing else to do.

Well I am certainly going some   in with a good gang   we are at one of the swellest Hotels here and <u>Champagne</u> flows like water   we took in the swellest variety show last night   where I will probably play if I take an engagement there later on.

But say the <u>Grub</u>   it might be because I pay for it that it is so good   but on the dead   it is the best cooked stuff I ever eat   when you can find a guy that can savee

"AND HOW THEY DO SIT AND DRINK AT CAFE'S . . . ."

Will mailed Betty six postcards from Berlin: one posted April 12, two on April 19, two on April 28 and one on May 3. On the last one he wrote: "Hello Kid. Well the old things are going fine and I guess will go to London May lst. So any light mail matter will reach me there from now on. Province Hotel Leicester square London. Will" Of the Kings Museum in Berlin, Will wrote to Betty: "This is one of the largest Museums all kinds of old junk in here see the old fashioned Busses that go about town."

~RC

enough to know what you want   oh it has made an offul hit with me   they do know how to cook.

I wired to Berlin yesterday to see if my pony had got there but they say <u>no</u>   he is now two or three days overdue and I am a bit uneasy and will leave here tomorrow direct for Berlin   still all the boats have had rough passages and are more or less late.

If they had landed and anything had happened to the pony why the Man would have wired the Garden   I know they are at sea yet

They tell me Berlin is as swift as this and then some   but I will quiet down up there   Wont know a thing about how long I will be over here till after a week or so more

I want to put in 3 or 4 weeks when I am not working traveling and seeing several different places

Heres a post card picture of the ship which by the way is the same one I and Dick Parris come over on 4 years ago.

Well I will close   please dont think hard of me for not writing sooner but I was only waiting till I landed   did you get that Bill Bailey song I sent you

I will write you after I open and tell you all. Now listen Kid write to me often for its mighty good to get your letters. Be good and dont hand out too much of that <u>Con</u> of yours to all those guys.

My very best to all the folks. All yours. Bill

Wintergarten

Berlin

Will seemed much more concerned about Teddy, his horse, than he was about his partner Buck McKee. Perhaps he thought of the two of them —rider and horse—as one. Buck was a married man and didn't attempt to join the fast set. Will was booked into the Wintergarten with Buck and the horse for a salary of $3,700 for the month of April.

Berlin
April 17 [1906]
My Dear Dear Betty

Good old Pal   your letter of April 1st landed this morning and say old hand I could just love you to death for writing it for I hadent got anything from out west since I come

Well things are going on nicely   half of the month has passed and it wont be long till I am done here   I am still the hit of the Bill and have been offered several engagements but I got a letter from my N.Y. agent and he says No, to come straight back and then we can book the work for future time at a big salary. My agent is coming over himself in a few weeks and he will fix it all up   he already has me booked in America for 36 weeks all in the East   so you see I am all fixed but I am coming home July and August and start work in September

I am going by London on my way home and may put my act on there just to show it for a week at one of the best theatres

Well this is the fastest 2 weeks I ever went in my life and thats saying something   It seems that it is a fact here that people dont sleep   why I never get in till 8 or 9 or 10 in the morning   everything is wide open all night and we just go from one Cafe to another and all over town then in a Cab and drive awhile and then out and drink and its that day and night.

There is quite a bunch of English girls and a few of us boys and I dident think it was possible to go such a clip   oh we do have some great old times but I will be glad when it is all up and I get back to America again   They talk of Gay N.Y.   why N.Y sleeps more in one night than Berlin in a week.   Honest I havent had my eyes closed here while it was dark   what sleeping I have done has been in the day.   Oh I have met the <u>Kaiser</u> when I was out exercising my pony in the park and he rides every day   he always <u>salutes</u> as he gallops past   oh he is a dandy good fellow

Well I guess you have got the letter I wrote you from Paris and the other one from here by now

I think I will go direct to London on May 1st   I will write you on a card where to address my mail   as a letter here would not get

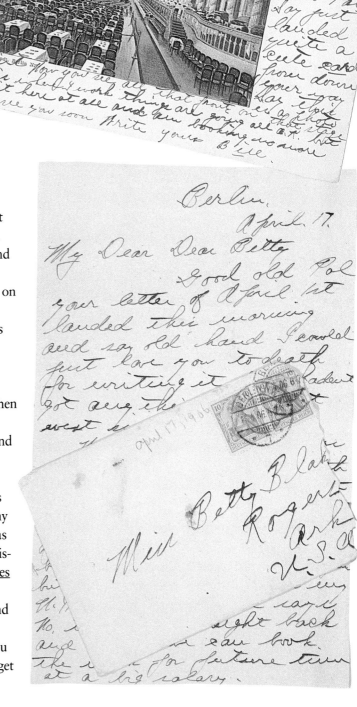

me now   I wont be in London longer than two weeks   I dont think

Well I will close   I hope you are having a good time and dont forget your old Cowboy   I will see you before long

I have wrote to my Music publisher friend in N.Y. to send you some Music

Solong regards to all and lots of love to you

Old Bill

Reviews from the Berlin papers which Will himself clipped and pasted in his own scrapbook have been translated for this book by Emil Sandmeir who managed the household for the Rogers family before Mrs. Rogers died in 1944. He is a native of Switzerland.

From Berlin, April 12, Will sent a postcard to Betty with a picture of the Wintergarten on one side. Around the edges he wrote her a message:

"Hello Pal / Say just landed quite a cute card from down your way/Say this is a photo of the joint/ Now you see all the front of that stage/

out there is where I work/ things are going all O.K but I dont like it here at all and am booking no more work. Will see you soon. Write Yours

<u>Bill</u>. <u>Keep</u> <u>these</u> <u>and</u> <u>I</u> <u>will</u> <u>send</u> <u>you</u> <u>a</u> <u>lot</u>.

PROVIDENCE HOTEL
LONDON

May 10. 06

My Dearest Girl

Say I am here and have been for over a week and not a line has come from you or any one in America and I know I wrote all of you and gave you my London address   but perhaps the letter went astray

Well I come right here and put on my act for a trial just to show them and I am working at the most select vaudeville theatre here at more money than I ever got before any place and my act has not only made good but it is said to be a sensation and they want me for 3 or 4 more weeks   oh it simply knocked them a twister and its all the very swellest London society people that come here but I think I will sail for home in a week   but I have wired my N.Y. agent for I see I can get all kinds of coin out of these people to stay on longer   but at any rate I will be out there about the 10th of July   even if I go home now I have 5 weeks work down south before I could come home and if I stay here I will cancel that. oh this is a great show place but very slow   otherwise   I was kinder glad to get away from there   it was to swift   oh Kid I am <u>dying</u> to get home and I sho do want to see you

Well I have a lot of stuff to tend to and I will write you more   now Goodbye dear

Yours   Will .

His reviews in London were excellent. He played to "swell" audiences, and he was invited to the exclusive Ranelagh Club where he roped and did his stunts before the king. Quite a different reception than he'd had with Dick Parris just four years earlier!

Palace Theatre
London
May 14. 06
My Dearest

Well here it is Monday and not a line from any of you people   had a bit of mail
that has been forwarded from Berlin. I got your letter with the photo in it before I
left there   It was good   send me some more.
Well I am starting in on my second week at the Palace here but think I will go
home next week and will get out west about July 10. Oh Kid I am homesick and I
sho do want to see you

Please write me often

Yours   Will

Held over at the Palace for a third week and finally for a fourth, Will forgot his
previous experience with the British in the Argentine. They loved him in London!

He was full of Christmas-morning surprise. But when he didn't get replies from
anyone—not even his family—he found friends to share his excitement in London.

Nina Gordon, a mimic on the same bill, was one such friend. So was "Eltinge, the
sensation of the American Vaudeville Stage" with his feminine characterizations. Life
was full of adventure, but Will soon tired of it and longed to go home.

It was the middle of June, and he had certainly earned a vacation. He left for Italy
and stayed at the Grand Hotel Continental in Rome, then went to Naples, from which
he sailed first class on the S.S. *Konig Albert* for New York. No more "third class,
wearing overalls for underwear," as he had returned in 1904. He had come a long way
in just two years. He clipped many excellent reviews for Betty to share—they just kept
getting better—and she must have wondered herself what he did to deserve such
accolades from the reserved British.

The reviewer at *The Era* said Will "brings something of the wild, breezy life of the
prairies across the footlights in his unique way. . . ."

The *Daily News* called him "a genuine Yankee with a quaint method of expression
which is hardly less interesting than his clever manipulation of the lasso."

The Referee noted his roping feats of a "really startling character, . . . taking care
all the while to crack many a quaint jest couched in the very broadest 'Amurrican.'"

From Europe, Will came home for a vacation. By now, his sisters knew of his
pursuit of Betty, and they wanted to know her better. Maud and Cap Lane planned
a house party for Will and they invited Betty. Hoping to have a little time alone with
Betty, Will took the train to Vinita where he met Betty's train on its last leg.

Alas, when he boarded, he found her seated with some stranger. He could only
shake her hand and take a spot by himself. He escorted her to the Lane home—an act
of favoritism that caused the other girls to tease him endlessly. To hide his shyness,
he clowned around with all the girls and seemed to avoid his one love. Betty was
puzzled.

Will could wax poetic on paper from long distances, but he was tongue-tied when
they were alone. On his way back to New York, he stopped over in Rogers, Arkansas,
and urged Betty to marry him at once. But she was not ready yet. The courtship
progressed slowly.

Betty received postcards from more than one "friend." Flowery suede postcards were the vogue of the time and Betty saved them all.

GRISWOLD HOUSE

Detroit. Sept 6.07 [1906]

Dear Papa

I got your letter with the two letters in it. good   send me any mail that comes for me

Well I got here and started to work and my act was a bigger success than last year and I am going fine   finish here Sunday and go to Cleveland. Ohio.   They are having the Michigan State Fair here and the City is full of people

[William Jennings] Bryan spoke here Monday.   it is getting cool up here on the lakes   we go from here to Cleveland by boat Sunday Night

. . . . buy anything you see there that looks cheap and borrow the money for me to pay for it. . . .

Well I will stop   where is Parris.

Lots of Love Willie

THE COURT INN

Buffalo, N.Y. Wednesday
[Posted September 27, 1906]
Dear Papa

Just got your letter about Spi   Now I think we should give him something even if he did say you could have the land   why I will give him half of what ever you think is right   for if he acts square why I will give him and you ought too.

Here is $100 makes me $1650.00 I left and this is $300.00 makes $1950 in all   I am doing fine   it is getting cool up here   I go to Toronto, Canada. Sunday to play all next week.

Say make that old Mc whats his name pay rent on that house if he dont get out of there

Well I will close   write soon
Love to all Willie.

B.F. Keith's
International Circuit
Theatrical Enterprises

Boston, Mass. Oct 30, 06

My Dear old Kid

Say I just got your letter forwarded from N.Y. in reply to my message   I had been here for two days and no letter so tonight after I went home from the Matinee   I sent you a wire asking you if you were sick and could <u>not</u> write for it seemed ages since I heard from you

Yes the opearator got mixed for the message said Big success here this time. You seem to have your trouble with agents   Operators and all those   still they are in your line. . .

Listen Kid I dident like your last letter I got just now   you said you wanted to consider me your best friend   Now dont be silly   you know what you are to me and dont say those things   oh one little letter you wrote said "I will be happy if you love me"

Now I sho do keep that letter with me for I like it and if that will constitute your happiness you are the happy Kid for I sho do love you, old Kid

Say dont say I have been bad for the only reason I did not write was that I waited to hear from you before I wrote   I was as good as could be and not <u>lushing</u>. and not for a minute did I forget you or never shall for you are <u>mine</u> and you know I am yours   you just keep on thinking that over for you will find me the most persistent Lover you ever saw. I just cant help it Dearie   you must write me at once Kid   I havent any <u>plans</u>   my plans are in your hands   shape them to suit yourself.

       Your Will

Next Week
Moores Theatre
Portland, Maine

Baltimore, Md.
Dec. 5th. 06.

My Own Dear Betty

Your letter just come and old Kiddie   I was just afful glad to hear from you but you kinder waited a while dident you

I kept waiting till I heard from you all this week

I will send you that letter   it is from a nice little girl friend of mine whom I met She was playing in a girl act and I happen to be on the bill with them 3 weeks and lots of times after the show I used to ask her out to have a little lunch as I always go out after and have a bite to eat and she was such a nice lady like smart kind of a girl and she got a bit stuck on me   and in N.Y. she was at one Theatre and Me at the other and cause I dident come around she wrote me and told me a lot of what she thought of me and I wrote her and just told her exactly how things was and that I liked her fine as a good friend and would do anything for her I could for she was a grand fellow but that she could never recall me having told her that I was stuck on her for I admired her in a different way and that I had a girl that I really loved and this is the letter from her which will go to show you that I am not (as bad as I <u>have</u> <u>been</u> and as you think I am   Honest Kid I am trying (and doing it) to be as I think you would like me to be. I have friends that I jolly along with and go around and have a drink (only beer) with. but only to kill time and be friendly   Now dont get sore cause I send you this, or dont think I am four flushing trying to show you what a good fellow I am. I only do it cause I want you to know.

Listen Girlie you are real mean   you wont tell me how old you are <u>not</u> <u>even</u> <u>me</u> why I dont care if you are a century plant   you are no "<u>lemon</u>" in my estimation

Yes still got that   those songs   have just neglected sending them. some are from Mr and Mrs. Van Alstyne   he's the composer of Apple Tree   Navajo   and all those and some are from Mrs. Josephine Gassman   The Lady with the <u>Picks</u> 4 negro Kids. Oh! yes and a book "Richard the Brazen," wild west and far east. its pretty good

I have no doubt told you of a dear friend I had in Washington a jewelryman and Wife. Well he come up this eve (you know Baltimore is only 40 miles from Washington) and he is taking me back home after the show tonight with him and I come back tomorrow in time for the show

Hurrah! got a wire today to play Hammerstein N.Y. Xmas Week   guess I aint glad   it is on the opposition circuit   but it is absolutely the leading Vaudeville Theatre of the <u>world</u> and all performers are tickeled to death to get to play it. You know its where I made my first hit and played so long and I am a favorite there. but I cant see how Shea got the Keith people to stand for it as they kick on acts playing for the other side.

Well Kid I go on in a little while   my act is doing great here as Baltimore is one of my best towns   I will write you again in a day or so and send you that stuff also and you must write me <u>every</u> <u>day</u> if you can   for I am certainly loving you a plenty now Kid

Please write me a long good <u>loving</u> letter

from your everloving Kid,   Will

Next Week.

Keiths Vaudeville

(I dont know the theatre but that will get it)

Altoona, Pa.

HIPPODROME

THE LARGEST PLAYHOUSE IN THE WORLD

New York, Friday. Dec. 21. 06

My Own Dear Girl.

Well my pal heres hoping you have a glorious Xmas and a plum good New Years   I know you will have a good time there at home   I am so sorry I could not come out but I only had the one week and I could not get next week booking set back. You know I am laying off this week because Wheeling W.Va. house is not open yet   that where I was to of played. I could collect salary and they told me so themselves but said that if I would release them this week they would see that I was well taken care of and would consider it a personal favor and Shea said if I

TELEPHONE – 3400 BRYANT.

CABLE ADDRESS – HIPPODROME.

NEW YORK
HIPPODROME

THE LARGEST PLAYHOUSE IN THE WORLD.

Entire Block 6TH Ave. 43RD to 44TH Street,

MANAGEMENT
Messrs. SHUBERT & ANDERSON.

New York, Friday, Dec 21. 06

My Own Dear Girl.

Well my pal heres hoping you have a glorious Xmas and a plum good new year. I know you will have a good time there at home I am so sorry I could not come out but I only had the one week and I could not get next week booking set back. you know I am laying off this week because Wheeling W. Va. house is not open yet that where I use to of played. I could colfect salary and they told me so themselvs but said that if I would release them this week they would see that I was well taken care of and would consider it a personaly favor and Shea said if I should hold them and make them pay. that I might should hold them and make them pay. that I might loose out in the long run   so I wanted to be in N.Y. this week if I did not go home   so I have had a great time going to all the best shows   you know its the only chance I ever had to go to them for its my first week off

Have been to the Hippodrome   my friend another cowboy   works there and we live here togeather   oh its a great show   also went to "The Rose of the Rancho." the new one   its good. "<u>The Great Divide</u>" oh its fine. saw it last night. and Montgomery and Stone in the Red Mill.   its great too. going to see Lew Fields in About Town and a burlesque on The great Decide, tonight. and Madam Butterfly tomorrow and I go to Matinees to all the vaudeville theatres. And oh how I did wish for you here this week to go to all these shows and enjoy them togeather, but we will sometime wont we Dear?

Oh you should have seen me shopping here in these big shops and then is when I did need you   had to fix up a box for home and that would of been your job. so get ready to perform that next year   you hear me shout?

Kid I sent you a little Xmas remembrance in the shape of a coat. and a muff. you should get it as soon as this letter. Now I dont know if it will fit you and that it is just right. but I hope it will suit you and prove serviceable for there is such a skin game in buying furs   it may prove to be a <u>lemon</u>. but it is the only thing I could think of that would do you any good and that I thought would please you.

Well Dearie I will jar loose   have a good time and think occasionally of the Kid in the east who loves you best of all else in the world

By-By. My Darling
Your loving Kid
Will .
237 W. 43rd St. N. Y.

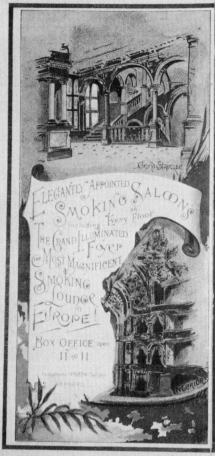

Manager   Mr. ALFRED BUTT.

Programme   6d.

1.	March	"Guards to the Front"	Trotère	7.50
2.	FRED. FRAMPTON, Burlesque Entertainer.			7.55
3.	ETHEL NEGRETTI, Comedienne.			8.3
4.	CAROLA JORDAN, Trapeze Artiste.			8.13
5.	JENNIE JOHNS, Comedienne.			8.24
6.	FRANK LYNNE, Comedian.			8.36
7.	DAISY JEROME, Comedienne.			8.46
8.	NINA GORDON, Mimic.			8.57
9.	DE GRACIA'S ELEPHANTS.			9.9
10.	LOUIS BRADFIELD, Assisted by Chorus, will sing—			9.27

(a) "Charlie, who's your Friend?"   (b) "The Lady Chauffeur"

| 11. | HANSL SCHON, Vocalist. | | | 9.37 |
| 12. | ROSE STAHL | | | 9.47 |

and her own Company in a One-Act Comedy of Stage Life, entitled—
"The Chorus Lady," by James Forbes.

Tommy Noonan (Property Man)   Mr. JACK DENTON
Una Hion. Miss Prudence Montague   Miss ELMA MORRIS
Miss Patricia O'Brien (one of the Chorus) Miss ROSE STAHL
Scene—A Dressing Room in the Royal English Opera House.

| 13. | Intermezzo | | | 10.7 |

(a) ENTR'ACTE FROM "L'Amico Fritz"   Mastagni
(b) TARANTELLE FROM "The Gipsy Suite"   Ed. German

14.	WILL ROGERS, Cowboy Lassoist.			10.17
15.	"ELTINGE"			10.29
16.	LES TROMBETTA, Grandes Originalites.			10.39

Dans leurs Œuvres et Creations

| 17. | THE BIOSCOPE. | | | 10.57 |

Arrival at the Prince and Princess of Wales,   Eruption of Mount Vesuvius.
4th May.   Humorous Phases of Funny Faces.
The Olympic Games.   Italian Cavalry Manœuvres.
The Music Composed by HERMAN FINCK.

MATINÉE OF THE FULL PROGRAMME EVERY SATURDAY at 2.
SPECIAL PRICES TO ALL PARTS. SEATS CAN NOW BE BOOKED.

Treasurer—Mr. THOMAS MILLER.   Stage Manager—Mr. FRANK DAMER.

NOTICE.—The Public can leave the Theatre at the end of the performance by all exits and entrance doors
which open outwards. Where there is a fireproof screen in the proscenium opening, it must be lowered at
least once during every performance to ensure its being in proper working order. All gangways, passages
and staircases must be kept free from chairs or any other obstructions, whether permanent or temporary.
The order and composition of this Programme may be varied as circumstances require.

DOORS OPEN 7.45.

BOX OFFICE open from 11 a.m. to 11 p.m.   TELEPHONE No. 6534 (2 lines) GERRARD.

The Pianofortes used at this Theatre are by Messrs. JOHN BRINSMEAD & SONS.

POPULAR PRICES:—PRIVATE BOXES, 1, 2, 3½ and 3 Guineas. FAUTEUILS (numbered and
reserved) 7/6. ORCHESTRA STALLS (numbered and reserved), 5/-.
ROYAL CIRCLE, First Two Rows, 5/-, other Rows, 3/-. (all Seats numbered and reserved),
FIRST CIRCLE, 2/-.   AMPHITHEATRE 1/-.

Musical Director—Mr. HERMAN FINCK.   Assistant Manager—Mr. FITZROY GARDNER.

"You Was So Wise You Couldent Be Showed. . ."

In many ways, 1907 was not a good year for Will Rogers or for Betty. It was the year he almost lost her for good.

It was the year he branched out with a bigger show and nearly lost his shirt before discovering that his own stunts and personality were what folks paid good money to see, not the massive productions which gained fame and fortune for Buffalo Bill and Pawnee Bill and to a lesser extent Colonel Mulhall.

It was a bad year for the country economically, climaxed by a panic on the stock exchange and a run on the banks in October.

It was the year when vaudeville moguls battled each other. Some went broke and others consolidated. A performer who attached himself to the wrong circuit found himself in deep trouble.

But 1907 had its exciting moments. Peek-a-boo waists—blouses made of fabric with tiny holes embroidered into patterns. The first all-steel Pullman sleeping car. In Washington, D. C., the elaborate new Union Station opened. Out on the Plains, Oklahoma finally claimed statehood, though not a mention of the destruction of Indian Territory or the establishment of the new state appeared in Will's letters, in spite of his father's involvement.

Onstage it was Gus Edwards and "School Days, School Days." Daring young men sang "The Peach that Tastes the Sweetest Hangs the Highest on the Tree," and everybody loved "Harrigan."

Will worried about the feud among the vaudeville lords and the uncertainty of the future. He joined the "White Rats" to protest some of the rules—"Rats" was "Star" spelled backwards. Yet he was one of the few who managed to get steady bookings and was able to "cross the lines" between vaudeville competitors.

Mail from home and from Betty only increased his insecurity.

As he told a Hollywood reporter later, "I'm not foolin' myself like a lot of these people around here, countin' on the good things to come. No siree! Just now things

Noisy partygoers at the Palace in London became quiet enough to hear Will's natural voice when he stepped onstage. Even the "percentage girls" selling drinks stopped and listened. At left are theater programs from Will's performances.

are breakin' fine—but every day I say to myself, tomorrow may be the last. The public's bound to catch on in time. . . . Just now doin fine—but it ain't goin to last—all luck! And luck don't last. . . . The public's goin' to get sick of us trick actors. We're just a fad and fads dont last. . . ."

Even though he was somewhat superstitious, Will was not the kind to sit around worrying. He constantly worked to perfect his act, to try something new. And he never gave up on Betty. Someday she would see it his way.

She was not sitting home twiddling her thumbs. She said later that Will had left her totally confused after the Lane's houseparty. He'd seemed to ignore her while he cut up with every other girl there. They never had a chance to be alone, not even when they were out riding. He didn't act like a man courting a woman at all.

Besides she had other beaus. The big white house on Walnut street rang with music and laughter. Her married sisters were often there with their families. Theda—the sister called "Dick"—broke off her engagement with a West Point cadet, took a job in Stroud's Mercantile and taught school. They sold her engagement ring and bought a horse called Moses and a buggy to drive around the countryside. They fixed picnic

lunches and went to Monte Ne where they swam in the covered pool.

Betty worked at various jobs when she felt like it or when money was needed. She set type and made up ads for the newspaper, worked in railway stations and sometimes at Stroud's with her sisters.

Will performed at the Gayety Theater in Brooklyn on New Year's Eve, where he saw the beginning of 1907. From there, trains took him to Baltimore, Pittsburgh, back to New York, to Boston and to Washington, D.C.

It was in the nation's capitol that his father and sisters got to see him perform on stage for the first time, and things looked up—for awhile, anyway.

But existing letters are scarce for 1907. His father spent most of his time in Guthrie, and may not have kept Will's letters. His sisters may not have written as much, or he could have been temporarily estranged from them for some reason.

We know he had another girlfriend—maybe more than one. He was a healthy young male and "needed a woman," as he told Betty.

Possibly he latched onto one who didn't want to turn loose in 1907. In any case, there was a problem. Perhaps that was why his family came to Washington, D.C. to see him perform. It might also have been his reason for going abroad again.

These are intriguing questions not answered in all the years since. They may never be. But it's plain Will never really gave up on Betty.

The local papers reported that Maud, Sallie and C. V. saw the closing days of the 59th Congress the first week in March and visited Will Rogers at Chase's Theater. Then Clem went back to Guthrie to attend to his duties.

The utopian community of Monte Ne was a favorite resort spot for the seven Blake girls. They traveled there frequently on the Frisco railroad that ran through Rogers, Arkansas, to Lowell, where a four-mile spur headed for Monte Ne. Betty's special friend Tom Harvey was engineer on the Monte Ne spur-train, pulling one passenger car with a caboose for luggage over the four miles from the main Frisco line to the resort. The resort offered many amenities, including an indoor-outdoor pool that provided spectators a shady spot while swimmers caught the sun. Huge log structures named for nearby states went up at Monte Ne before 1910, serving as hotels and recreation centers. "Oklahoma Row" (above left) was dismantled in the 1970s and restored about half a mile away, north of the banks of Beaver Lake, which now covers much of the original utopian site.

HOTEL PUTNAM

New York
April 18 [1907]
My Dear Papa

I got the letter and the money all O.K. and am off in the morning for England as I think I can do pretty good over there for a short time   I am taking over two other boys and three horses   I bought two ponies from a boy   they are polo ponies   it makes 4 of us and three ponies

I am going to put on a bigger act   I dont know how I will make out   it will take a lot of money but I think it will pay me in the long run

Dont know how long I will be over there   only going to England   I will write you as soon as I get there
> Write me to
> Hotel Provence
> Leicester Square, London
Lots Love to all
Willie

Will was disorganized, underfunded, and out on a limb when he took his little troupe to London. He sailed on the S.S. *Kaiser* on April 18. The troupe worked on an act and finally found a couple of bookings—at the Empire in Coventry and at Liverpool the first week of June. Fortunately, Palace patrons remembered Will from the previous year. He gave performances there and at Kettner's restaurant, barely making enough to get the group back home. By the end of June, he was booked into the Chestnut Street Opera House in Philadelphia as "The Cowboy who has astonished the world with his Lasso."

Variety reported that "Will Rogers was given the place of honor on the bill, and held it down in fine style. Rogers closed the show, but everybody waited for him, and his act went with a hurrah."

In early fall he rehearsed for a role with "The Girl Rangers," a George W. Lederer production with three acts and five scenes. It was to open in Chicago. Rogers' contract called for twenty-five consecutive weeks at $300 per week.

"Incidental to Act I, Mr. Will Rogers, universally conceded to be the greatest rope thrower in the world, who has just returned from his European triumphs, will introduce his famous exhibition of artistic lariat manipulations." He roped to "The Carnations' Waltz."

A lengthy review in the *Evening News* (city unknown) included raves for Will Rogers:

> The one restful, amusing and delightful quarter of an hour in the great big show was the specialty of Will Rogers, the 'plum good' rope thrower from Texas. Mr. Rogers has a set of teeth which carry him through an Indian massacre without a scratch, so attractive are they in a rakish smile. He is tanned-up, a lean and richly witty cowboy who does not lose his ranch manners in an op'ry house. His act was considerably lassoed itself by the scenery and Mr. Rogers impromptu monologue was deliciously witty and acceptable and his rope throwing wonderful.

Another clipping sent home to Betty said, "His part of the show is worth the entire price of admission." A notice from the *Journal* of Monday, September 2, 1907, went further:

> The authors of this sizzling show ought to write in a part for Will Rogers. That is, incorporate Will into the story and let him talk. Isn't that the greatest line of ranger conversation ever heard? That plumb good lingo of Texas and the plains. The man has temperament, too, and magnetism and every word he says, every glance of his keen eye, ever swift curve of his magic rope comes over the footlights with a flash of power. It would be too bad to spoil a good vaudeville act, but Rogers ought to be in a play. He is a whole show himself . . . but Rogers is a genius and has a kind

of shaggy romance about him which is attractive. He is the great big hit with the big show and it does not seem to have interfered with his chest measure. . . . [The second night] Rogers is given fewer fence posts to lasso when he wants room to do wonders. He ought to have a play written for him, with a playwright who could sit and drink in some of the Rogers talk and that Texas Drawl. He has temperament, ease, grace and unconscious dramatic talent for splendid comedy. . . . He is a big hit.

THE SARATOGA

Chicago, Sep 19, 1907
My Dearest—
 Well have waited two days for that other letter you said in the last one that you would write tomorrow. Why dont you keep your word for I looked for it now for two long days
 Well just found out that we do not go to St Louis but to Philadelphia and that I am to remain with the show—aint that good—eru-errr. (growls outside) But I dont think I will be east but a short time and then the first open time I have I will be home and if not till Xmas. Oh, I am coming then show or no show.
 Got a dandy letter from Mr. [Tom] Morgan today. . .
 We finish here Sept 29. would stay longer but the house is rented and they have to move.
 Now I am only writing this to tell you about that letter so I will stop—Now listen Dear   please write often—to the Hotel here.
   Yours now   Billie

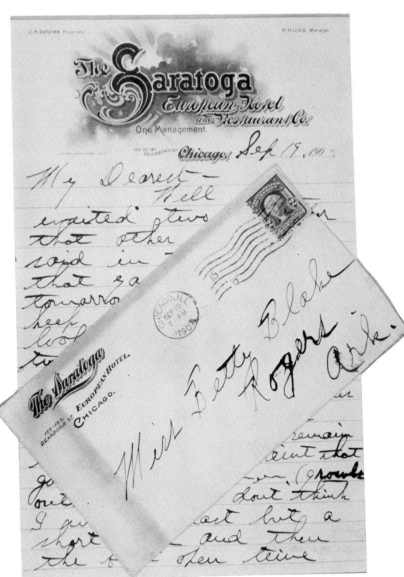

 Wow! Suddenly he is calling her "Dearest" and signing himself "Billie." Clearly they have had some time together and patched things up. But a couple of letters are missing from this year—possibly destroyed by Betty because they were too personal to keep.

 By mid-September Will managed some time away from the show for a visit to his father who had been ill. He also managed to spend a little time with Betty. Then he was back on the vaudeville circuit by the last of October, in Philadelphia. The "Girl Rangers" folded. He must have seen it coming.

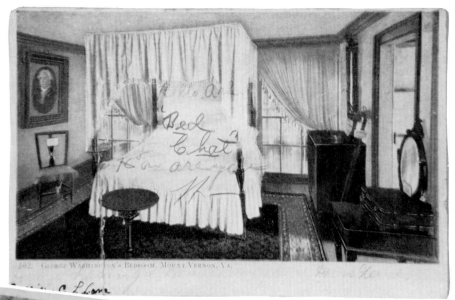

Philadelphia
Peoples Theatre
Thursday Aft. [Posted November 7, 1907]
My Dear Betty.

Well you dont seem to be writing so offul fast after me asking you to forgive me for my long delay   now I thought you would write me a few by now— Now listen Betty that was not my fault and besides I am just supposed to be a bit mad at you for awhile yet for you know you did not just do right when I wrote you from Chicago   But let it go and you get busy with the stationary and lace a few pages out to the old dog for he is just as strong for you as ever. and always will be. Well how are things breaking for you in that land and aint it about time to make up your mind to get out and see something

Oh tell Morgan I am <u>Headlined</u> over our friends Hymus and McIntyre this week and that Hymus is high on Tom, thinks hes great.

Well I go to Brooklyn Grand Opera House next Week. I am glad to get back in Vaudeville again   Well I have not got a cent of that $1,275.00 yet and dont think I will.

I am planning on seeing you Xmas if things break right   "G" but I been away a long time aint I. and I will be so glad to get back again.

Well I will have to stop   I am in my dressing room writing this

Now you write me a nice long letter at once to Grand Opera House Brooklyn.

I will certainly get St. Louis and K.C. this winter soon for they are on this circuit

Well <u>Idios</u> my Girl and you be good down there for I know you all are having one big time this winter

Yours as ever.

Billie

White Rats of America
Mon- Night [Posted November 19, 1907]
My Dearest Bettie

Well I got your letters last week and of course was glad to hear from you and that you was not sore at me—honest I aint so bad if you only knew me better—oh girl you dont know how I do think of you and if I dont write it or show it—I think it I think I will be able to get home either Xmas or about Feb 1st as this contract runs out then and I will get to come then sure

Tell Morgan thanks for his letter and will write him. I cant write you much Bettie for I dont know what to say but hope to get to see you and tell you a lot.

Write me a nice long letter. This week I am at Shubert Theatre till Saturday. 23. Newark, N.J.
Next Week. Tremont Theatre   Boston. Mass.
<u>Be a good girl</u> and just remember who loves you.
Billie
Goodnight.

HOTEL RALEIGH

Baltimore, Md. Dec. 6 [1907]
Well My old Pal

I got a letter from you in Boston and it seemed a bit queer   (you said you had written or was going to write three)   I only got one as I have been traveling to fast for my mail lately   I am in Baltimore this Week and go to Washington Next week—Write me there—General Delivery and I will be surer getting it.

Now I am going to ask you something Betty   if I act queer dont <u>think of it</u>—I aint treating <u>you right</u> and I know <u>it</u> but I will later on   I am doing the best I can under the circumstances   <u>I am in wrong</u> and will tell you all about it when I see you which might be Xmas and not later than Feb. as my contract goes till then.

When you still refused me last spring—<u>We both will regret that</u>. for we would of been happy and a thousand times more prosperous. Still you was so <u>wise</u> you couldent be showed. Now you see what it has led too. I have not been worth a <u>dam</u> since and you are the <u>direct</u> and unwilling cause of it. still I dont blame you   only I wish you had not been so
<u>Bull headed</u>

Now thets [lets] hope all will come out O.K. Now you be a good girl and always remember that I love you more than all   when you know all you will say I aint such a bad fellow and will always do what is right.

Think lots of me and write to Washington
<u>Yours</u>
Billie.

In Rogers, Arkansas, Miss Bettie Blake's complimentary pass on the Monte Ne Railway operated by Tom Harvey expired December 31. We don't know how often she used it or whether it was renewed.

Facing page: Two postcards sent by Will from the home of George Washington in Mount Vernon, Virginia. On the card at the top, Will wrote: "Hello, Ark. ['Bed for Chat'] How are you   W—" and at the bottom "We are having a houseparty here Mrs Lane." The card below he sent to Betty, writing "Hello Pal. We are right in this place now inside Washingtons old house big time." On the reverse of this card is a one-cent stamp, the name of the publisher, Foster & Reynolds, 1 Madison Avenue, New York, and Will's handwritten address to "Miss Betty Blake" in "Rogers, Ark." In 1907 no further address was needed for the card to reach her. The postmark reads "Mount Vernon on the Potomac, Va., Feb 27, 1907, P.M."

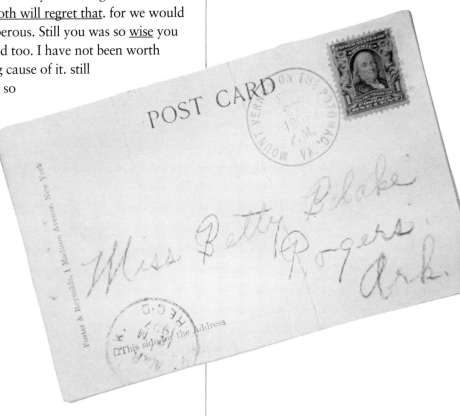

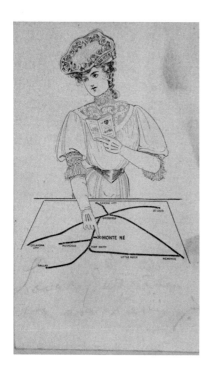

The courtship of Will Rogers hit rough seas during this period, just when it seemed that the young couple understood each other and could use endearments with ease. Will readily admitted he was jealous, but Betty still dated other men. She claimed that she wanted to remain just friends and that she was not jealous. Will promised to be open and honest—to reveal all— and asked Betty to do the same. He sent her a red-hot letter from a "showgirl" to prove he was immune to advances from other women and that he was open and aboveboard. But she still would not tell him about her friend Tom Harvey, or about other men in her life.

He had probably already told her—as most men did in those days—that a decent man courting a good woman wanted her to remain pure, but that he needed "the other kind of women" for physical reasons. Will wanted Betty to understand that he didn't go out with them for "marrying" purposes.

Because of the mail and traveling involved, Betty did not get the letter sent to Will by Mamie—which he included in his letter to her— for several days. He had two good letters and a few days of grace before it all broke loose. The letter from Mamie upset Betty. How dare he! But it has remained in the Rogers collection all these years.

Will poses with a friend for this snapshot postcard that he sent Betty from Portland. "Cute (yes-no.) NO" he wrote on the card between the two men's photographs, and above their dapper hats (Will's on the right at its characteristically extreme slant), "imitation of a smile— almost a grin." The inscription to the side reads "Taken out at a park in Portland after getting one of your letters, 'aint that some smile Kid' That other boy is Gibson boy and knows Sandy name Alexander. Well you are dandy now, and I am ashamed cause you are doing great just keep it up and I will do better. dont hardly think I will get there though still I hope so."

THE WALDORF

Hamilton, Ont.
Jan. 23, 1908
My Dearest Betty

Well I got your letter which had been sent on to me from Montreal . . . .

I am playing here in Hamilton, Can. this week and go to Toronto Can. next week so you can nail me there with a letter. I did not write you on your trip cause I knew you would . . . not have time to be messing with letters.

Well I am up here and just about froze say Kid but it is some chilly I havent seen a wheel only on trains Its all <u>sleds</u> and snow and skates. I will get back in the U.S. after next week if I dont freeze.

Well I had my first little sick spell last week in Montreal and it was kinder like a very hard or congestive chill and I went on Matinee then to my hotel and was very bad called a Dr. and he came 4 different times before 12 at night I missed only the one show as I felt better the next day but I sho got sorter scared and some way I kinder wished for my Betty and would of got well quick. Its all alright away off all the time till you get to feeling bad and then it puts you to thinking and you wish you was home but I feel good now and am all O.K.

Well I hope you did enjoy your trip and wish I could of been home to went around with you in some of the places for I am beginning to get to feel homesick.

Well my present contract will be up in a short time and then I will get home and down to see you the 1st thing

Now I hope you was a good girl on this trip and did not make any new mashes and you are still <u>heart</u> <u>free</u>

Now write me a long letter and all about your trip and tell me <u>all.</u>

Well its late at night just come in from my usual night <u>feed</u> its about 2 A.M. so will be <u>beating</u> <u>it</u>.

This is a "lousy" town will be glad when Sat comes.

Write often and long Your old boy

B__

Gaiety Theatre
Toronto, Can.
Wednesday [Posted January 24, 1908]
Dear Kid

I am very sorry you dissipointed me this afternoon had you come round where I asked Brown to tell you, you would have been quite safe as it is the back entrance to the Hotel and nobody would have seen us. oh my darling I am dying to see you. Sure I know you will laugh at me saying that but it is true all the same. I suppose the boys told you what had happened up there so of course I will not go there again. Now darling will you do me this favour and come here tonight about an hour after show or say half past twelve then I will come out to see you. Instead of going up the street that the tram runs turn off the other street you will see a lane wait there fore me I will not dissiapoint you now will you my darling? I know you will my darling old Kid

yours loving   as always
Mamie

p.s.

I just almost forget to ask you this, you seem to have cut me since last night and I heard you remark this morning about looking for a boat   well darling if you wish to cut loose from me come tonight and tell me so even if it is a great blow to me anything would be better than for to look at me as you did this morning   it does hurt me because I love you more than I can ever tell anyone   perhaps it is not my place to tell you how I love you but I cant help it   I must let my mind out to some one and I trust you more than anyone else

now sweetheart write me a note and let me know if you will come   Bill will give it to me

     M.S.

Will was performing at Hamilton, Ontario, and staying at the Waldorf that week. Then he went to Toronto, to Worcester, Massachusetts, and back to Brooklyn, New York. He had a little reprieve before the letter reached Betty and in all innocence he wrote her as if nothing had happened.

NEW PARK HOTEL

Worcester, Mass.

Feb 6th. 08.

My Dearest—

Well your letter finally got here it   did not get to Toronto till away after I left and was forwarded on here and reached me today just <u>now</u>   it was written on Jan 27. and get here Feb. 6. I was just going to send you a wire tonight and tell you where I was at. I am here this week and go to Brooklyn next week.

Well old pal I was cert glad to hear from you and more so to hear you was having such a good time but you always do, do that   you are a pretty lucky girl and a lot of ways   did you ever think it <u>over</u> "<u>Well</u> <u>do</u> <u>you</u> <u>are</u>"

You have a lot of good times and no worry at all

No that was all right to tell Mary [Gulager] anything and I am glad you did   I wish you could of gotten up to see the home folks and I know they would have loved to had you come for they think you are a fine girl.

Well I will kinder know next week about just when I will get home as I have not heard from my agent for several weeks but will see him next week. I dont hardly think I will get there by the 1st but will perhaps by the last   still I dont know a thing till I get to N.Y. I am getting kinder homesick and am in a hurry to come and am liable to get in at any time from the 1st on.

Well I was glad to get back to the U.S. after three weeks in Canada and will be glad to be back in old N.Y. again next week as N.Y. and Brooklyn is all one

Well I am all well and have not been sick anymore and dont think I will as that was cold more than anything.

     It seems that I cant get west at all   they keep playing me <u>over</u> and <u>over</u> again around here and never do send me on one of the western Circuits.

So you <u>snared</u> you a <u>promising</u> lawyer   What all did he promise you. and you him.

Now you better slack up on that <u>stuff</u> for it gets you in bad and I will be getting

"NOW YOU BETTER SLACK UP ON THAT <u>STUFF</u>. . . YOU KNOW HOW JEALOUS I AM . . . ."

pretty <u>sore</u> some time   you know how jealous I am and what a lot you have to tell me when I see you all about that what you said was too long to tell one time   I still have all that up my <u>sleeve</u> and am still a bit leary on just how you stand and if you dont tell me all these <u>things</u>, Well <u>I might find out otherwise</u>

Now you better deal square with me for I have with you as bad as I have been. You could of prevented it

Well Betty I sho would love to see you and oh what a time we would have   talk about staying up late we never would turn in   we would have so much to tell each other wouldent we.

Well I must stop or I will be getting sentimental and I cant afford to do that you know.

You write me a nice long letter and just <u>hope</u> and <u>pray</u> that things turn out all right-   Tell Tom [Morgan] will send his photo soon as I get it

With a lot of love to the best Girl I know ever knew.

     Your old Boy
     B___
     Orpheum Theatre
     Brooklyn

The Henking Hotel
Springfield, Mass.　　　　　　Feb 20, 1908.
My Dearest Bettie

Well your letter finally reached me   your letters always seem to reach the theatre just after I have left it but they are certainly appreciated when they do come

Well I am on what is called the Poli circuit   he has 7 houses and this is my second one and guess I will play the other five in rotation   I go to Poli's Hartford Conn. next week   it is only a little ways from here.

Well I got a little letter from old Mary told me about seeing you and you being a fine fellow and all that   I am going to write her and also send her some pictures and some <u>Music</u> and you by the way   I will go out and see if I cant dig you up something in the music line and I will send Tom Morgan the pictures   now they are not those large ones but these are all I have but will send him one of each   I only had just yours and Papa's and Sisters of the large ones   the others all the other size   yes he is a good fellow and I certainly would love to see him succeed for he is certainly bright and to see some of these <u>hams</u> back here that do get on is a wonder to me for he has all of them tied to a post.

Well I think I will land up there about May the 1st for I am getting pretty homesick but I better get this while I can.

I look for a bad year next year   I have made no plans at all for them   I may stay home if things are any ways bright out there as I am crazy to get another little bunch of cattle and get back on that old <u>farm</u> and tend to what little I have got. still its hard to give up the money one can make but at the most one more year will let me out   I am still offered that play for next year   that is the most likely thing of all

You never do seem to understand me when I ever make any allusion to that which you once wrote and told me was too long a story to tell. "You know what I

"I AM CRAZY TO GET ANOTHER LITTLE BUNCH OF CATTLE AND GET BACK ON THAT OLD <u>FARM</u>. . . ."

For all his talk about ranching, he forgot it in a minute when the new offer came. After that taste of show business, he lost his desire to be a rancher. All of Dad's life he talked about getting a real ranch. He looked at a million of them, but could always find something wrong with them. A ranch was just a dream—something to talk about or maybe thought he should have—but he really didn't want one."

~James Blake Rogers

mean in regard to your <u>Dearest</u> <u>friend</u>. T. H. [Tom Harvey]   you remember what we had our troubles about before I went to Europe. Now you never did care to tell me what there is or was to it, but me like a big <u>rummy</u> I up and told you a lot of stuff (that I had never ought to of told anybody in the world.

Well I am just living life as she comes and havent much confidence in anything we all make mistakes but as long as we live to the best we know how they cant be considered against one can they?

By the way how are you doing with your lawer [lawyer] Well its <u>even</u> for I have fell in love with an <u>actorine</u> and <u>gone</u> <u>plum</u> <u>nutty</u>

Now you see if you cant get a line or two there on time

Be good and I hope to see you soon   I liked the picture great and it was so thoughtful of you to send it.

Well show time

     Lots of Love,

     B___

Poli's Theatre

   Hartford, Conn

Because of his work schedule, Will took advantage of his late-night hours. Betty too knew the small town excitement of dancing the night away and going home by daylight. It was socially acceptable, and, after all, they were not yet engaged. Neither was supposed to get upset over such things.

Oneco Hotel

New Haven, Conn.

[Posted March 2, 1908]

<u>My</u> <u>Dearest</u> (and that goes)

Well Betty I received your crazy letter and honest it knocked me a <u>twister</u> You could not of been your same dear old self when you wrote it.

Now I want to not only tell you were wrong in most all you said but I will show you that you were and prove it to you

Now in the first place if you remember <u>rightly</u>, this <u>coolness</u> of which I fully admit started when you refused to tell me of that T.H. thing

Now you know that and I have always treated you coolly since   Not because I felt like it but because I just felt that I was <u>getting</u> <u>back</u> at you and I done the whole thing purposely and intended to do it in a way till you did tell me, for I honestly felt and do feel that it was <u>due</u> me

That last letter remined [reminded] you of that and you know they all did.

Now <u>secondly</u> as to any other girl it is foolish to think of them <u>ever</u> in the same breath with you

Now you say about my regretting telling you all of that stuff I did one time. <u>Yes</u> <u>I</u> said I felt like a <u>rummy</u> to tell you all of my past and then you not tell me one little thing   I said it was not fair cause I told you all and you still would not tell me a thing

No I am not ashamed of a thing I ever told you and feel <u>proud</u> of it   I thought it showed <u>manhood</u>   It only hurt me so bad cause you could not trust me with a

"YES I GOT A LOT OF GIRLS NOT ONE AS YOU SAY   BUT SEVERAL <u>ON</u> AND <u>OFF</u> THE STAGE."

measly little old <u>love</u> <u>scrape</u> cause I know that was all

I told you I had always been a <u>bad</u> <u>boy</u> and guess I will continue to be one till you are with me and then its all over   I will put all of this old life behind and I think I am man enough to do it too.

Yes I got a lot of girls   not one as you say   but several <u>on</u> and <u>off</u> the stage. I dont mean this as <u>sarcasm</u> or conceit   its just to put you right.   several <u>girls</u> <u>not</u> <u>sweethearts</u> or girls that when it comes to settling down I would consider for a minute   I kinder always thought I knew about where my love and affection lay. And I gave you credit for not being a jealous girl and take a thing that was put in a letter just for a little <u>sting</u> the same as you had put in mine several times   the last in regard to the Lawyer   Now I am the jealous one of the two. And yet I took it as it was meant and come back at you with the actor gal one, but no you size it all up wrong and write that afful letter.

You say I spoke of it as a mistake   yes so they were <u>lots</u> of them   I have done nothing all year but the wrong thing and then you say <u>thank</u> <u>goodness</u> it was discovered in time

You speak as if I had a dark plot to decieve you and you (<u>old</u> <u>sleuth</u>) had discovered it. Now when I tell you I have made a mistake I mean what I say and I intend to tell you all about them when I get home. Not in regard to you or nothing that concerns you   but if its necessary I will explain them to you. The mistake I spoke of was for telling you all and then you telling me nothing and if you read your letter properly you will see it as its meant. Now if I wanted to break off with you I would do in a great deal more gentlemanly way than that and one that I think you would not lose respect for me for it would be to tell you the <u>plain</u> facts, whatever they might be but I hope that will never come to pass on either side I wouldent beat about the bush trying to save your feelings but out with the whole truth   if you think other wise you got me sized up wrong.

Now Betty comes the thing   the whole thing   in your letter that certainly did <u>hurt</u>, and I dident think you could accuse me of such.

You say,—"I was idescreet [indiscreet] and for that you have never thought well of me. or at least have never believed me and when I refer to other boys, you invariably grow suspiciously <u>sarcastic</u> <u>and</u> <u>throw</u> unpleasant insinuations."

Now Betty plainly, <u>that's</u> <u>not</u> <u>so</u> and its the worst thing you could say, for of all the things I admire and love you for its for you being <u>good</u> and <u>pure</u> and not silly and <u>spooney</u>

Now I never in all my life insinuated a wrong thing in regard to other boys   it would be the last thing on earth   why I would fight any one that would insinuate as much to me as that you acted the least bit unladylike at any time. <u>Why</u> girl thats why I <u>love</u> you. thats why you are different from the rest   Why <u>what we done</u> I <u>love</u> <u>you</u> <u>for</u> if you had not of done it I would of known you did not <u>love</u> me. I dont think bad of you for that, cause I knew you was a girl that if you hadent of loved me that wouldent of happened   Why I would trust you every way in the world

You size me up cause I showed you a silly letter once   my good girl   to show you how I knew her to be only fooling   she was <u>mixed</u> up with to my own knowledge, with three fellows perhaps writing worse ones to them. No I know these girls in this business <u>a little</u>, and I think there is a little difference between you and them

Now as you have said you would love to tell me that little story why then I know you will when I see you and for the 1st time in a long time I feel that you are dealing as square with me as I am with you. I came very near closing and coming out there this week but it would of been very foolish for I would of got in bad here as I have this time to play.

Now Betty I want you to cut out all of this foolish talk for when I tell you you are the only girl for me I mean it regardless of how I act sometimes   Now I think I will see you some time soon and oh wont we have a jolly time and wont it be great

Must go do my show now and mail this. Write at once

Your same old boy

This Week   Billy,

Poli's Theatre, New Haven, Mass.

Variety reported on March 2 that Will Rogers had received a telegram saying his father was dangerously ill and had left for home at once. His father's illness may have been his reason for returning, or it might have been just an excuse. Will knew he and Betty were on dangerous ground, and he needed to be near her to work things out. From the relaxed tone of the next letter we can guess that he succeeded.

THE CONVENTION TO FORM A CONSTITUTION FOR THE STATE OF OKLAHOMA

CLEMENT V. ROGERS

MEMBER SIXTY-FOURTH DISTRICT

CLAREMORE, I.T.   GUTHRIE, OKLA.

Friday Eve.

[Posted April 18, 1908]

My Dearest Betty

Well on my arrival home this morning and did not get a letter from you I felt offully disapointed—but I guess I expected a little more than I should and after due consideration I know that you are right and if I had of deserved a letter I would of got one so I guess I did not deserve one.

Now I was offul busy at McAlister [on Masonic work] as we were kept in and did not get a chance to ever get out from the work till late at night and that was not my fault.

Well I go back east in a few days I think I will get by your house either Monday or Tuesday I cannot get there Sunday as all of the family are having a dinner at Mauds and all the Family will be there and then I will come by and see you on my way east and do you know I just hate to go some how or nother and I feel kinder blue and I just want you to <u>cheer</u> me <u>up</u> for you are the only one that can do it. you always do have a clear conception of everything and I do so trust you and believe you. I dont know why but I do   honest I do.

Well I am a <u>Mason</u> Are <u>you</u> and I tell you it is great and it should make me a lot better boy—Well there is plenty of room for improvement.

Well dearie I will have to stop as the train is coming soon and I want you to get this tomorrow

Papa, Maud, Sallie. Cap, and I are down here spending the day and will stay till the late train and see the <u>Holy City</u> played tonight. I bet its great

Well Betts I will let you know when I come   I think it will be Monday on the <u>Noon</u> <u>train</u>

      Your old ever loving Kid
        Billy.

There was a popular song, "I Am a Mason, Are You?"

Arcade Hotel
European
Bridgeport, Connecticut April 29 1908
My Dear Papa

    Well I got Mauds telegram saying you were just doing <u>fine</u> and I am sure glad —Now you just stay most of the time up at Chelsea and take your medicine and take good care of yourself and you will soon be all right

    I am getting along fine since I opened up here   my act is doing as well as ever. I will send you some money at the end of the week as I want to start in to pay off that note. . . .

    I seen the Buffalo Bill Show in New York as I came through.

    I guess I will get that <u>Grip</u> Maud sent about tomorrow.

    It is as hot as summer up here and I sho do sweat when I work   my old pony is fatter than ever   he is so fat he can hardly walk.

    Now I will write you often and will let you know later where to write to me at

    Lots of Love to all and you just look after yourself good and when you git able and can I want you to come east and stay a few days with me in each place   you could spare a couple of weeks

      Your loving son
        Willie

[Posted May 3, 1908]
Arcade Hotel
European
Bridgeport, Connecticut
My Own Sweetheart

    Well here it is Friday and do you know I do believe I will have to lay off next week   after already having my agent book me now I find myself that there is a hitch some place cause Scranton. Pa. where I was booked is to change for the summer and play <u>Stock</u> instead of Vaudeville   it changed one week earlier than had been expected. Still I am to hear from my agent today by <u>phone</u> and I may land something yet   I hope I do but I am not <u>raving</u> about it cause they tell me you are luckey these days to get anything at all. I have a good offer for next season   15 weeks at $300 per. and 25 at $250.00 per   that is great   40 weeks   open Sept. 1st, on the Keith circuit   that's the people I generally play for. Week after next I think I play 5th ave. Theatre New York and am offered two or three weeks on Hammerstein Roof Garden again. Thats the candy place to work and where you

Many times he could have been with her, but he didn't go. Sort of like the song—He "Had It His Way."
    ~James Blake Rogers

"I HAVE A GOOD OFFER FOR NEXT SEASON 15 WEEKS AT $300 PER."

Will poses with a friend for this snapshot postcard that he sent Betty from Portland. "Cute (yes-no.) NO" he wrote on the card between the two men's photographs, and above their dapper hats (Will's on the right at its characteristically extreme slant), "imitation of a smile— almost a grin." The inscription to the side reads "Taken out at a park in Portland after getting one of your letters, 'aint that some smile Kid' That other boy is gibson boy and knows Sandy name Alexander. Well you are dandy now, and I am ashamed cause you are doing great just keep it up and I will do better. dont hardly think I will get there though still I hope so."

get all of the out of town managers to see you.

This letter is all business but I want to tell you all for <u>you</u> <u>should</u> <u>know</u>

I got your letter you wrote yesterday. Sunday and it was great and I just love you more all the time and want you to tell me everytime I do wrong cause I am very careless and dont think

If I should lay off I will be in N.Y. and tend to a lot of business I should do. My address will be care of.

White Rats Club 47th St. Broadway New York

Now if I wire you I am not working you write to me there and a dandy long letter cause I sho do love to hear from you   and say <u>Hon</u> it seems a year since I saw you and I just want to go right back down there now.

Will write and wire later. Yours any old time

B___

[Posted June 4, 1908]
St. Louis Hotel
Duluth, Minn Thursday 1908
My Dear Papa:

I got your letter all right and am so glad that you are doing so well now   you must keep up your medicine and take good care of yourself

Well I finish here Sunday night then I dont play next week as it takes most of the time to jump to Butte, Montana. where I play the week after. I am going to go by the Yellowstone Park and stay a couple of days as it is right on my road.

Papa I guess my note there is about due and you better get Godbey to renew it for another 60 days for in a couple of more weeks I will be able to pay a lot of it off. so just renew it for me for 60 days

Got a letter from Mrs Gibbs but tell her I am out of Canada now and don't know when I will be there again and cant get the Gold coins she spoke of.

Write me for the next 10 days to Grand Theatre Butte, Montana

Love to all   Willie

Evidently Betty told Will again that he must leave vaudeville and settle down in respectable work before she could take him seriously. In the next letter, he made a strong argument for staying in show business. Probably when he got back on stage where the crowd loved him and returned to old friends who thought he was great, he felt much better than when he was home as the errant little brother and the guilty lover.

[Posted June 5, 1908]
St. Louis Hotel
Duluth, Minn., Thursday Eve
My Own Dearest—

Well Sweetheart your letter came yesterday and say you did take your time about writing   I thought you had lost the address.

Well I will try Dearie and tell you a few of the things you asked me about. Yes it is very lonesome sometimes but as for hating the work and wanting to give it up, No not as long as you can get booked and get a good salary for there is no work in the world as nice and easy as this business when things are coming right.

It beats that old farm and ranch and store thing.

Now the time to stop is when you have made enough to live without it and when they cant use you any more

Now I am going this summer and next year to make a good little bit of money out of this bar [barring] misfortune of course and how could I do better at home I will go there in time enough and have my good place to live and wont have to depend on a business.   thats my dope on this thing.

Now you are wrong about this trip. this is one of the best paying trips I ever took for the time. I will be $1500 or $2,000 ahead of what I was when I left New York. it will keep me away from those cheap summer houses and parks all summer where $200 is the best I could of got. it will put me in a new country that I never played and may want too again. it is great   my salary as [is] great $275. for this circuit. it keeps you away from N.Y. during these dull times. in fact it is lucky all around. Now I will be able to go back next season new and fresh and at a good salary   you must remember I played 3 years right around those same houses so it does one good to give them a rest.   yes last Sunday I spent all day on the train   on this circuit all the acts jump togeather   this same bunch will be togeather till after Seattle.

We finish here Sunday Night as we have to work here on Sunday and then we lose next week jumping to Butte. I will go by the yellowstone and spend a few days   leaving here Monday morning   wont get to see a lot but will get an idea of

"NOW THE TIME TO STOP IS WHEN. . . THEY CANT USE YOU ANY MORE. . . ."

it. We open a [at] Butte on Saturday. Write to Grand Theatre there for the next 10 days and I will get your first letters on my arrival there

Will leave there on june 20th. for Spokane. then Seattle. Would like to meet your friend and say its funny you did not let me meet Tom Morgans Sister   I could not <u>savy</u> that at all.

No about Tony [probably Coin Harvey's secretary] I only told you that he acted quite a bit different the last time from the first and thats all. Now please tell me what you mean by him trying to <u>sting</u> you. and why. and what kind of an understanding did you have with that other fellow. you know that all seems queer to me but you never tell me.

Say by the way do you know that there is always these lines in all your letters "Cant write you as long letter as had planned too. the house has been full of company all day." Thats old <u>stuff</u> kid and has been done to death   get a new <u>line</u> of stuff or either dont plan so big.

Well I will stop the Hotel is full of <u>Guests</u>.

Now write me lots and long cause this is a lonesome old trip.

Enclosed find a <u>picture</u> cartoon and a Nell Brinkley drawing I just happen to see here on the desk.

Your Boy All the time
Billy

No I never did try any of TM [Tom Morgan's] stuff yet.
[Gags written by Morgan for Will to use in his act.]

YELLOWSTONE PARK ASSOCIATION

Yellowstone Park, Wyo.
Friday noon [June 12]
My Own Sweetheart

Well old pal I am now at a lunch station for dinner   just drove in from the Grand Canon about 15 miles and will go on back to the <u>Mammoth</u>   thats where you start from   its 20 miles from here   will go there   then on out 5 miles to Gardiner   the entrance to the park and where you take the train. I have been in the park three days counting today   leave tonight at 7:30 from Gardiner to Butte. and dont know if I will make it or not as I have to open at Matinee tomorrow and I just hear there is a lot of fresh washouts on the line so I may not get there,   but it cant be helped   if I cant I cant   thats all   and will open when I do get there. But I think I can make it allright.

Did you get some cards [Playing Cards] I sent you and a folder postal and some others.

Well this is a great place   wish I had had time to take the regular tour of 5 days but I only had 2   so I got me a special rig and they layed out a special trip for me and I have been all alone   only the <u>driver</u> since yesterday noon   I was with a bunch the first day until noon yesterday. By making this special I seen a lot and most all of it but the big lake and a few Geysers. I seen the Canon   stayed there last night at the big Canon Hotel. The first and only Guest. Oh it did seem funny A tremendous big hotel. All the clerks and Waiters and servants and all ready as their first bunch will arrive there tonight   so I had the whole Hotel to myself. They

Will and Betty stand at the tent opening with Betty's guitar preparing to entertain the picnickers. Note how the ladies dressed, even on a hot day in the country.

even had the Orchestra to play while I was in a big dining room that would seat 300. All alone but them.

Oh I was the "<u>poplar</u>" Kid for fair once in my life.

This hotel is away out all alone just up on top of the Canon and last night all kinds of big game were playing around out on a big level place there and some Bears come down at the back hunting up where they throw out all the Garbage. Oh there was 50 or 75 elk. A lot of young ones and Deer and Mountain Sheep Antelope. The buffalo are the hardest to see but there is all kinds of game here.

That Canon is great   the most beautiful coloring and the falls are 360 ft and the rocks all different colors   the Canon is about 1500 or 2000 ft deep, but its the coloring they rave about. not being an artist I dont know   it looked fair   not as good though as that big rocky ditch down back of your house   But they rave over it almost as bad as you do those <u>trenches</u> down there.

Where I am now is Norris Basin where a lot of the Geysers are (you know what they are dont you) "I dont"   I dont mean "<u>Geezers</u>" of course you've seen lots of them   <u>One</u> in particular

Some of them play every few minutes and shoot up 100 ft and this whole hill where this place is is just steaming and smoking and holes blowing off steam in <u>jerks</u> just like an Engine and different colored hot pools all with boiling water   hot caves and   oh

Well I wont tell you cause you wouldent enjoy it as much when we come back and see it all and go horseback riding and fishing   they limit you to 25 at a time, guess that's poor, eh!

There is a big Military post up at Mammoth and you see the Cavalry drill and the whole park is patroled by Soldiers and also scouts.

They carry all the Tourist parties in big 4 and 6 horse Coaches. You go so far eat dinner at a lunch place   then on to the 1st hotel and complete a trip of about 150 miles in a big circle in 5 days   of course you can stop over where you please by paying your extra hotel fare and take up the trip the next day with the next bunch or stay a week   the Hotel bills are American plan $5.00 a day   my little trip of 3 days special rig and all will only cost me about $40 dollars. "G" that would of bought you a swell hat wouldent it   and I could of paid 25 cents for a book and read about it. (and perhaps known more) What am I telling you all about the cost and all that   I just caught myself doing it. And I dont know   it just seems as natural and not improper. does it to you   No its all right   you should know all I do and all about it.

Well I will have to stop as my rig is coming (a swell team and buggy by the way) its kinder raining too but I have no more sight seeing and its great to drive through the rain. Hope I get a lot of <u>mail</u> from you tomorrow in Butte. it seems a month.

> Your only Boy
>
> Aint I.   B___

(Next Week Sullivan and Considines Theatre, Spokane, Wash.)

Will always had the ability to write as if he were at the scene—writing as he rode along through the hills and canyons! There is not a shred of proof, but he protests so much about being alone on this deluxe tour that one wonders if he had a woman friend with him. If so, it would be easier to explain why the hotel rolled out the red carpet for him—especially if he told them he was on his honeymoon. Not long after, he was making apologies to Betty again for what we do not know.

It might have involved this trip.

THE BUTTE

Monday Eve. [Posted June 15, 1908]

My Betty—

Well say Girl are you sick or have that <u>bunch</u> prevailed on you to see differently and you are so occupied with your Banker Boy that you have no time for your Cowboy boy.

Well I am in the great Mining town of Butte. and it is <u>sho</u> a hummer. they just throw the <u>keys</u> to all the places away and never close up   there is some life to this place

Well I got caught in a washout coming from the Yellowstone and was delayed and missed 4 shows   it could not be helped   I dont know what they will do about it only take out Salary for the time I missed I guess   but my trip to the Park amply repaid me for all I lost as I enjoyed the trip fine.

Well the old Act is one big hit out here in the wooly   where people are supposed to know   it is better than the east and think it will be a success all the way

"... YOU ARE SO OCCUPIED WITH YOUR BANKER BOY THAT YOU HAVE NO TIME FOR YOUR COWBOY BOY."

out   I go to Spokane next week   Sullivan and Considines Theatre. then the following week opening June 29. Oh yes the Coliseum Theatre, Seattle. would be glad to see your friend while there.

Here is a picture was in todays Butte Paper   good cut don't you think   I like this picture best of all. it was taken just after receiving a dandy letter from <u>Ark</u>

Now say away out here where it takes a year to get a letter you better not be waiting till you get an answer cause it takes too long   you must write every day or so cause I know I write a lot more than you do   why I would of <u>bet</u> there would of been a letter here for me when I came but here I have been for three days and not a sign   its been almost 2 Weeks.

Look out or you will make a <u>3 Weeks</u> out of it. <u>Did you ever read it</u>. "Of course not."

Well I wont write so "offul" (<u>Note</u> spelling) much now. You get busy.

With all my love to the dearest <u>Girl</u> I ever knew. (<u>aint</u> <u>that a pretty little speech</u>) and it mean it too

<u>Your Regular Boy.</u>

These mean Good wishes xxxxxxxx)   Billy

Betty was evidently giving Will some spelling lessons, and he kidded her by spelling *awful* incorrectly on purpose.

THE BUTTE

(Butte, Montana, Wednesday)
Wednesday, noon [June 17, 1908]
My Dearest Sweetheart.

(I have several)

No <u>hon</u> I have not   you are the only one and always will be <u>the</u> one and today I just got your letter the only one in 2 Weeks and I aint a bit <u>sore</u> and I am writing just as soon as I got it and I have written you every day or so for the last few weeks and just thought of you all the time

But you must not worry about me Girlie cause I am always all right and get by some way cause I have knocked around so much that I just take it as it comes   yes the flood knocked me out of 4 shows and I guess will greatly reduce my salary this week but lord look what it has done to everybody all over the country.

We have to close here one day early to get to Spokane cause ordinarily its one Night run   but we will have to go away around and will be two days and two Nights getting there some of these lines will not be running for months.

Now listen dear you seem to think I blame you cause I asked you about all that you told me   why I dont   Why I trust you more than I ever did or ever will a soul on earth and I know it was just as you said and you of course were perfectly right in telling me about it.

How was it if you dident like this Harvey Girl and did not trust her that you spent so many nights there supposedly to be her friend   was it only to be near him. I know you will not like this but honest Betty I am just so rotten jealous that I am <u>mean</u> and cant help it.   I just found a lot of great post cards lots of them marked C.M.R. are by a man I know   a cowboy   C.M. Russell (The Cowboy

White man's skunk wagon no good heap lame

Me and my Squaw giving you are _____ _____ the _____ _____

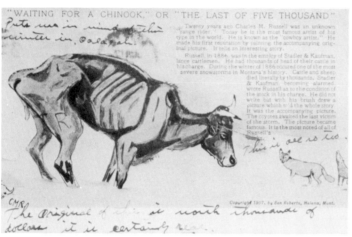

"WAITING FOR A CHINOOK," OR "THE LAST OF FIVE THOUSAND"

Puts me in mind of this winter in Colorado.

The original of this it worth thousands of dollars it is certainly _____.

This is all so too.

This one is a peach.

I wonder whats the matter with them fool hounds?

I aint wonderin' from looks them hosses is wise.

Sun shine and shadow

"I JUST FOUND A LOT OF GREAT POST CARDS. . . BY A MAN I KNOW A COWBOY C.M. RUSSELL (THE COWBOY ARTIST). . ."

Artist) he is the greatest artist of this kind in the world   Remington is not in it with him   he lives just above here in Montana but is becoming very noted   had a studio in N.Y last winter and has been at my flat there lots of times

And I just sent you a book <u>Paid in Full</u> I have seen the show and I think its great   hope you like it if you have not read it and I have now two books <u>Lure of the Dim Trail</u> by <u>Bowers</u>. and will send it later and did I ever send you the Book the <u>Round Up</u>. if I did not will send it also. Cause you would like it

Not much chance out here to get much late music but if I find any will ship it on.

Are you all living at home now and did you get the house fixed up   I'll bet its dandy   I'll tell you that was lovely of you girls to do that   "G" now look at me with all [I] make and all   I never yet done a thing for a soul but myself and dont reckon I ever brought any one else a happy time   I sometimes think I am the most selfish boy alive   I spend all of my money but its all on <u>Willie</u>. I could do oh so much if I only knew how or was not so mean. some day I will wake up and have some <u>sense</u>.

Well I must keep of [off] that sentimental stuff.

Now see if you cant write longer letters cause 'G' its afful out here and I should get a letter every day.

With all my Love I am
your same old boy. B___

The "Harvey girl" is Annette Harvey, daughter of Coin and sister of Tom Harvey.

THE SPOKANE
Sunday Night. [Posted June 21, 1908]
My Own Betty -

Well listen dear I did think I would get a nice dandy letter or two from you on my arrival here but not a line   in fact I have only had one letter in 3 weeks now

Well <u>hon</u> I was the biggest hit here today and tonight I ever was in a long time   Oh I went great just got in here at 11 today after being 3 days and 3 nights on all kinds of roads   come away down near Salt Lake and then away out towards Portland just to get a 12 hour run from Butte to Spokane   but thank the lord we had our tickets through and the expenses was on the Northern Pacific railroad   only of course our sleepers and food on the diners   Oh it was the <u>affulest</u> trip I ever had and I have had some trips too. Well sir in the last town where I missed two days on account of going by the park the Manager on Friday when I left paid me in full and did not take out a cent he could of taken out about $75 or 80. dollars. wasent that good of him.

here I go again telling you all my financial troubles.

Here are a bunch of cards from the hotel here where I am at   it is swell but the rooms are <u>bum</u>

I am going in the Silver Grill room pretty soon to get my little night lunch and oh but I am tired after that trip and todays work and say it gets you up here in this high Altitude   I find myself almost out of breath when I finish

I sent you a card from Pocatello, Idaho where we "laid" <u>is that right</u> over. Say did you ever get a deck of cards from yellowstone   tell me cause they were paid for and he was to send them.

We finish here next Saturday Night and then go to Seattle where we open at Coliseum Theatre there   so address there please [write] at once and see if you cant get me a letter there so I will get it on my arrival cause its lonesomer then

I hope I can be this big a hit in Seattle and Frisco.

I dident mean only to write you a short note and here is a letter   I'll bet I have wrote you 100 to 1 in the last 5 weeks   I will slow up for a spell now. . . .

Be good and write often to your old boy who just loves you to death and does love to get your letters.
Billy.

THE SPOKANE
[Posted June 24, 1908]
Tuesday. Eve. 5 p.m.
My Only (honest) Sweetheart

Well my Gal I got your first letter written here also one forwarded on from Butte and say but they did seem good to me and by the way I am <u>loving</u> you some at the present time <u>also</u>.

I am only writing you this little note as I want to send you these three little clippings from Spokane papers   my act is certainly a success here   if it will

The postcard at the top bore a Charles Russell illustration and was imprinted "Here's how to me and my friends, the same to you and yours, I savvy these folks." Will inscribed it with a comment about Russell: "he always wear a sash" and to the side, "these are the characters that he draws. this is him and his friends." On the center card, he wrote jokingly, "imitation of <u>you</u> on your arrival in the <u>yellowstone</u>. . ."

only be half as good in Seattle and Frisco. Yes I would like to meet your friends out there.

today is pretty warm   the only warm day I have seen all year.

This place is a beautiful little city   one of the best in the Northwest   a lot better than Butte.

Oh how I do wish I was home this summer and oh what a time we would have and how I would enjoy it   and we would certainly get <u>good</u> acquainted wouldent we   But I think I will get there the latter part of August or Sept 1st and will see that you get more than two <u>Sundays</u> as the <u>song</u> says.

"<u>Well, you'll get all thats a coming to you and a little bit more.</u>"

I will stop cause I am so far ahead of you in writing I fear you will never catch up.

     Your old ever loving Kid
      Billy

Back home, C.V. Rogers was getting ready to go to the Democratic convention in Denver. Will must have been neglecting his correspondence with his family. Or else his letters were not being saved.

THE SPOKANE

Spokane, Washington
[Posted June 27, 1908]
Saturday Eve.
My Sweetheart—

Well my gal I got your two letters today and they are all the candy. and I just would love to drift into old Rogers now on one of those <u>almost trains</u> and not have to dig out at all   just drive out and on and on and tell each other how nice we are with all the <u>accompanying trimmings</u>. Oh well when we can it may be nicer so why <u>rave now</u>.

Well this is a dandy country up here and a beautiful city and everything nice   I like it cause my act is such a hit   guess I will be a frost in Seattle for unusual success only comes about every other town   I will just about scratch through in Seattle, and to make it worse the nice theatre where I was to play is closing tonight for repairs and they switched to [the] show over to an old bum place and I am afraid your friends will think I am a <u>kinder shine act</u>   You see people out of the profession dont know a lot of things about why or what and they think if an act is in a big Theatre it is good and if in a small it is bad   they dont know that the salaries are sometimes just reversed   of course this is the best circuit in the Northwest but some of the houses could be better but it is delightful to work for   they certainly do all they can to make your stay pleasant from the Manager down and you are treated with more respect than on the Eastern circuits.

I dont know where I go from Seattle but I think Vancouver   will let you know or you can write to Seattle and it will be forwarded on without any delay, as Seattle is the headquarters of all this circuit—

. . . . I wish I was home and we would all have one more time cause Ada, Scrap, Nell and you are all there and still "<u>single</u>" <u>I hope</u>   and I really believe you and I could get on better than before and would both enjoy it better. but the great American public need enlightening on the sports and pastimes of our great American Cowboy so I guess it <u>behooves</u> me to act out a spell for them and postpone the hilarity for an endefinite period.

Did you get the book and have you got <u>Lure of the Dim Trail</u>. or the <u>Round Up</u>.—tell me   if not I will send them cause I have both of them

The weather up here is delightful and not at all hot.

Well my gal I must stop cause this is gettaway Night   we catch a train 30 minutes after I come of [off] the stage and I will have to go some   will perhaps work in my Street clothes, travel all Night from 11. to 3. P.M. tomorrow—Sunday to Seattle, open Monday Matinee and close there the following Sunday Night.

Keep on loving your old boy cause he is a fool about you.
Billy.
Star Theatre.
Seattle.

"KEEP ON LOVING YOUR OLD BOY CAUSE HE IS A FOOL ABOUT YOU."

Palace Hotel
Seattle, Washington
Sunday. [Posted July 5, 1908]
My Own Girl—

Well _honey_ I was out to your friends   Miss Randolph and spent from about 11 A.M. to 2:30 and had a dandy lunch and they just treated me fine   went out with Mrs. Eaton and family and all had a great day   it was the 4th. they have a nice big old country looking place   lovely trees and grounds and the girls are great   so is Mrs. Eaton   they are all jolly and I felt right at home They had all seen my Show one Night   6 ladies in a box   and they seemed so to enjoy it and they are allright a little different from what I expected I have promised to call up Mrs. Eaton today and run up to her house a little bit. do you know she reminds me a lot of _you_ and she is just like I imagine you will be when her age and all that (just grand)

I promised to come back by if I can and spend next Sunday as I will not be working and will pass through on my way to Tacoma from Vancouver.

They laughed about you saying it was 40 miles out to their place   its about 4. right in the edge of the city   Well I will stop. One letter all week. leaving here tonight at 12 on the boat for Vancouver. Week 13. Grand, Tacoma. Love Love Love.

I sent the 2 books.
                    Billy.

Palace Hotel   Seattle, Wash
[Posted July 4 or 5, 1908]
Dear Papa.

leaving in a few minutes for Vancouver B.C. play there next Week at Orpheum Theatre and open Monday july 13. at Grand Theatre. Tacoma. Washington. so write to me there

Love to all   Willie

Will be by home for a few days about August 17 or 18 on way back east

Tacoma
Thursday [Posted July 16, 1908]
Dear Papa.

Guess you are home from the convention now and guess you had a big time. I . . . go to Portland Ore. next Week then I lay off a week and jump to Sacramento California. so you better write to me there. I play the Grand Theater. Portland. Ore. next week. but by the time a letter got there I would be gone so address "ACME." Theater Sacramento. Cal.

Love to all   Willy.

HOTEL TURCLU
Sacramento, California August 8, 1908
My Dear Gang

Well, I got a few letters from some of you and you seem to be getting on pretty good and having a time.

Dad wanted everything right now! One time he said he wanted trees around the Santa Monica ranch. He got home and saw they had planted little saplings and he said he wanted TREES! The gardener had to get full grown trees and plant them.
~Will Rogers, Jr.

I sho wish I could join you for a short spell but it just looks like I cant cause I am signed for the time out here at a raise of salary, so I will just have to take it. But I will get there a little later on before Xmas.

I will perhaps have some open time   you see I am not overlooking any work when I can get it cause I need all I can get and have great prospects of a good year. This year I only lose one week jumping from Frisco to Detroit and then guess I will go along pretty steady for while. But the first time I cant get booked I will jump right home.

Well so old Mary [Gulager] is there   well I sho would be there if I had a Ghost of a chance and am glad she is up and going   honest you couldent kill her with a stick   she is too game. Well I go to Frisco next week   play one Week, then Oakland one Week, then back to Frisco for one week more, then I jump to Detroit, Mich. on the old Keith Circuit again. . . .

Just write for the next two weeks to the National Theatre, San Francisco. I will get them even if I am in Oakland or at a different theatre   there it is the one I play next Week   opening Monday, l0th.

Would send you post cards from out here but Sallie and her Gang and May know more about this State than I ever will know   I am close to Mays old stomping ground aint I.

Well I will stop   write all of you <u>lazy kids</u>, if your Mamas havent time. Love to all. _____old Uncle E.

Got me a little cheap Kodak   will send you some picures at <u>once.</u>
Will Rogers
Oakland Cal.
Aug 18 [1908]
Dear Papa.

Well I am playing here in Oakland this week and go back over and play Frisco next week and then that finishes me out here and I have only six days to jump back east to Detroit Mich where I open for my season   but have some weeks open around about Christmas and will be home then.

after you git this <u>you</u> all can write to me to Temple Theatre. Detroit Mich, and I will get them when I git there   but I dont open there till Sept 7th. I am sorry I wont get to come by home but I cant spare the time just now and I am under contract. I am at the Wigwam Theatre. Frisco. next week.

Lots of Love to all
Willie
[Note by C.V. Rogers]
This is Willie's letter   Sav letter for "Mary"   I feel fine   Love to all   Your Pa   I wrote Willie today   Will drive Roger K this afternoon

Clem's buggy horse is "Roger K." He sent the letter to "the girls" in Chelsea, and they are to save it for their sister May. Note absence of letters to Betty
~RC

Hotel Antler
Sept 21 [1908]
Pittsburg, Pa.
Dear Papa.

I got your letter to Rochester last week   I did not know I was to play here till

Friday I open here today and close Saturday Night

Here is $100. Now you get Mr. Godby to send me a statement and tell me how I stand Now in regard to selling the farm I dont like to do it but if you can do it for $20,000. twenty thousand dollars You said there was 350 acres at $50 an acre at least that would be $17,500 Well I wont take that but if you can get twenty all right and I dont care much about it at that. Write to me here before Saturday.
Grand Opera House
Pittsburg. Pa. and next week ARMORY. theatre Binghampton. N.Y. please send this up to the girls so they will know where to write.

I will close Love to all.

Willie.

Without Betty Will had no reason to keep the farm. Mary Gulager was a friend of Betty's and she may have been passing along to her the attitude that prevailed in Chelsea and Claremore—that Will needed to settle down in Oklahoma.

Whatever it was, she must have forgiven him. He was very close mouthed about any girlfriends, and we certainly never heard about them when we were growing up.

~Will Rogers, Jr.

"I HAVE <u>LIVED</u> A <u>LIE</u> AND NOW I AM REAPING THE HARVEST OF IT. . . ."

Hotel Antler
Pittsburg, Pa.
Wednesday [Posted September 23, 1908]
Dear Dear Betty

Your little note just come and it has made me feel terrible

honest Betty I feel offul

I know you thought from the way I wrote in the last letter that I loved the woman No you were all wrong I wrote that way cause I did not want to appear like I was <u>knocking</u> her after all that had happened. Still you are right when you say that I have not treated you square. No I have not Betty it seems that I havent treated any one square. I have <u>lived</u> a <u>lie</u> and now I am reaping the harvest of it please make a little allowances for me dear I am not myself now and seem to have no mind of my own

I am <u>scared</u> and dont know what to do.

Betty this is all of what comes of doing wrong I done the greatest wrong that any one could do and I have wished and prayed a thousand times since that I had not done it.

No I am no man I am the weakest child you ever saw if you knew me better I am easily led and can be pulled into almost anything. I have no mind of my own I just drift and drift. God knows where too.

Now listen dont you think of deserting me in all this. I need you and want you and I am hoping that this will all soon be at an end and I will be my own old self again.

I'll admit I havent treated you right honest if you know how that hurts me Betty you wouldent say it, but its the truth.

Well I will stop its show time. Im <u>bad</u> dearie <u>all bad</u> but I am trying to do better and live better.

Write to me girl.

Your Billy.
Armory Theatre
Binghampton, N.Y. next week.

No one living today knows the truth of what happened at this low point in Will's life. It involved "another woman," as he states. But which woman and in what way? And how did Betty know about it so fast? Were her friends he visited in Oakland involved? Did he run into an old flame? Did he get engaged? We simply do not know. One or more letters must have been destroyed. In Betty's book about her husband, she omits all of the letters and most of the details during this period. It must have been painful for her. Yet she didn't destroy the letters.

ARLINGTON HOTEL

BINGHAMPTON, N.Y.

Thursday [October 1, 1908]   My Dear Folks-

Well I guess you all think I had deserted you but I been pretty busy and only got a chance to write to papa. I got Mauds letter yesterday. Well I am just kicking along same old way and going pretty well things are none too good in this business this year still I will be all right if I can keep working It is raining up here for the first time in months this country was all about to burn up with forest fires. the fair is on here now.

I am sho sorry I missed the two big fairs down there I will get those things yet some day.

So May has a boy and is getting on fine well I am so glad. So Johny [Yocum] has gone off with a show Well I'll be the ruination of my Nephews yet. they will gradually gather in after they get a little wiser and find out where and what is best You know that prowling and show off feeling is just like a case of biliousness if its in your system the quicker you get it off the better. At any rate if the son and Nephews of our dear father accomplish nothing besides a roaming disposition. We can always rest assured that the opposite sex of the family will follow in the beloved footsteps of the _dear mothers and grandmother. that being accomplished is all that can be asked   Well now to dispose of seriousness and come back to every day life again I got the much sought after Bank Statement. You have often heard of a fellow looking for trouble and then finding it. Well there was the most striking instance of it you could find.

It looks like a plot to a jewish play. or a Chinese Laundry bill. I am going to publish it as a Rebus in the paper. I think they made a mistake and sent me the clearing house sheet. or some of Godbeys livery stable statements I either am the poorest mortal in Rogers County Cooweescoowee district. party of the first part heretofore mentioned. sign here his mark (EASY) (that is my mark all right.)

or

I have a mortgage on the aforesaid bank and a balance so big that a horse couldent jump over it.

I dont know what it is but think I will wind up by owing myself money and to cap it all it seems that my dearest friend Morgan (Wonderful man)is going to stand by and see me enter bankruptcy and not even offer a helping hand

He is looking out for my interest so well that he wont pay me money cause he is afraid I will drink it up and ruin my young life. Now in return for his generosity and sincere affection I am going to reward him abundantly by issuing him a life time lease on the old Homestead and also paying him a small bounty of some 500

"THAT PROWLING AND SHOW OFF FEELING IS JUST LIKE A CASE OF BILIOUSNESS"

shekels a year for the privilege of having him and it shall also be in the agreement that I shall defray all expenses of an exploring party to penetrate the <u>deepest depths</u> of those weedish jungles once a year to ascertain if my victim still survived and if not by what means did he pass away. was it by <u>overflow. house falling on him.</u> or was it seeing so many people passing along all those much traveled roads. or a mosquito bite.

thats the only way I can ever hope to get even with him is by making him stay there forever.

You know papa wrote me I should sell the farm and I told him yes for 20 thousand. Well I never heard from him since that was a month ago. I'll bet he is besieged night and day with men laying the 20 thousand at his feet and he dont know which one to take and rather than make them mad he wont accept any of them.

I am writing him now that I meant <u>20 cents</u> instead of 20 thousand. and does he think 20 cents will be too much

Well I will have to stop and go fool the unsuspecting public for a brief space of 12 minutes as long as they dont catch me at it its all right

Will I will stop again
Write me Next Week
      Grand Opera House   Syracuse New York
Lots and Lots of love to all
    Your old bro. Bill

Syracuse, New York
[Posted October 11, 1908]
My Betty—

Well dear just a line as I am getting out of here tonight after the show at 11:40 and get to Montreal at 10 in the morning this is one of the towns you have to play Sunday in but not in Canada only 6 days

Well <u>hon</u> I just think of you all the time and am just most crazy to see you and it wont be so long till I do either.

I cant hear yet just where I go after Montreal but will wire as soon as I find out.

Now you write all the time. Say are you in the store (working at Strouds) you did not say, tell me.

Aint it funny this is the town I sent you the little Hdkf. [handerkerchief] from that time. I kinder have a warm place in my heart for it when it does what I <u>hope</u> it <u>will</u>

Well By By my Darling Sweetheart. I hope you may never regret sticking by a <u>bum</u> like I am.
    Your own Boy
      Billy

Betty has evidently pledged her allegiance to Will. In return, he sent her a letter from Nina to prove that he had broken any ties with her.

The Gerard
New York [no date]
Dear friend Will

Am very glad you wrote me as you did as it was just what I needed to restore to me what little common sense I ever had. I hope you will forget that I have been such a fool as I do not care to loose all your respect and no one apreciates a good, true friend better than I do and they are mighty few. The girl that wins your love may consider herself very fortunate, only wish the average men were more like you.

Well be good. trusting everything is going fine
I remain
        Sincerely Yours
           Nina
We are changed to Harlem next week.

The letter from Nina indicates he was considered a great catch in show business, just as he was at home. Her full identity is not known by anyone in the Rogers family nor by researchers at the Will Rogers Memorial.

The Osborne House
Auburn, New York
Monday [Posted October 19, 1908]
My Own Betty.

Say <u>Hon</u> what is the matter   I did so expect to get a letter when I got here this morning but none came and last week only one in reply to the first wire I sent from Syracuse, Did you get offended at anything in my letter. I cant imagine it at all.

I am just now sending you by mail three separate <u>parcels</u> two of them containing Books. <u>The Devil "Togeather"</u> and <u>A little brother of the Rich</u>."   Hope you will like them if you havent read them before as they are the three books of the year. And in another parcel 6 pairs of gloves and 6 pairs <u>of Female Hosiery</u>. Now the reason <u>one of them,</u> of my getting these is that I bought them last week in Canada and are supposed to be cheap up there

I hope you wont be offended at me sending you the Stockings. They are <u>bum</u> and I dont think you will like them but you can try and give em away.

I hope they fit. I mean the gloves as I thought I remembered your size as 6 1/2.

Now let me hear from you kinder often wont you dear   will wire you next weeks address.

Your same old Billy.
THE OSBORN HOUSE

Auburn, N.Y.
Oct. 24. 08.
Mr Dear Papa

just got a long letter from Maud and told me all the news   I finish here tonight and go to play next Week at Willksbarre, Pa. I am planning on coming home Christmas or a week or so before and am pretty sure I will be able to come

Pay all the money I have there and all you collect and get from Morgan and the

"... I WANT SOMEONE THAT I CAN LOOK UP TO AND NOT A BUM LIKE MYSELF."

Will is certainly making up for lost time in romantic writing.
~Will Rogers, Jr.

houses on that note of mine and make a new note for the balance and only make it for a short time as I will be able to pay it off soon. Why is $100 all that I can get out of all that stuff   I have a Mortgage on all of Morgans   why its on all his hogs Wagon and all he raises. looks like it should be more than $100.

I wont be able to send you any money for a week or so as I owe some here and am getting paid up

Write me this coming Week. Poli's Theatre. Willksbare Pa.

Love to all

　　Willie

HOTEL REDINGTON

Wilkes-Barre, Pa.

<u>Tuesday</u> [Posted October 27, 1908]

My Gal Betty.

Well my own sweetheart your dear letter come yesterday and I just love it and you more all the time. you always kinder cheer me up with your letters and I will sho be glad to see you and I am crazy for the time to come.

I am so sorry you say you wont get you a <u>pony</u> now cause I do so want you to have one. but you keep on the lookout for one and if you see one why that offer always holds good and you must <u>buy it</u>

Yes dear those books do show a lot of heart aches and misfortune and it makes me sad to read them but it is just all what you make it as you say and God and Love is all there is after all

"G" hon you are a smart girl and I have read so little and really dont know a thing and I will just love to have you tell me oh so many many things that I dont know cause I want someone that I can look up to and not a <u>bum</u> like myself. I just know you will be disappointed in me cause you think I am wise cause I have traveled but I dont know a thing only the bad side that I should not know.

Well this is the jumpiest season   I still dont know yet where I go next week and may have to lay off but I will wire you later on.

Did you get the last book I sent you and the letter in it

Here is a little clipping from todays paper here   my act is going pretty good This is a new Theatre and the first time I ever played here.

I hope I get a letter from my girl tomorrow   I am getting crazier about them all the time

I am going over tonight and see the first part of a show as I am on late. Robert Edison in, "Call of the North."

I always hate to tell you about all these cause there is my girl away out there and has to content with an <u>Uncle Tom</u> show

Nevermind Kid   this aint <u>dog days</u> but still every pup has them so yours is coming.

Well I will stop as there <u>aint much news in town</u> and I must eat a little   even if I am in love I do occasionally eat.

Write me a long letter all about "<u>Togeather</u>" and tell me your view.

　　Your own old Bill.

But she didn't get a chance to write him. He got some time off and made a surprise visit home. As Betty told it later, he just showed up on her doorstep saying he was going to marry her, and wouldn't take no for an answer. On November 4, he would be twenty-nine years old. Betty was his real birthday present. . . .

WESTERN UNION TELEGRAPH COMPANY

K.C. MO Paid   147 PM Wilkesbarre PA 10/31/08
Miss Betty Blake   Rogers, Ark
Laying off nest week address hotel Preston fourth Avenue twenty sixth street
New York

Billy

ST. LOUIS & SAN FRANCISCO RAILROAD
EATING HOUSES
FRED HARVEY, MANAGER

[Posted November 11, 1908]

My Intended Wife.

Dont that sound great   it will sound greater when that middle word is <u>disected</u>.

Well Hon I got in all O.K. but my train was 40 Min late out of Rogers and I come near going back up there and annoying you for a little longer

Well I get out of here at 11:15.

Aint that a fine wait   wish I could get you by long distance Phone   I would just spend all my money telling you how much I love you, cause I sho do <u>feel good</u> and I dont feel so lonesome either cause I am just living on expectations and for the future and <u>you</u>

Well Sweetheart I sho do sympathize with you about now cause I can picture you having your <u>trouble</u> and a lot of it at that

Well I wish there was some way old Bill could help you through it but guess you will have to go it alone in this <u>news breaking</u> business cause I would be of no use.

I do so hope and pray you make it all right. its <u>you alone</u> that I want but at the same time I should hate to cause any of your folks any worry or uneasiness cause I know how they all love you and want to see you happy. I will tell the folks at home and know all will be fine cause they all like and love you

Here is that clipping I forgot to give you   Now you take <u>heed</u>. And here is <u>your</u> 50. not mine, yours. Now dont you <u>utter</u> a <u>murmur</u> cause what I have is "yourn" and you might need this little bit for something   but what you havent got you wait till you get east and get. You must remember all the fine clothes in the world on you could not make any more of a hit with me. dont worry about your <u>waist</u> not coming   you can get one in St. Louis. thats only one day longer to wait and just what you have looks might good to Willie. You always did hear my views on this clothes thing for a wedding and I always did express them long before we knew when ours would be a bit <u>hurry up</u>

I hate the sound of that preparing thing   I want <u>you you</u>   not clothes   I will let you get all you want when we get east

Betty's "trouble" would be convincing her family that she was doing the right thing by promising to marry the "Injun-Cowboy-Vaudeville performer" who had courted her since January 1900. She was old enough to know her own mind, but she knew that opposition came from nearly every direction.

~RC

". . . I AM JUST LIVING ON EXPECTATIONS AND FOR THE FUTURE AND <u>YOU</u>"

I dident see Harry Osborne   his store was closed before I got here.

Guess I wont cause a disturbance at 2 a.m. tonight when I arouse the McSpadden or Lane domicile and have them slaughtering the fatted <u>rooster</u> for breakfast.

Just think I wont get your letter tomorrow   not till Thursday.

Hope all the folks are well   you see I havent heard from there in over two weeks

I must run down and see the Gulagers one night while here and have a <u>chat</u> with dear old Mary   She will be the most pleased person cause she always did <u>boost</u> you great. really more than _____[Tom Morgan]_as I was saying before.

Well my own Sweetheart, its getting along late   will send you a line tomorrow and all other days and you must too. Goodnight Darling   just think in 16 more days. Bill loves you oh just lots, lots, more all the time.

<u>Your own Billy</u>.

Wednesday [Posted November 11, 1908]

4 P.M.

My Own very own Betty

Well Sweetheart I got in at 4 o'clock this morning. train two hours late   I walked up to Sister Sallies and sneaked in and they did not know I was on the place   I went up and went to bed and early this morning Sallie come in the room to get something and found me in bed.

We phoned Papa and he came up from Claremore and is here   the whole two famalies all stay all night over at Mauds and then tomorrow we will all drive out 8. miles to my other Sister May's [Stine]. she lives out in the country   you never met her did you

She is dandy just like the other two   I am the only <u>bum</u> in the troop. Well I told them all about it at dinner in a kind of a kidding way   I started it and then told them I just know they will be pleased as they like you and think that you will take good <u>care of me</u>. Well, I will get your letter tomorrow and will be so glad to hear from you. Oh! I got your letter sent on from New York.

the folks are outside waiting in the buggy for me and I want this to go on this train.

I will write you tomorrow after your letter   still I go to the country all day but will write late tomorrow night.

<u>With all my love.</u>

Billy

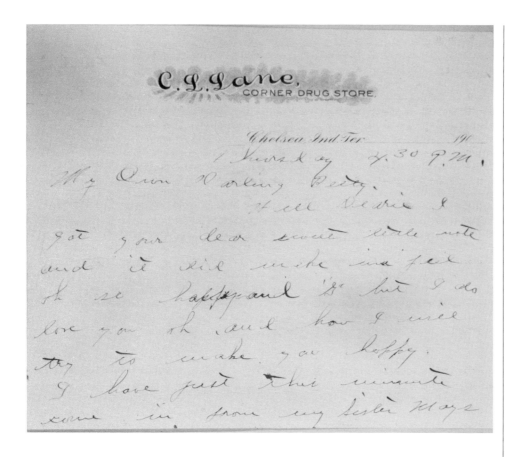

C. L. LANE
CORNER DRUGSTORE
CHELSEA, INDIAN TERRITORY

Thursday, 4:30 p.m. [Posted November 12, 1908]
My Own Darling Betty,

Well Dearie I got your dear sweet little note and it did make me feel oh so happy and "G" but I do love you and oh how I will try to make you happy.

I have just this minute come in from my sister Mays where Maud, Sallie, Papa and I all drove out and spent the day, oh, Betty I am so happy and so glad that it is so soon now, aint you. Cause I just could not wait long for you the way I want and love you now. My folks are so well pleased and just think it fine and love you and think you are grand. They have always been kinder afraid I would grab on to some old show girl or some bum and now that they know it is you they are tickled to death. I dont know now about just when I will get over there. I do so want to come Sunday and am very apt to do it. I will wire you Saturday if I do and if not I will come about Tuesday or Wednesday and we will plan just <u>what</u> - <u>when</u> and <u>how</u>. I will go down to Claremore tomorrow and spend the day and I want to go up to the farm some one day. I am going south by Tahlequah from your home this time will spend a day and night there and go south on that No. 5. Then I will come in on the day before. I am just crazy to come Sunday and will I think. Now listen Sweetheart dont worry and feel bad cause you have not got things just as you would like but what do you care. Dont you think old Bill will understand and I want you all the more and <u>not clothes</u>. You can get just what you want in St.

Louis and New York. Say that day we had planned on is Thanksgiving a fine day and I think it would be good just like we had planned dont you.

Well Dearest, Sister is waiting to take me home up to Sister Sallies. I will be so glad to get your letter tomorrow.

Well Goodnight my own very own two weeks from Today.

Your own Billy

“My Almost Wif”

Western Union Telegraph Company

10:50 am 11/19 1908 Chelsea Okla

To Miss Bettie Blake Rogers Ark

Sending you package today by registered mail was traveling all yesterday and not able to write write today love Billy

Chelsea, Oklahoma

November 19, 1908

My Almost Wif

Well hon your little letter come today and it was just like you and I loved it even if it was short.

I got in last night or rather just this a.m. at 4 o'clock. I stayed over in Muskogee a few hours longer than I expected and then come home last night by the way of Vinita. I did not get to see Sandy in Gibson and I wish I had but I had some Business with the Trent boys in Muskogee and had to go there. I will write to Sandy today.

“. . . Say guess what we will see in St. Louis Thanksgiving afternoon, a great football game.”

Say hon, your ring just come and I am sending it on to you today by registered mail. It is not as large as I wanted but it is a pure white, perfect stone. You see I told them by all means that what I did get I wanted to be perfect and not some big yellow thing. You can exchange it if you like when we get back there. I want to have one of those pins made into a ring and if I can have it done in Claremore today will send it to you also.

Form No. 1.

THE WESTERN UNION TELEGRAPH COMPANY.

INCORPORATED

23,000 OFFICES IN AMERICA. CABLE SERVICE TO ALL THE WORLD.

This Company TRANSMITS and DELIVERS messages only on conditions limiting its liability, which have been assented to by the sender of the following message. Errors can be guarded against only by repeating a message back to the sending station for comparison, and the Company will not hold itself liable for errors or delays in transmission or delivery of Unrepeated Messages, beyond the amount of tolls paid thereon, nor in any case where the claim is not presented in writing within sixty days after the message is filed with the Company for transmission.

This is an UNREPEATED MESSAGE, and is delivered by request of the sender, under the conditions named above.

ROBERT C. CLOWRY, President and General Manager.

NUMBER	SENT BY	REC'D BY		CHECK
		a	19 Paid	

RECEIVED at 1050 am 11-19 1908

Dated Chelsea Okla 19

To Miss Bettie Blake

Rogers Ark

Sending you package today by registered mail was traveling all yesterday & not able to write writing today love

Billy

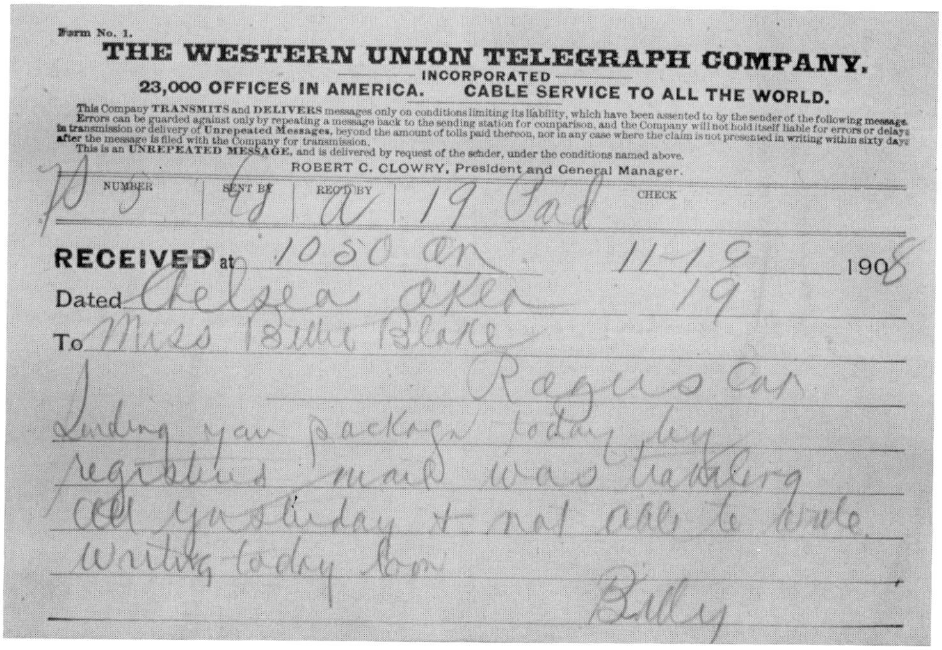

Say what do you think? sister Sallies children or one of them have got the Scarlet Fever and of course could not be able to come. They are hardly in bed but the house is all quarintined and no one can get in or out. I will write you tomorrow and tell you something more definite but perhaps Maud and Papa can come. I am running down to Claremore this eve for a few hours.

Well old Mary [Gulager] was just tickled to death and so is all the people I have seen. Oh I sho am proud of my <u>wif</u>, and cant understand how this did not happen long ago. It was all your fault that it did not.

Yes Sweetheart we will get that first train and say guess what we will see in St. Louis Thanksgiving afternoon, a great Football game. Carlisle Indians against Washington University. I have always wanted to see those Indians play. They are one of the greatest teams in American. Wont you like it.

Well I must stop. "G" I dont think of a thing but you all the time and oh girlie how I do love you and how I will try and make you happy. You are just the grandest girl in all the world. Oh I love love Love you with all my heart and am so so happy.

Your Billy

Chelsea, Oklahoma November 20, 1908
[To James K. Blake, Betty's brother]
Dear Sandy:

I passed through your town yesterday going from Tahlequah to Muskogee but had to be in Muskogee on business or I would of stopped off and seen you.

Well old boy I guess that Dear Sister of yours has made known to you <u>our</u> desires and should you approve of it I just want to tell you that I will do all in my power to try and make her happy and will try to live up to the high ideal you have set in caring for her as you and your dear folks have so well done in the past.

I sho do admire you Sandy for the unselfish way you have cared for your folks. And she certainly does appreciate it and loves you as well she should.

Now I will just try and take up the part of caring for her and looking out for her where you have done so well. Now if I do what you have done you wont ask for more cause there would be no more to ask for.

Perhaps you are not aware of the fact that I have loved that girl for many years since Oologah in fact. And I have been all over the world and she is the only <u>real</u> girl I ever saw.

Now Sandy our home wherever it may be on the road or at home is always your home and you can come once a year and stay a year if you will. And we not only ask you but <u>want</u> you.

I wish you could come over. I know I would feel some better if I had you there but if not we hope to see you back east on a trip to see us real soon. We will show you a time.

Well I better quit before I get sentimental (and that dont take long either when I get strung out about Betty.)

I will try and prove myself a <u>real</u> brother to you.

Will Rogers

Dad always said, "From the time I saw her, I knew she was the only girl for me." And that was true as long as he lived.
~James Blake Rogers

"Announcement is made of the approaching wedding of Miss Betty Blake and Will Rogers of Claremore, Okla., at the home of the bride Wednesday, November 25. . . . The announcement has created much interest owing to the prominence of the bride in local circles."
ROGERS [*Arkansas*] DEMOCRAT

Friday, 2 P.M. [Posted November 20, 1908]
My Almost Wife

Well Sweetheart, it is only a few more days and you and I will be "1" and I will be oh! so happy and I just think of it all the time and just want my own Girl, oh how I do want you Sweetheart.

Now Betty I dont know just who will be down with me besides Papa and perhaps Maud and Cap. Sallie dont know yet and hardly thinks she can come. Her children are just doing fine, still they cant let them out and my Sister May will be in town tomorrow and dont hardly think she can come on account of the baby and really I dont know but will let you know. It will perhaps be Papa and Maud and Cap and perhaps me if I can possibly get off.

Say Hon about those announcements - "G" I dont know I have so darn many friends or supposedly friends all over the Universe and I would not know where to stop or dont remember half of them and all my vast army of connections and if I should overlook a cousin or a dozen then the devil would be to pay and I have thought so little of who to send them too that I dont see any use of it now. I know I should only send them to my dearest friends but I have been away so much and all that   I dont know who they are and do you think that it would be all right to let it go. Honest dear, I dont know who I should tell you - I dont remember even half of my near relatives.

Now hon I sent you a package by registered mail today containing a little bunch of pins and diamonds. Is there a jeweler there that can do that for me. The cluster pin I want you to make a ring; the Horseshoe you can do with as you think best; a bar pin of some kind for your collar and the locket for your chain around the neck. Have that Masonic charm taken off, it is only stuck on and if you have one of your little pictures, a good one, put it in there. I only had that little post card one in there of me and on one side for yours. Now I wanted you to have that done there and you will have them on the trip east. I hope you can get that one made into a ring cause it will be swell. I wish you could have some kind of a ring made out of that horseshoe pin cause it would be fine. The little pin of mine I just sent you to look at not for you. Wear that locket, he can take off that Masonic pin for it has been commented on more than all my other stuff put togeather.

I sent the cuff buttons and two rings back to _____[Will left it blank] and wrote and told her I did not care for them just as I had told you I would and I feel good over it now that all that dreadful thing is over.

Yes, the plans you spoke of are all O.K. Anything you plan is good. Yes, we will get that first train out. I wrote Sandy yesterday. Wish he could come over I wouldent mind him. Is that Lee Adamson there. Just poison him for a few days with my regards will you. Thank the Lord, Bill Marshall cant be there. Have you a suit case hon. By putting in there just what you want you will not have to get into your trunk till N.Y. I will get you a dandy little traveling bag and you can discard the big grip or suitcase. Did you mean to come direct from the train up there. By, By, My love I will write you tomorrow, with all oh, just all my love.

Your Billy.

FIRST NATIONAL BANK

Claremore, Okla. [Posted November 22, 1908]

Claremore Saturday. Eve.

My Own Betty

Well, hon I am down here on a little visit for a few hours and go back on the eve train.

Well <u>hon</u> I am sho a loving you these days and will always   oh I just know it and oh we will be so happy and just happy all the time.

Well Sweetheart it is only a day or so and we will be all for each other

I will be up at Chelsea now till Tuesday Night when we will leave   I think it will be Maud, Cap, Papa and ___ I wont know if Sister May can come and of course Sister Sallie cant come   still the children are not sick at all.

Did you get that bunch of stuff and could that fellow, jeweler fix them for you. if not can have it done in N.Y.

Well hon I must <u>get</u> this off on this train and you can get it tomorrow and how I do wish I <u>was</u> down there tomorrow (Sunday) and the long old quiet drive·in the hills cause it will be some time before we get to go again and how I did love those drives and I think you did too.

I do hope your mother will not go to a lot of trouble because that is the very thing I wanted to avoid.

By, by, My Very Own
    Your Billy.

WESTERN UNION TELEGRAPH COMPANY

615 PM 11/23 1908   Oologah, Okla
To Miss Bette Blake   Rogers Ark
Back to the scenes of our childhood wish you was at this old depot now love
    Billy

"OH BETTY I AM SO HAPPY AND I DO LOVE YOU WITH ALL MY HEART. . ."

On November 23, 1908, two days before his wedding, "Billy" made a sentimental journey alone—to the depot at Oologah where he had seen Betty Blake for the first time nine years earlier. He had come a long way, but essentially he had not changed. Nor would his feelings for Betty change as long as he lived.

~RC

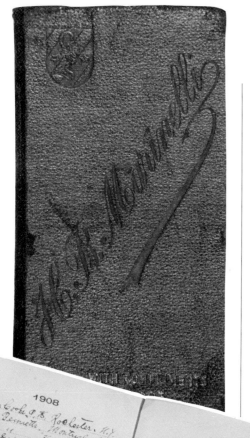

Will's vest pocket datebook from the year 1908. In capital letters he wrote the entry "GETTING MARRIED."

FIRST NATIONAL BANK

Claremore, Okla. [Posted November 24, 1908]
Monday. Eve.
My very very Own.

Well my Betty it is only two more days and "G" this has been a long old Week about the longest I ever saw

Well I come down last night from Chelsea and up to the farm today at Oologah went up on the train and drove out from there and back in time to get the local back to Claremore and will go up on this afternoon train to Chelsea. Say but I did think of you a lot while up at old Oologah and I sent you a wire from there did you get it and think of how I used to see you at that old Depot those were fine old days

Say but it looks lonesome up there. The old farm is looking pretty bad but I dont want to sell it and will keep it and think it will still be all to the good for us yet. I have turned the management of it over to Buck Sunday that Injun boy you remember him in the store. He is a good business boy and will see to it all for me and it will relieve papa of it all cause he is getting so he cant do business anymore.

Well we will go up to Monette on that tomorrow afternoon train and will get a good nights rest and feel refreshed for a strenerous day.

Are you scared, hon I am not. Maud and May are coming and perhaps Cap.

Say how do we go from the train to your house and be married right away is that the way I understand it to be. if it is as soon as we get there I will not change my clothes just have on a dark traveling suit that I will be married in. remember no dressing up. My sisters will just have on what they wear down there, so dont let those sisters of yours be all dressed up

Just think Sweetheart in two days from now how we will be and I just know we will be happy and I will just do all I can to please you and try to make you love me more and not let you ever feel sorry that you left home for me. Oh Betty I am so happy and I do love you with all my heart and just want you more all the time

I hope I get a dandy letter from you when I get to Chelsea this eve do you know it seems that you have kinder neglected me since I came away but I know you thought of me lots and that is just as good.

Well Goodbye Sweetheart My Own, my own. Only a day after you get this and I will be yours forever and you all mine.

Your Billy.

They took the evening train to Monett, Missouri, changed to a compartment, and went on to St. Louis. On Thanksgiving, they went to see the Carlisle Indians play football against a St. Louis team. The Indians won. That night they had dinner in their room —with plenty of champagne—and went to see Maude Adams in "What Every Woman Should Know." Betty regretted the champagne throughout the first act and Will teased her about it. The marriage was off to a laughing good start.

MARRIAGE LICENSE

STATE OF ARKANSAS   **COUNTY OF BENTON**

To any Person Authorized by Law to Solemnize Marriage—Greeting:

You are hereby commanded to solemnize the Rites and publish the Bans of Matrimony between Mr. _William P. Rogers,_ of _Claremore,_ in the County of _Rogers,_ and State of _Oklahoma_ aged _29_ years, and M.iss. _Hattie Blake,_ of _Rogers,_ in the County of _Benton_ and State of Arkansas, aged _28_ years, according to law, and do you officially sign and return this License to the parties herein named.

Witness my hand and Official Seal this _16th._ day of _Nov._ A.D. 190_8._

N.E. Hill Clerk.

D. C.

CERTIFICATE OF MARRIAGE

State of Arkansas,
County of _Benton_ I, _John G Bailey_ do hereby certify that on the _25_ day of _November_ 190_8_, I did duly and according to law, as commanded in the foregoing License, solemnize the Rites and publish the Bans of Matrimony between the parties therein named.

Witness my hand this _25_ day of _Nov_ A.D. 190_8_

My Credentials are recorded in County Clerk's Office _Bentonville_ County, Ark., Book _B_ Page _129_

CERTIFICATE OF RECORD

State of Arkansas,
County of Benton. I, _N.E. Hill_ Clerk of the County Court of said County, certify that the above License for and Certificate of the Marriage of the parties herein named, were, on the _26_ day of _Nov_ 190_8_, filed in my office and the same are now duly recorded on page _396_ Book "G" of Marriage Records.

N.E. Hill Clerk.

D. C.

"I DIDENT KNOW I WAS SO STUCK ON YOU, HON"

he long honeymoon for the carefree Rogers couple continued through early 1909, first in the New York-New England area, then on a two-month Pacific tour beginning in March. Will played in Butte, Spokane, Seattle, Portland, Salt Lake, San Francisco, Oakland and Denver. They took in the sights, spending nearly all the salary Will made, except for the one dollar Betty dropped into a rainy-day box each day.

Where Betty came from people didn't bother locking their doors, but on the road she was very careful to lock the hotel room door. There were about 125 silver dollars in the locked box when the couple arrived in Butte. They went out skating before the show. Cold and tired when they got back to the room, they discovered that someone had broken in, pried open Betty's trunk, opened the steel money box with an ax and taken all the money as well as some personal items.

Shocked and angry, Betty went to tell hotel authorities about the theft. They seemed to feel it was her fault for being careless about locking doors, and that made her furious. But she and Will never saw the money again. Years later, her family said, she still fumed when she thought of the treatment she received. That hurt her more than the loss of the money.

Will had bought himself a large diamond ring and diamond scarf pins when he was still single, but he never wore them. In Betty's book she wrote that in their early days the couple often had to hock the diamonds for emergencies, even though Will was making about $300 a week. Of course, out of that he had to pay Buck McKee and take care of expenses for the horse.

In April, the newlyweds completed their Pacific tour, came through Colorado where Will performed in Denver, and proceeded on to Rogers County, Oklahoma, where they had a brief visit with family and friends.

I'll bet Mother told that story about the Butte incident a hundred times! And she would add that when they went down to the dining room that evening, she felt that everyone was staring at her because she was to blame for the theft. Then, she was so shaken that she dropped her plate! She was so humiliated!

~Will Rogers, Jr.

Then it was Betty's turn. For nearly four months she had been a good trouper and lived Will's lifestyle in vaudeville. Now she wanted to go home to Arkansas—to bask in the love and friendship of family and friends, to have some new clothes made by her seamstress mother, and to shop where she knew everyone.

Will readily consented, promising he would not be jealous or worried about her seeing old beaux. She promised to have complete faith in him. (But he had to promise to avoid drinking parties, gambling and after-the-show dinners with female performers.)

He put her on the train for Fort Gibson, Oklahoma. She would visit her brother Sandy there, then go to the Blake home for two or three weeks. After that, Betty planned to rejoin Will for the rest of his tour.

It was the first time they had been apart since the wedding. Be good for both of them, Will agreed, but almost at once he regretted the arrangement.

THE SEELBACH HOTEL

Louisville, Ky.
[Posted April 25, 1909]
Sunday, 10.30 a.m.
My Own Own Dear Wife,

Well hon, here I am and say but it is lonesome and I sho do miss you all the time and more than ever now since I got here and it is as lonesome as the D

Well old hon, after you left I got off the train and Dr [Jesse] Bushyhead was out on the Platform waiting for me and I was with him up to 11 oclock when my train left [Claremore]. we just sit around down at the Drug store and talked. . ..
Got to St. Louis it was about noon [Sunday]   train a little late. Went down on the stage at the American Theatre and saw all the boys and at 2 oclock out to the Ball Game   saw the Worlds Champion Chicago team play St. Louis and beat them too then back and sent you a lot of Music   sent the Real Slivers Rag. learn it good so you can play it when you come   couldent get the words to Loving Rag. then had Supper. then back on the stage behind and saw part of the show at the American and left at 10.10 P.M. on the Southern Railway sent you a wire from Depot   did you get it. got here at 7 a.m. and there is no Hotels in this town but this big one so I finally just come here and got a nice little single room for $1.25 a day. not with bath of course and I can only have it till Tuesday as they have a big Convention of some kind but I will find me one by that time and I dont mind moving as I have nothing but comb and brush and collar. it is a nice hotel   nothing like the Baltimore though

Buck [McKee] had got in yesterday all O.K.
It is nice and warm here. I am billed second up next to the Headliner. The Country Kids   that Kid act from Newark   you remember that was with me are the Headliners.

Well I'll bet you are just getting ready to have one glorious feed for dinner today and I sho would like to be there too and after dinner we would go for a good old drive but I'll bet it wouldent be as good as the one we took at home would it   I enjoyed that more than any drive I ever had. and we were looking at our own things then.

The Indian-Cowboy has come a long way. He's learned to call Betty's mother "Mama," learned to spell awful, *and is trying awfully hard not to be jealous of his bride!*

~RC

I know you had a good time with Sandy [Blake]. hope he got to go home with you and you all will be having a big reunion today. Give my love to Mama [Amelia Blake] and Dick and all of them and tell them how I wish I was there and that I will be before long.

Old Honey Bug I got that Dandy picture of you just right here in front of me and it sho does make me wish for you. I feel "awful" lonesome today   its been such a long old day and it is not noon yet maby it will be better after I get to work. I got me a lot of Sunday papers and I will read till Show time   Now if they have any dances and card parties you just go to all of them cause I want you to have a good time and you must get you some new clothes too   I will send you the money   I want you to look nice   Get Tom Morgan to Show you the Variety. last weeks of the Denver shows. and see what it says about your old <u>Hubby</u>.

Well my Sweetheart Wife I must close cause you might want this long a letter all the time. With all the Love of your old Husband   I sho do miss you and love you a lot. your only,

Billy

Nic Bosler's European Hotel

Louisville, Ky.
[Posted April 27, 1909]
My Own Darling Wife

Well Sweetheart your first letter come last night earlier than I had expected and I sho did love it and you too.
I am sorry you got so scared in Ft Gibson but I cant blame you for that is one tough town   you should of made Sandy [Blake] have you put up stairs

Well I am down here at a kind of an Actor Hotel and have a very good room at $1.00 a day and it is very good   several of the boys are here   it is a <u>Stag</u> Hotel.

Well yesterday after I wrote you I went down on the river and it is away up and a lot of those little tough Kids they call River Rats were playing there and I sat and watched them for a long time   they were the toughest customers I ever (saw) <u>not</u> <u>seen</u> then had dinner and went to the room and read and then to the show and straight home   had Milk and Pie and did not even have a glass of beer all day   then read and played Sol and went to bed and got up at 11. but it sho is lonesome in an old room and in an old bed   I look around all the time thinking you are there.
Oh I tell you hon, I sho do miss you and will be glad when you come back but I want you to have a good visit and you can come to Indianapolis   I guess I can stand it that long.

I am going to send Shea [his agent, M.A. Shea] that $150 tomorrow as he is going to go to Europe Saturday. . . .   Now hon you get you some clothes while you are home   order them and tell me and I will

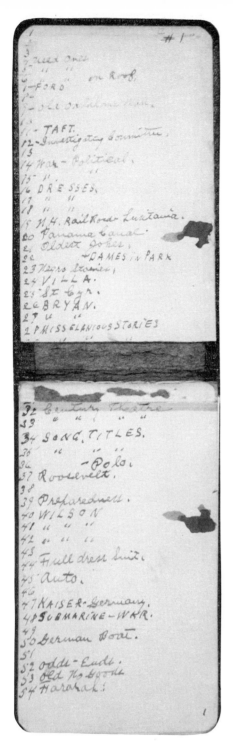

One of the world's great ad-libbers, Will still felt better if he had a word or a phrase to remind him of a gag he'd planned. The worn leather notebook from which this page came was with him constantly.

send you the money to get just what you want.

I sent you the clippings yesterday   did you get them

Now you have a good time hon but you must write often cause I love to get your letters.

I am just home after matinee.

With all the love and a million kisses to my own dear Wifey.

Billy.

NIC BOSLER'S EUROPEAN HOTEL

Louisville, Ky.

[Posted April 28, 1909]

My Own Wife,

Well hon it has got only to Wednesday and it seems like it should be Saturday this is one long week   and I did not get a letter all day yesterday or today but know I will get one tonight   this is just after the Matinee.

I am sure tired and all in as I got up this Morning and thought it must be at least 12 or one oclock and when I come down it was just 9:30 and I wired Shea that $150.00   I got it from the Manager last night. I wrote him the right kind of a letter too. then went to the Theatre and got to Practicing and worked hard from 10 to 1 P.M. then played Ball till 2:30 and I am all in and am going to go up and go to sleep or read   I am going around tomorrow and see a bit of the town I havent heard from papa or a soul since I got here only the one letter from you and I have read it through a dozen times. I dident know I was so stuck on you hon, but I sho am. and I think of you all the time and will be offul glad to see you I tell you   Do you think you can get Dick [Theda Blake] to come back with you for a while   I hope you can   it would do her a lot of good.

Did you get to see Virge [Virginia Quisenberry, her younger sister] before she left. I wish I was there to get <u>filled</u> <u>up</u> good   I expect to see you come back <u>plum</u> <u>fat</u>.

Well Baby I will stop   write me a line and tell me all you do.

All my love to my own Sweetheart Wife

Lots and Lots Love and Kisses

Billy.

NIC BOSLER'S EUROPEAN HOTEL

Louisville, Ky.

[Posted April 29, 1909]

Thursday eve. 5 P.M.

My Own Wife

Well hon your two dandy sweet letters both came at once last night and they were just fine   you know I just love to get letters from you cause you certainly write dear sweet letters just like you are — <u>and</u> thats no <u>opera</u> <u>house</u> <u>joke</u>.

I am so glad you are enjoying yourself and will be able to see all the folks   hope you get to see Mrs. Marshall [Betty's sister Cora] too

I havent had a letter from Papa   I guess he did not know where to write   which theatre.

It seems like I have been here a month and still I have two more days.

Hon as for news   I dont know anything   I am just dragging on   there is several of the boys stop here and I am sitting down in the office and we kid around talk and I go up to the room and read and play Sol. I got up today at 10:30 and went to the Theatre and worked. I have every day since I came

Now hon if you get your visit out a little sooner than you expected why you just come on home   it would make an offul hit with me to have you come in any day now cause I am getting very anxious to see you. We dont know how much we are to each other till we are separated for a little while Its just like summer here and it is certainly getting hot working in the old <u>Show</u> <u>Shops</u>.
I hope I get another letter tonight when I go up cause I sho am foolish about my wife.

Well Hon I will stop   Give my love to all the folks   tell them I will see them some time soon and I would love mighty well to see you the latter part, at least, of the Cincinnati week

Bushels of Love and Kisses to the dandiest girl in the world and I sho do love you dear.

your Billy.

All my love to my Own Sweetheart Wife
Lots and Lots Love and Kisses
Billy.

NIC BOSLER'S EUROPEAN HOTEL

Louisville, Ky.
[Posted April 30, 1909]
Friday Eve. 5. P.M.
My Dear Sweetheart Wife,

Well last night I got your short letter and looked for another but none came but I will get it tonight

I got a letter from Papa and will enclose it. tells about his trip. you must write him every day or so for he does love to hear from you. I did not think Spi [Trent] would be mean about those deeds   I wrote him a long letter last night and thanked him   also wrote to Papa about some more land I wanted to buy up around the old place   I want all I can get reasonable cause it will never get any cheaper

Well old pal it has finally after about a month got as far as Friday on the week I was in bed just after the show last night and up at 10:30 and practiced hard till show time   They are having big Ball Games here but I am on so late I cant get out to see them. suppose it will be the same way in all the towns.

Where are all those drives and horseback rides you had planned [?] get you a horse and fly at em.

I am going to get up at 7 oclock and go out to the big race track where they are training all the fast horses for the Kentucky Derby which will be run here Monday. The old Millionaire who owns this Theatre, Cincinnati and Indianapolis has a fine bunch out there and his Trainer who has been in to see the show asked me to come out and see them exercise them. The Track is quite a noted one in America

Home must be wherever he is.
~Will Rogers, Jr.

C.V. Rogers was helping Will buy up allotted Cherokee land which adjoined the Rogers ranch. Will's cousin Spi took part of his allotment near C.V.'s land, and was supposed to sell it back to the Rogers. Evidently he had stalled on selling, but the deal had been made by this date.
~RC

and is called Churchill Downs. Wish you was here to go along.

There was a big wind storm here all yesterday and last night   done a lot of damage all over.

I got me a lot of papers and will go up and read for a while then eat and go to the show and will get a letter from my own wifey and it will make me think of her more than ever and wish she was here.

Now you write long letters and tell me all you do. All my love and kisses to my dandy sweet Wife.

Billy.

HOTEL HAVLIN

Cincinnati, O.
Sunday 5:30 P.M. [Posted May 2, 1909]
My Own Sweetheart Wife

Well here I am in the Germany of America   got in at 8 oclock this morning   left last night at 7 P.M. and the best part of all of it was that your dear sweet letter was here and I went right to the Theatre at once cause I expected it and I was sure glad cause I was afful lonesome   I did not know a soul and the show did not start for hours and if I had not of gotten it I dont know how bad I would of felt

I am at this hotel   pay 1.50 a day for a nice little front room without bath but there is one next door It is a pretty swell place. I eat at a nice little restaurant across the street   have had about 6 dishes of Strawberries at different times all day   just finished a couple just now

Well the old act went great this afternoon   they were great laughers   I am billed about third or fourth here as there is a big show.

Buck today as he reached down off of the Pony to pick up the rope out on the stage   the strap that he was holding on too with his other hand broke and he fell all over the stage on his right _ear_. of course it did not hurt him cause he was right at the floor any way but it was sho funny. The stage is very slick and old Teddy like to fell twice.

That Woman mystifier Irma Eva Fay is the Headliner and she does all that stuff having the audience write on a tablet questions and later on she tells them the answer. so she closes the show. she goes on No. 6. then has to have time to frame up the answers so she always goes on last again   she does like two acts. I have a dandy place No. 7. I am glad I am not closing cause it is a late, long, show.

Hon the little Pictures are dandy and just as cute as they can be of my Gal and I have looked at them a thousand times

There is another big Kid act on the bill just like the one last week with 10 Kids in it in a schoolroom scene.

This being Sunday I dont know if this letter will go out at once or not. I wonder what you are doing today. I'll bet you are having such a good time you dont think much of the time of me   I wish Sunday would hurry up and pass cause its lots more lonesome than the other days.

Well hon I will mail this. With all my love I am always your

Billy.

HOTEL HAVLIN

Cincinnati, O.
Monday 5 P.M. [Posted May 3, 1909]
My Darling Wife,

Your letter written Saturday came this morning and it was a dandy

Well say I just got a letter this morning from the office and my route has been changed from Indianapolis to Forest Park Highlands, St Louis. I leave here Saturday Night and open in St Louis Sunday afternoon at Matinee. so you wont have so far to come   the rest of the route is left as it was.

I just come over from Matinee and it has started to rain.

I am glad you are having you some clothes made   you can get what you want there   Will send you some Money   tell me how much you will want   now <u>hon</u> you get you just what you want and as much as you want.

Now dont as you say "ruin your <u>rep</u>" by coming back until three weeks cause you dont want people to <u>get</u> <u>wise</u> that you care for or want to be with your husband that would be a disgrace.

Here are a couple of clippings from two papers today   all there was in it seems that the papers have had a fight on with the Theatres and they dont advertise in some of them

I done a bad act last night and should of been roasted for it but I did great today and it goes good with the audience here. . . .

Well hon I will stop   hope I get that nice long letter that you said you would write Sunday

My love to all the folks   Write lots   all my love to you dear Girl and lots kisses
                    your own
                         Billy

HOTEL HAVLIN

Cincinnati, O.
Tuesday, 2 P.M. [May 4, 1909]
My Own Dear Wife,

Well this is earlier in the day than I usually write as I generally wait till after the matinee But I got up at 10 oclock and went to the Theatre to get a nice long letter from you before breakfast—but I am sorry to say I was disappointed as I only got your <u>note</u> and it was ab out the chilliest little thing I had ever gotten from you in a long time. I am afful sorry hon you felt bad but am glad you know it was not about me and that you are so perfectly at home and feel that you had never left.

But dont worry dear I am not silly enough to think you mean all those things you just felt a little upset when you wrote and you dont mean things like you say them I know and its mean of me to tell you of them but you had promised to write a long letter Sunday and I guess thats why I noticed it so much

I am sorry now that I sent you the letter from Sister Sallie cause I know you did not like the little part in there where she says Betty she thinks will be ready to join you in Cincinnati because your whole attitude seems to be to give people the impression that you are not in love with me and you do hate to have them think that you are   But I dont think you really mean it its only that you are afraid

"YOU DONT WANT PEOPLE TO <u>GET</u> <u>WISE</u> THAT YOU CARE FOR. . . YOUR HUSBAND. . . . "

Much as he loves her and wants her to have a good time, Will still smarted from the early distrust of the Blake family. It was probably sarcasm with a grin, but the grin didn't come through on paper.

                    ~RC

someone will tease or kid you about it. Well after breakfast this morning I went back to the theatre a[nd] worked for three solid hours and I am just about all in but will go over and do my show pretty soon

Here is the paper telling of the big race and my friends horse won it the one I had breakfast with and that is this horses picture that I sent to you, Wintergreen I was in his stall and met the jockey and all The race was run yesterday I could of won a bit of money on it for I knew this horse would win but I knew you would not like me to bet and I did not bet a cent That Owner Respass in the picture is a fine old fellow and I am glad he won.

This is actually a more lonesome week than last week (I did not think it possible) I dont know a soul and there is no one but me stops here

Hon here is $20.00 I will put in this letter it is all I have and I know you need some I will send you some more in a few days I just happen to have this and will send it now.

Say where is that letter you was going to send me that you got from some one.

Now dearie you write me a nice long letter and if you feel like saying a little sarcastic thing just leave it out and see how much nicer it will sound. My letters may not have been as long as you would of liked but you must remember I have not a thing in the way of news to interest you all days are the same to me. and at that I have written more and also <u>more</u> <u>letters</u> than you you spoke of writing twice one day but I notice you dident do it. The day you said you staid home from a club to write me you wrote <u>4</u> little Pages—just think it over and see

Well must get to the show shop I do hope you feel good by now and wont feel bad any more and write and lots to the old boy who takes things as he knows you mean them and not as you do and say.   yours always the same
Billy.

HOTEL HAVLIN

Cincinnati, O.
Wednesday 2 P. M. [Posted May 5, 1909]
My Own Dear Wife

Well hon I went over to the Theatre today and I <u>almost</u> got a letter.

I dont know what you mean in your letter where you refer to my good time in Louisville and hope I have as good time here you wrote as if I had been having a gay time and all I can recall is going to the track to see the horses and I dont know that it was a particular good time. I enjoyed it yes But I dont know where the good time come in Louisville nor have I discovered it here either.

Are you sore about something I did or havent done or what is the matter I dont understand the peculiar little chilliness of your last three letters My Lord I am not doing anything and have tried my very best to write you often and tell you all I do. and to not do a thing that would displease you.

You knew when you went home you could stay just as long as you wanted to or come back just when you wanted too and you know I how glad I will be to have you back. without you saying "if you want me back that week."

I want you to come just as soon as you can—and have had your visit out I know you are having a good time and are enjoying yourself cause you dont even

My sister Mary said Dad was inherently a selfish man. He did exactly what he wanted to do. She remembered how Mother loved the really nice home we had in Beverly Hills, a bit more formal than the sprawling ranch house we ended up with in Santa Monica. She wanted a nice home, a place for her silver and crystal, but in the end, it was Dad's house, not Mother's. Mary had a lot to say about this, but of course the ranch suited me just fine. Dad did want things to go his way, to live life as he wanted. Many of his trips were not as vital as he made them out to be—his trip to China when there was a war on . . . the last trip, to Alaska. But Mother never really put her foot down. Maybe most "stars" are self-centered like that. The rest of the world centers around their wants and needs.
~James Blake Rogers

have time to write.

I am just home from a long practice and oh but it is hot   I will now go over and do my matinee. dont do a thing but eat-sleep. read—and play a little Sol—till I get sleepy at night.

Now Betty dont feel sore or hurt about anything—I havent done anything "G" I dident think you would mind me going out to that track and I just happened to meet those men. My I am not having any good times I never was as lonesome in my life

If I do anything you dont like tell me about it   dont take it out in not writing and in saying sarcastic things

Must get over and do my stunt. Now Sweetheart please dont be this way with me   I am trying to do the best I know how to please you and you know I want to do anything that will allow you to enjoy yourself. Now come up to St. Louis any time of the week you want too. your old boy who loves you more than all the world.

Billy.

Betty still resented Sallie's letter. How dare her sister-in-law criticize her for spending some time at home! Especially after all the years that Will had stayed away from her. Although both women tried very hard to get along together, their relationship was like that between a wife and a mother-in-law. Sallie loved her little brother dearly and wanted him to be happy above all else. Betty wanted to be number one in her husband's life, and of course she was.

Betty was at home, probably getting kidded about her new husband running off and leaving her. Her sisters' husbands stayed at home. These were but little lovers' spats. Obviously their love remained strong.

Mother had a great sense of humor, but she could also be sarcastic. She'd throw a little zinger in there sometimes.
~James Blake Rogers

Both Sallie McSpadden and Betty Blake Rogers were very strong women and there was some friction between them throughout most of their lives. Sallie had written Will that she felt sure Betty would join him soon, implying that a wife's place was with her husband. If Will had understood women better, he would not have sent Betty the letter!
~RC

Will Rogers and Betty's mother bundled up at the sea shore.

HOTEL HAVLIN

Cincinnati, O.

Tuesday Night,11:30 P.M.[Posted May 5, 1909]

My Dear Sweetheart Wife,

I wrote you once today but I have just come in to the hotel after the show   I was in a saloon and had about 4 glasses of beer and am home ready to go to bed—but I dont know I feel so lonesome some way tonight (I do all nights for that matter) but more than usual tonight and so I will write you just a little note

Oh here is a little Kodak picture those two little Milch Sisters in Denver took they sent them to Buck   they took a lot of him and the Pony   they took this out in the alley by the stage one day as I was going   I was reading a paper

I leave here Saturday Night at 1 oclock and get to St Louis at 10:30 Sunday morning and open at Matinee   I think I will get a place to stop out near there if there is a hotel in or near the grounds and they tell me there is

When will you be up. dont make it too long cause I am sure lonesome for my little girl

Well hon I will stop and go up and see if I can go to sleep and get up early and hope I get a nice long letter from my own wife "G" but that seems great just to know you are all mine and I do love you oh, but I love you. Goodnight

My only only Love,

A million kisses, your boy,

Billy

HOTEL HAVLIN

Cincinnati, O.

Thursday 2 P. M. [Posted May 6, 1909]

My Dear Wife,

Well hon I did not get a letter today cause it come last night and I did not much look for one.

Here is $25.00   now I dont know if this is enough   you would not tell me what to send but if it is not we can send it to Dick as soon as you come

. . . .

Oh but it is hot here today and we are having a Womans Matinee. No Men admitted   this Anna Eva Fay is going to tell them a few secrets   I guess it is one grand Bunco I got a letter this morning from the Press agent at Indianapolis and he said I was to be there the week after St. Louis. the week that I was to be in Milwaukee but I have not been notified of it from the office so I dont know which one will go to   it dont make any difference anyway   I dont know yet just what will do after Chicago   have got a couple of agents hustling for me some parks and may get them and then I may not   so it might be possible we would be open after Chicago   still you cant tell yet.

They all say that Grand Rapids week is great   right out on a lake-fishing-rowing-and lots of fun   I want to get us a place to stop out near or in the park in St. Louis next week   wouldent you like it better than in town   I have been over to the Theatre and been practicing working and oh how I did sweat   it sho is getting hot on these old stages now when all those lights are up.

Well only three or four days and I will be with my own little wife and I will sho be glad cause it is certainly lonesome.

You decide yourself what trains to come on and I will sho be glad to see you cause I sho do love you a heap, your own   Billy.

HOTEL HAVLIN

Cincinnati, O.

Wednesday Night.11, P. M. [Posted May 6, 1909]

My Own Darling

Dear Sweetheart Wife,

tonight just after I come off from my act your <u>dandy</u> <u>good</u> <u>regular</u> letter come and I feel so good and love you so much and oh how I wish you was here   I would just love you to death

I just went right straight and sent you a wire and told you to leave no later than Sunday cause I want you quick <u>right</u> <u>now</u>

Now dear if I said things in my other letters you dont like they dont <u>go</u> <u>now</u> cause since I got your dear sweet letter oh! I am sorry I wrote the other

Now you better leave there in the morning   if you dont like the idea of being on a sleeper all alone you could leave Monday morning as perhaps you would like to spend Sunday at home   I will get in and have <u>us</u> a place located and could meet you even though it was late. I am so afraid you would not sleep on a sleeper <u>alone</u> aint there a train leaves at 9 oclock in the morning   it must get in around 10 at night. I think you would like that better   still you know and do just as would suit you best.

if you should be coming while I am working I would have some one meet you and take you to the Hotel   I expect you will need some money so will send you some tomorrow   I dont expect I will get a letter tomorrow cause this one was written Tuesday. I will stop and go to bed   all my love to my dear sweet little wife and love to Mama and Dick and all the folks. Goodnight, Love and Kisses,

Billy   This is the 2nd letter and a Telegram today.

HOTEL HAVLIN

Cincinnati, O.

Thursday Night 11:30 P.M. [Posted May 7, 1909]

My Own Darling Wife,

just a little note before I go up stairs cause I am lonesome and wishing you were up there waiting for me. and you will be in a few days wont you <u>hon</u>. "G" I sho do love you and I miss you oh so much and think of you all the time and I said some mean things in some of my letters and I did not mean a one of them. you are so good to me and I am the one who is wrong and you must forgive me cause I dont mean a bit of it and I will show you when you come "<u>home</u>" I hope I get up and go over and find a dandy good letter in the morning cause I dident get one all day today   it come last night the one that should of come today—

Well Goodnight my own my love you are the best and dearest wife in the world your Billy.

Tuesday, July 13th [1909]
My dear Mr. [C.V.] Rogers

We leave tomorrow afternoon for New York. We have had such a good time here [Atlantic City] that we sorter hate to leave. We have been going in the water every day and its great. I'm not afraid now and I go out and swim with Billy. He has taught me how to float and swim on my back. Oh, we have had some great times and are both as black as niggers. Im so tanned you would hardly know me. There are hundreds in the water every day. Its the greatest thing here.

Billy thinks he will work next week. He has several weeks booked for summer but they all come later. I will let you know at once if we leave New York next week. The weather has been so delightful here, cool and a good breeze all the time. We have not felt the heat once. But will in New York I bet. We were going to take a boat trip today, dressed and went down to pier to start but the sea was so rough the boat did not go out. I was sorry. We had counted on it so and some way I wanted to get <u>sea sick</u> just so I could tell about it sometime.

Married less than a year, Betty Rogers became a "woman of property." That was something to make folks in her hometown sit up and take notice.

~RC

Will ready for a night on the town, in Atlantic City, 1909.

Billy gave me, for my very own, one of the little rent houses he has in Claremore. He said I could have the nicest one. So I want you to take care of it for me. You pick out the best one for me and every month I want you to put the rent in the bank in <u>my name</u> and don't you let Billy touch it. You tell me which one is the best and all about it. Im greatly interested in my new possession and just tickled to death to have it for myself. Wasn't it good of Billy to give it to me? When I'm home sometime I'll fix it up and make a real pretty place out of it.

Lots of love from Billy and your daughter

Betty

New York, July 19 1909
Preston Hotel
4th Ave and 26th St.
My dear Mr. Rogers

Your letter written July 13th came a day or so ago. We came in here last Wednesday night. We are at this "Preston" hotel, small but very nice. Billy thought it would be cooler than at the Albany. It is very pleasant, we have a big room, big windows. We are only 4 blocks from river and get such a dandy good breeze all the time. We have not felt the heat once since we came here.

I have just come in from a long walk. Im sorter lonesome today. Billy left about ten o'clock to go down to Long Island to see his lots down there. He has never seen them you know, and I was sorter anxious to have him go and look them over. He has 3 lots near Hampstead and 2 (almost 3) acres of land at Deerpark. Hampstead is quite a place you know and I think he should sorter know what he has there. He will get back about 4 or 5 o'clock this p.m. Hampstead is only 20 miles from New York but Deerpark is farther and sorter hard to get too so I don't expect Billy back until later this afternoon.

This hotel is directly opposite the Madison Square Garden, and is the same hotel Billy stopped at when he was here with Mulhall the first time. It was the old Putman Hotel then, but has been improved since and the name changed to Preston. We were over to Madison Square Gardens last night and went up on the roof and also up on tower. We had a fine view of the city from there.

I hardly think Billy and I will get home this summer. . . . We are coming home late in the winter and fix our home up and next summer will find us there keeping house and living like <u>white folks</u>. We are just crazy for it and plan all the time just how we are going to fix things. Won't it be dandy. We will all have the best time and we can see you and be with you every day.

Billy has 4 weeks work—Newport, Brighton Beach Rockaway. We are laying off next week and may go up in the mountains and spend the week.

Lots of love

Betty

Sadly, the week that Will and Betty went up into the mountains, Will's sister May Stine, thirty-six, died unexpectedly at Oologah. It was July 25, 1909.

Will was grieved beyond words—he took his family responsibilities very seriously. But he could not get home for the funeral. He and Betty both corresponded with the

Will kept his own scrapbooks, carefully preserved, beginning with his first vaudeville days in 1905. Such items could serve as references if he should need them. Here he also cut apart the program from the Memphis Orpheum so it would fit on the page. The photos were sent by Betty to remind him he had a wife waiting during their first separation as a married couple.

family, telling them that he wanted to do something, at least to support one of May's children and to help with their education.

Both Sallie and Maud were with their younger sister at the end, as were May's children. They had about two hour's notice that she "probably would not live through the night," and they all had a chance to kiss her goodbye, Sallie said. "Poor little sister May" was conscious until the end.

Her husband Frank Stine survived as did her son, Johnny Yocum, sixteen, Jacob (Jake) Stine, nine, Mattie ("Lanie"), six, and Owen Gore Stine, six months. Sallie and Maud each took one of the younger children, and Jake was permitted to stay with Frank for awhile. Later, Frank Stine's mother in Texas took the children, then Frank remarried and they lived with him again. But Will Rogers did keep his promise. He paid for Lanie's education through Ursuline College, after which she taught school for fifty years. He also helped Jake Stine get a ranch in California.

[New York]
July 27, 1909
My Own Dear Papa.

You cant imagine what a shock it was when we got Sallie's telegram [about May's death] We did not even know she was sick.

Well this is certainly a sad blow to all of us and I do wish I could of gotten there for the funeral but as I could not get there I guess there is little use of us coming as I have to go to work again next week. but we will be there before long.

Poor May she had had a lot of trouble in her life but it seemed to of been all over and she was getting along so happily and well the last few years and it seems too bad that it come so soon but God knows best and all things are done for the best. But it will be hard on all of us to give her up We were always such a happy family and so enjoyed all being togeather, and all loved each other so much. Poor Sallie and Maud I know they are just heartbroken.

Well we have all of us children been wonderfully fortunate in having such a kind and loving Father as you have been to all of us--not only financially but by every word and action. and though our dear sister has gone--she is happy and you should be happy to know that through all of her life you and Sallie and Maud have done every little thing possible to help her and make life more pleasant and that should be a great consolation to you all

I dont know what arrangements you all will make about the children but I want to pay for the schooling for at least one of the boys

Well I will hear in a day or so telling me how it all happened I know that everything was done for her that possibly could of been done and I do hope she did not suffer

Well I will stop. and write again as soon as I hear With all love and Sympathy. Your loving son and Daughter

For the remainder of 1909, Will was on the move. Through July and August he was close enough that Betty could remain in New York most of the time. The temperature climbed and the heat was hard on business. Will suffered during his strenuous activities on stage. In August, he was in Philadelphia, Newport, then New York for two weeks. In September, he played Waterbury, Connecticut, Buffalo, Niagara Falls and Toronto. Betty went back to Arkansas to be with a sick sister.

LISEES'S HOTEL

PHILADELPHIA, PA.

[Posted August 10, 1909] 12:30 P.M.

My Own Darling Wifey

Well Dear here it is another old lonesome night   have been sitting down stairs for a long time talking to a gang (not drinking much) just <u>blathering</u>

Well I got in all O.K. today on the same train   had a shave and a bite to eat and then to work and tonight we had the best audience of the whole week and the old act went great. Donnelly has not come back from Atlanta yet Well I guess May and Tom have seen all of N.Y. by now   Dont you go prowling around too much   you just stay close home and let them do all the going you dont kneed to go. Well old baby Doll it looks lonesome tonight and I wish I was there but I will be tomorrow but tonight I feel offul tired and sleepy and think I can go right to sleep and dream of my own Dear little wife   I wont write you much   will see you so soon Goodnight my old Dear

I sho do love you

a million kisses and all my love

your Billy.

Jake married Mary Allen and they had one daughter—Betty Pauline Stine—who was the first woman to receive the uniform as a WASP [then Women's Air Ferrying Service] during World War II. She was on her last solo flight—1,000 miles across country—returning to Sweetwater, Texas, when her plane caught fire over Quartsite, Arizona. She bailed out but was killed when her parachute dragged her through the mountainous terrain. Her wings were granted posthumously, and she is honored as the first woman killed "in action" in World War II. She was 22. May—and Will—would have been proud."

~RC

202   WILL ROGERS

LISEES'S HOTEL
PHILADELPHIA, PA.

Night about 11:30 P.M. [Posted Aug. 12,1909]

My Own Darling Wife,

I should of wrote to you this afternoon and you would of gotten it the first thing in the morning but I did not think of it not getting there but now I see that this will not get there till tomorrow eve.

Well Dear I opened up O.K. done a pretty good act both shows and went good got a nice hand tonight on my entrance.

Tonight was Baseball Night   had the two teams there Philadelphia and Detroit and I used several ball gags in my act and they done fine   I have a good place on the bill early but a good place and I am sho glad   Say Hon but it sho is lonesome here tonight   I am in my room writing this and I sho do wish for you   I dont see how I could let you stay in N.Y. next year   its too lonesome   I'll bet you are lonesome too aint you dear   I hope you dont get afraid. I will be there tomorrow night about 1 oclock. and it is lucky that I am on early cause 10 oclock is the last train out   if I was on late I could not come   aint you glad I sho am

I am here for the night at the old hang out. have met a lot of people I knew and have been sitting down talking to them   Donnelly is in Atlantic City   will be up tomorrow. Wish he was here tonight   I would make him sleep with me   it is so lonesome.

Here is a Programme see how the way I am on the programme   Dear this has been the hottest day of the year here   oh but I am about roasted now and at work oh but it was fierce oh! got a wire today from Casey to play the Alhambra, 125th St., N.Y. August 30. pretty good eh.

Well Dear I must stop or melt.

With all my love to you my own Dear Wife I do love you so and miss you so much. Goodnight Dear your Billy. XXXXXXXXXXX

LISEES'S HOTEL
PHILADELPHIA, PA.

[Posted August 14, 1909]

My Own Dear Darling Wife

Well here it is about 12:30 and I want to drop you a little letter tonight. cause hon I dont like this alone thing and I will be glad when tomorrow night comes. I got over all O.K. today and spent the day as usual. I hope you all had a good time today.   I am going to take this letter over to the P.O. myself tonight and mail it and it will get to you in the A.M. they say if I mail it by 1:30   its only three blocks
. . .

Well old baby Doll I will be there at about 1:20 tonight cause this is Saturday now Donelly is not here yet   I wish you was over here right now cause I sho do miss you and want you bad   I dont think I can spare you to stay in N.Y. this fall   its too lonesome

I can only write this note hon as I want to write to Shea and get them both off So goodnight my own Dearest   will see you soon and I sho do love you   your own boy   Billy.

"TONIGHT WAS
BASEBALL NIGHT
HAD THE TWO TEAMS
THERE
PHILADELPHIA AND
DETROIT. . . . "

Facing page: At Will's request, Betty had this full-view picture made for her new husband to take along on his travels in 1909, their first of many enforced separations when his show business career called him from her side.

Hotel Columbus
Harrisburg, Pa
Saturday [Nov. 7, 1909]
My dear Mr. Rogers

Your good letter came yesterday evening. We leave here in the morning for New York. We leave at 9:40 a.m. and arrive in New York 2 p.m. in the afternoon. Billy plays at Newark, N.J. next week. This is the first theatre he played after we were married. We have had a splendid week here, Harrisburg is such a pretty town. Yesterday we went through the capitol. Oh, its beautiful. The finest one in the United States, and it certainly is a beauty. The most beautiful decorations and we were told the dome is supposed to surpass (in beauty) the dome of St. Peters Cathedral in Rome. The grounds are pretty too. Billy and I have spent most all our time over there. The capitol is just across the street from our hotel.

I sent you $15.00 last week to put in the bank for me. You know Im going to give Billy a watch this month—the 25th is our wedding anniversary. The chain and charm and all will cost me $50, so when I get to New York Im going to write a check for that much. I don't want Billy to know about this. Im going to get him to give me money along for my bank account and soon I will make up the 50 dollars I will draw out.

I think Billys farmer did fine this year. I hope the corn turns out good. Yes 256 dollars would look mighty fine put in the books to my credit and I would take it away from Billy too but I want him to apply that to his note there at the bank and get that cut down some. . . .

We got a good long letter from Maude today and the picture Mr. Stine had made of sister May. Im sorry Mr. Stine took the baby, surely he will not try to keep it. We have had a nice letter from Jakes grandma. She must be a mighty good woman. She writes such nice letters. She says Jake is such a good boy and so much comfort to her.

I will stop now. Will write you again from New York. Lots of love to you from Billy and your daughter.

Betty

HOTEL PRESTON
NEW YORK

Tuesday [Nov 9] 1909
My dear Mr. Rogers

Your good letter came yesterday. I got the check you sent. The manager of our hotel said I would have to be identified at the bank here to get my money so he proposed that I just write a personal check to him and he would cash it without any trouble. I guess I had better do this as I don't want Billy to know anything about it at all you know. . . . I'm sending you a picture Billy and & I had made at Niagara Falls & I will also send you some good newspaper articles about Billy.

Lots of love   Betty

Mr. Glantz, manager of this hotel has just cashed my check for $50. I signed the check Betty B. Rogers and felt awfully big too. Im going to get Billys watch right away.

Mother knew she would have to bend her wishes. . . to permit Dad to have his way. . . when she married him. Helping him became her career and she was as dedicated to her career as he was to his. And I know she loved every bit of it.

~James Blake Rogers

KENMORE OAKS HOTEL CO.

Albany, N.Y. Saturday [Nov 27] 1909

My Dear Mr. Rogers

I came up here Thursday to eat Thanksgiving dinner and celebrate out wedding anniversary. Billy and I had a big turkey dinner in our room and so enjoyed it. We have been married just one year and a mighty happy year it has been.
I go back to New York Sunday and Billy goes to Boston. He will come to New York the following Sunday. I will write you next week from New York.

    Lots of love   Betty

During this period, Will Rogers tried again to realize his dream of having a big show—if not one as large as Buffalo Bill's, then one that would fit on stage and surpass anything of its kind ever seen in vaudeville. He hired three women riders and two more men in addition to Buck McKee and did the announcing himself. But he soon saw the difficulties, primarily with the size of the act. Not many stages would hold that many horses and riders.

He gradually had to cut back, and finally his agents convinced him that it was really Will Rogers and his humor that brought down the house, and it was foolish for him to waste time and money on larger acts. Just as it was when he took the troupe to Europe, Will had to do his own monologue and roping show to get money to bail his show out.

HOTEL ST. FRANCIS

Friday morning Dec. 2, 1910

My dear Mr. Rogers

This is just a note so I have only a few minutes. We got the letter from the express Co regarding the grip and are so glad it has been found. We sent for the things to be sent here. Billy had a suit in there and so many things we did not want to loose.

I will write you a letter tomorrow, this is just a note. Our big act will open Monday and I hope I will soon have some good news to
tell you.

    Lots and lots of love   Your daughter
                Betty

Billy is working like a Trojan getting his horses and people in shape for next Monday. He gets up early each morning and by 8:30 has every thing ready for rehearsal. He is awfully busy, I hardly get to see him.

      Love   Betty

HOTEL ST. FRANCIS

Friday Dec. 9th 1910

Dear Mr. Rogers

We are having pretty weather now, still have snow on the ground, but the sun is bright and warm and its just fine to be out.

The big department stores here are beautiful, the Christmas goods and display is so pretty. I wish each day the children could be here, they would so enjoy seeing the beautiful toys. I hope you can be with us Christmas

"WE HAVE BEEN MARRIED JUST ONE YEAR AND A MIGHTY HAPPY ONE IT HAS BEEN"

*A pretty Betty with her mother,
Amelia Blake, in their big turn-of-
the-century hats have a formal
portrait made in New York.*

The big act is going pretty good, its so big Billy is afraid now he will have to cut it down some to get it on the regular stages. He is working with it all the time and we both think that it will make money.

We got your good long letter and was so glad to get it. Im sorry for Lanie and Owen [Stine] and only hope that later Frank will let them go back to the girls [Sallie and Maud]. Im afraid he won't be able to care for them as they have been use to and as they should be cared for. Pauline is home today [from treatment of crippling effects of polio] and Billy and I can imagine the happiness in the McSpadden family. I should love to see Pauline and do so hope she comes home much benefited by her long course of treatment.

My love to you all

Betty

Monday [December 12, 1910]

Dear Mr. Rogers

Your good long letter came yesterday and was so appreciated. Yesterday was an ugly day, snowing and cold. Billy and I stayed in our room all day, reading the Sunday papers. It is some warmer today, not snowing now but lots of snow on the ground.

Billy will bring the new act into New York about Tuesday. He is out now getting his stuff brought over to get everything shaped up. The act is working fine but Billy thinks he will have to take out some of the horses. Its too big and hard to handle on the stage. He intended doing this any way where he took the act out on the road. Some of the managers want him to take out two of the horses and in this place add his own act. They would give him big money for this. Until we get the act in New York tho we won't know just what to do about that.

You never say anything about coming out to see us. Now we want you to come. Surely you have not changed your mind.

Lots of love from Billy and your daughter

Betty

The remainder of 1910 was just as busy as every year for Will Rogers. He was booked mostly in areas close to New York City so he and Betty could be together— Yonkers, Philadelphia, Boston. He was booked at Keith and Proctor's Fifth Ave., New York, with W.C. Fields, the greatest of tramp jugglers. He saw Buffalo Bill's show in New York, played baseball every chance he got, and tried to make some money.

In July, Will and Betty went to Arkansas and attended a big family reunion. In mid-August they went to visit the "home folks" in Oklahoma. Will performed at county fairs and roping contests, and he took his sisters and Betty to the circus. He also searched for more good horses before he went back to New York to try to perfect his "big act."

In October Will wrote home that his horse Teddy had been lost or stolen. The pony had been one-third of the show since 1905. He offered a $100 reward.

Will wired for Betty to come "home" to the St. Francis Hotel in New York. On November 4, 1910, when Will celebrated his thirty-first birthday, Betty was with him. In December "Will Rogers and His Bronchos" did a benefit at the Hippodrome for the American's Christmas Benefit.

Clem Vann Rogers celebrated his seventy-second birthday January 11, 1911. It was to be his last. Will and Betty sent a telegram of love and congratulations to Sallie's house where the birthday dinner was held.

Lawrence, Mass

[Posted January 5, 1911]

My Dear Dear Papa,

Your letter just come and we were so glad to get it cause you always tell all the news.

I am so glad you are getting all of your business straightened out cause then

---

"BILLY AND I STAYED IN OUR ROOM ALL DAY, READING THE SUNDAY PAPERS."

On February 13, 1910, Will paid $100 to Elks Lodge Number I in New York City for a lifetime membership. The Elks Lodges gave performers a place to stay at reasonable rates. . . a place where they would be accepted, in spite of their connection with vaudeville.

~RC

Betty and Will take turns photographing each other at a Sunday picnic with the papers, bottled beer, boiled eggs and sandwiches.

you will know just how you stand and wont worry about your different affairs. I am mailing to you today the abstract that Johnstone made and you can get the farm all straightened out too. Who is the lawyer that is doing it. Now we are expecting you back here right away and in case we go to Europe which we may do you are to go along for a few weeks any way.

We are thinking of going over pretty soon and have a trip mapped out for you and Sallie and Maud it wont cost much and we will all go over togeather and then you all can come back when you like it wont cost you all over $250 or $300 apiece now Sallie and Maud can afford that and we will just all go over and have one big time I will write them later all about it as I will know more when I get to New York next week. A little ocean trip would be the finest thing in the world for you.

Well the big act I put on did not do so well and I saw it at once and only played it one week then I took part of it out and put it in my act and I think I can get quite a bit more money for my act I have a girl from Pawnee Oklahoma and her

husband and she rides a bucking horse in my act and I still use Buck and three ponies besides the bucker 4 horses and 4 people. She is a great rider and I have a great bucking horse. I have 6 horses in all but I only use 4 of them in this act.

I bought a pretty spotted horse looks like Tom's old Spot and he is good and I have two buckers and the three ponies   they all work good. The little Blue Starr pony is just another Teddy, the other act was two big and they would not pay me enough money to afford to keep it on I got all the people other jobs and they are all doing well. I think I will get some money with this act, this is a bad year back here and its hard to get work but this act is certainly going great with the audience.

Now Maude you and Sallie this is no joke We will all just go to Europe I will find out all about the cost next week you could make it in 6 weeks Papa could stay with me while you all and Betty   and Bettys sister Dick may go If we do and you all could take in all of it, I am figureing on an engagement in Paris and if I get it it starts Feb. 15, so hurry up.

We could go by London as I want to put on a trial show for the managers so I could come back there from Paris. Now we all could go over togeather and then you could take a side trip up to Scotland and Ireland then all over to Paris and you could come home by way of Venice, Rome, Naples and perhaps the Holy Land all in three or four weeks over there. Papa could stay with me and Betty could go with you all then you could sail home from Naples he could meet you there and Betty come back to where I was. Now can you beat that for somewhere around $350 or what if it costs more, thats the trip of a life time for all of us.

Now I will write you all next week. Now Papa we are sending you by express a present for your birthday wish we were there to help you celebrate and eat a big dinner.

Say ask Mr. Godby to send me please a statement at the bank and see how I stand.

Well I must close write to the same address in N.Y. St Francis Hotel, as we will be there next week as I dont think we work.

Lots of love to all of you and go to getting your money ready cause this will be some trip.

What will Cap and Tom say?

With all our love

Billy and Betty

Reviews said the show was great but Will didn't feel it was doing well. He'd wanted to be producer of a big show, but somehow all the fun went out of it when he had to spend all his time and much of his money on other acts.

They were booked, but not as often as when Will appeared with just Buck and Teddy. Back then he'd made as much as $350 per week. April 27, 1911, his contract for four persons for one week was $600. Not much was left for Will and Betty. He was booked in Dallas at a summer theater the first of June, then he and Betty went back to Claremore for one day, and he left for Chicago. By July he was almost ready to call it quits and come back home for good.

Besides, Betty was pregnant—finally!—and she was ready to settle down with a family.

Claremore papers reported that Will had bought the "top of Prep Hill"—twenty acres across the street from the Preparatory School on a beautiful hilltop overlooking the town. It had a spring, a stream cutting through the lower part, and plenty of room for a playground for the children Will and Betty wanted. They were drawing plans for a home.

But first, Will had to go back for "just one more tour" to make enough money for his start. In August he was a hit at Hammerstein's Roof Garden—almost back where he started! And theatergoers loved him more than ever. Maybe the Oklahoma home would have to wait awhile longer.

August 21, 1911

My dear father Rogers

I have been so busy the past few days getting ready to go back to New York. I leave here tonight at 9:30 p.m. and get in New York City Wednesday morning about six o'clock. My sister [Theda] is going with me and we are at once going to get apartments and start house keeping.

Billy will come in to New York next Sunday and spend the day with us. We hope to be settled by then and have a good home cooked dinner for him.

Im feeling just fine and am sure I will stand the trip alright.

I have about all my baby clothes made. I am expecting the youngster about the fifteenth of October. Billy wants a boy of course, but I do not care which it is. If it is a boy I am going to name it after Billy. I would name it for you but there are so many Clems in the family Im afraid they would get mixed up.

I will write you just as soon as I get to New York. You write to me to the St. Francis Hotel. . . . We will stay there until we find suitable apartments.

Lots of love to you from your daughter

Betty

St. Francis Hotel

Friday August 25, 1911

My dear dear father Rogers

Your nice sweet letter just come and I am so happy to have it and to hear from you. We had a very nice trip in here and I am feeling just fine. We are looking for rooms now. Im so anxious to go to house keeping. Billy will not get in here this Sunday as he had planned. He is in Montreal, Canada and the trains do not run so he could come here Sunday and get back to Buffalo in time to open there Monday. He will come tho the next Sunday sure.

I am glad you are feeling so well, and that your health continues good. Did you sell your horse.

It is raining here today and is quite cool. We wear out wraps and feel very comfortable in them. I had a letter from Billy this morning. He said he had sent you the money ($141.00) for his insurance.

I hope Sallie is feeling better. I will write her a letter real soon. I will write to you often.

With lots of love to you from your daughter

Betty

Monday Sept. 18th

#203 West 94 Street

New York City

My dear papa Rogers

Last week I went up to Syracuse N.Y. and spent most of the week with Billy. It was only a few hours ride on the train. I went up Wednesday and came back yesterday. Billy and I had such a good visit and such a good time. The New York state fair was being held there and we went out to the fair grounds. I saw an air ship, it was fine and the finest stock I ever saw in my life. You would certainly have enjoyed the fine stock. Billy and I both wished for you. Col. Zach Mulhall was there with a wild west show. We saw him.

Your letter came a day or so ago and I was so glad to get it. It was such a good letter. I sent it on to Billy. Im so glad your horse is all right now. I know you enjoy driving him these pretty days. I feel so well all the time. I have real nice rooms and so enjoy housekeeping. We sure have lots of good things to eat. Im a pretty good cook. . . . .

I will write you again soon.

Lots of love from your daughter

Betty

Monday Oct 2nd [1911]

203 W 94 St.

My dear papa Rogers

It has been several days since I wrote you and I feel ashamed of it too. I should write you more often. I am feeling so good all the time and go out just as much as I can every day then what little time I have in the house Im sewing and making pretty things for my baby. I can hardly wait now until <u>he</u> comes.

My mother came last Thursday. She is so well and Im so happy and glad to have her here. We have real nice rooms and enjoy our house keeping. We have lots of good things to eat. We can get anything we want here. We buy potatoes by the quart and peaches too. It seems so funny a quart of potatoes. I wonder what the grocery man out there would think if one should go in and call for a quart of potatoes.

We had a nice letter from Mrs. Stine, Jake's grandmother. They were so glad to get the things Billy sent them.

Billy will be in town Sunday and will work here next week. Im so happy to have him home for awhile.

I will write you again soon.

Lots of love from

your daughter   Betty

Oct. 7, 1911

551 West 113 St.

New York City

My dear father Rogers

We are moving today to another house. We think it is much better than this one and think we will like it much better.

Billy will be here Sunday. . . . We are going to have a nice big dinner for him tomorrow.

It is raining today and the weather is quite disagreeable. I expect it will be getting much colder. . . .

Tell Maude and Sallie that. . . when we get straightened up I will write to them.

Lots of love to you

from your daughter

Betty

Will Rogers became a father— and fatherless—in just eight days.

~RC

Will Rogers, Jr., was born on Friday morning, October 20, 1911, at a nursing home in New York City. Will Rogers, Sr., was able to be there for the big event. He was the one who wrote *Will Rogers, Jr.*, on the birth certificate. No frills with it.

Excited finally to have a male heir named "Rogers," Grandfather C.V. bought some beaded moccasins and stockings and mailed them himself. But he was never to see his grandson. C.V. died in his sleep at Maud's house in Chelsea, Oklahoma, Saturday night, October 28. They found him at peace, still in bed, on Sunday morning.

Times Sq, N.Y.
[Posted Oct 20, 1911]
Saturday
Dear Papa--

Just a note we got your letter and the dandy little Moccasins and stockings and Betty and baby and I were tickled to death with them
    You all have sent him some awful pretty things.
    Sallie and Maud sent some beautifuil things and Spi Trents wife too.
    We are doing fine Betty will write you she sat up today.

            Love
            Willie

"Will Rogers, Jr." was the name Will told the doctor to put on his infant son's birth certificate on October 20, 1920 in Manhattan. Yet all his life, Will, Jr., has used as his full name William Vann Rogers, Jr., which included the middle name of his grandfather, C.V. Rogers, and the surname of his great grandmother, Sally Vann, who married Clem's father, Robert Rogers, Jr. Will, Jr., still does not know who gave him his middle name. He thought it strange that he did not get his father's full name—William Penn Adair Rogers—with Junior tacked on. Likely, Betty and Will wanted to honor C.V. who died just a week after the child's birth. As Betty wrote to C.V., she did not want to use his first name Clem because it had already been given to more than one family member. Presumably Will and Betty honored C.V.'s memory later by adding his middle name to Will, Jr.'s. Will, Jr., only learned of the variation in his name when I obtained his birth certificate for him in the 1980s so that he could obtain official listing on the tribal rolls of the Cherokees. A birth certificate for James Blake Rogers did include his full name. He was named for his maternal grandfather. But the certificate for the third Rogers son, also obtained in the 1980s, did not include the middle name his parents intended— Stone. Will and Betty's sons were the only descendants of Clem Rogers and the only descendants of Clem's father, Robert Rogers, to bear the Rogers surname.

                      ~RC

The letter posted by Will to his father from Times Square October 20 almost certainly reached him but was the last communication between Will and his "papa."

Will Rogers had become a father—and became fatherless—all in the same week. Betty's mother stayed with her, and Will left for home at once.

Betty grew more reconciled to show business and the planned return to Claremore was postponed again and again.

Will tried once more to produce a big show—and failed. Finally he saw that he himself was the real crowd pleaser. Just him and his rope.

After five and a half years, Will parted sadly from Buck McKee and Teddy, his original sidekicks in vaudeville. Buck McKee opened a riding school and later moved to California. Teddy was sent to Oologah to graze peacefully on the old Rogers ranch, tended by Sallie's son Herb McSpadden.

It had been some seven years since Will first hit the bigtime in vaudeville. Twice he'd tried and failed to put together larger acts. Salary increases plus the tremendous accolades from audiences and the steady bookings would have been enough for most humorists. But Will was never comfortable in a rut.

He was offered a role—playing himself—in a musical show, *The Wall Street Girl*, starring Blanche Ring. Again he was the favorite of the show.

The show was a success in New York. When it closed for the summer, Will and Betty took little Billy and returned to Arkansas. When Will rejoined the traveling cast of the musical, Betty stayed at her mother's home off and on for the next few years.

"ANDREW" IS JUST ABOUT TO IMPOSE A LIBRARY ON SOME POOR TOWN

Will wrote the caption referring to Andrew Carnegie for the picture of little Will Rogers, Jr., in the family album.

"I sure am glad the stork dropped me down the right chimney," said James Rogers when he was in his sixties. "It enabled me nearly always to do just about what I wanted to do, and mostly that was to cowboy."
Cowboying to Jim is the ideal profession. Relaxed in the saddle, with his lariat in place, little Jimmy waits for others to get-agoing. All the children had horses to ride in Amityville, Long Island.

Mary was "Daddy's darling" from the time she was born, and their mutual admiration can be seen in her young pictures with her father. She no doubt felt betrayed when he died in the plane crash in 1935—on a trip he really did not have to take, at the very time he had promised her and her mother that he would be with them at the Lakewood theater in Maine where Mary was playing, and where Betty had gone to visit her after Will's plane left for Alaska. In 1982, she came to visit the Will Rogers Memorial in Claremore for the first time in nearly 40 years—since the bodies of her parents were interred there in 1944. She said, "You know, I guess it was silly of me to stay away so long, but I didn't think I could stand it—to come to the site where they are buried. But now that I'm older and have had to give up several friends, I can understand death better. So I will be back." Her final resting place is beside her parents in the same vault just below where we sat that day.

~RC

Will was at the Rice Hotel in Houston where he was performing at the Majestic Theater when he received a telegram: "Little Betty arrived at 2 p.m." The date was May 18,1913, and Mary Amelia Rogers was named for both her grandmothers. Will read the telegram to his audience when he went onstage that night, and he gave one of the best shows of his life.

With two babies and a traveling husband, Betty decided she was better off at home where she felt safer and where she had lots of help with the little ones. As often as possible Will came back to her, and many times she went with him for several days.

Betty adjusted to their separations better than Will did. She was honored at luncheons and parties, in Oklahoma as well as in Arkansas. With built-in babysitters she had plenty of freedom for social activities. And she was by nature a happy person. She managed to cope with grace—no matter what happened. As James Rogers has said, she coped with being Mrs. Will Rogers and she loved every minute of it.

Will was in San Antonio when he wrote Betty that he would try to come to see her, and he probably did on his way to an engagement in Winnipeg in Manitoba, Canada, June 10. Claremore *Progress* dated July 18 said he was there for two weeks' visit with relatives in Chelsea. "He's with the Orpheum circuit, jumping from Portland, Oregon, to this city, then will return to Frisco." The *Claremore Messenger* July 18 said Will was starting that night for Frisco to join his show, then jumps to Sacramento, Los Angeles and to New Orleans where he would close the Orpheum circuit.

Variety reported in January that Rogers was at Hammerstein's riding a "single wheel," skipping a huge loop back and forth under it while balancing himself. It was the same month that he was caught in a stalled elevator with other people in the Longacre Building at Broadway and 43rd Street for two hours, 5:30 to 7:15 p.m. New York papers said Will threw a loop over the knob of the door and pulled the car to the upper landing!

By then, he made $350 a week—and he didn't have to support a horse and a rider. In February he appeared in Philadelphia, Columbus, Cincinnati, Syracuse; in March and April in Cleveland, Indianapolis and Louisville. Ads in the New York papers said he would be back in town in May.

In June 1914, Betty met Will in Atlantic City for what she thought was a week's vacation. He had booked them passage to England on the German luxury liner *Vaterliner*. It was Betty's first trip by ship. Will had no bookings abroad, but his English agent, Sir Alfred Butts, at once found a spot for him in the musical *The Merry Go Round* at the Empire Theatre in London, an enormous music hall.

Alarmed at the noisy banter in the audience as the "percentage girls" hawked drinks during the acts, Will was not sure his drawling, intimate talk would work. But when the girls heard him they stopped strolling and settled on the steps to listen and watch him rope. The act was so successful the theater offered him $400 a week to stay on.

While Betty was shopping on the continent with a friend Will decided that the international situation was so bad they had better leave England. They took the German liner *The Imperator*, and by the time they reached home World War I had begun.

By the end of July, they had returned to Claremore to look after property interests—again looking at plans to move back—and the *Claremore Messenger* reported that Will had "just returned from a European tour where he showed to millions of people . . . no roper in the world can beat Bill Rogers with the trick rope." After several days in Oklahoma they went to Arkansas, and from there Will left for Kansas City, Ogden, Utah and to San Francisco. Postcards from Sacramento, Los Angeles, Tijuana, Salt Lake City and Denver traced Will's route till he came back to Oklahoma in mid-November. He became a member of the Akdar Shrine Temple in Tulsa. His roots were still in Oklahoma, even though he found little time to be there.

In the summer of 1915, the Rogers family rented a house in Amityville, Long Island, across the road from their closest friends, the Fred Stones. Fred, a popular star of Broadway musicals, convinced Will that he should stick around New York instead of traveling the vaudeville circuit if he wanted to move up in show business. And it was paying off already. The *New York Times* July 19 reported that Will was quite the best number in the show.

On July 25, 1915, Will and Betty's second son, James Blake Rogers, was born and

Betty and the children spent time at her old home in Rogers, Arkansas, while Will was traveling with the musical, WALL STREET GIRL. Crowded into the tiny swing at "Mamoo's" house are Will, Jr., and sister Mary.

named after Betty's father. Writing about this event in his newspaper column in December 1934, Will sandwiched it into a piece about the death of "Dopey—the pony loved by the whole family."

"Jim and Dopey came that summer. Jim was a baby boy, and Dopey was a little round bodied coal black pony, with glass eyes, the gentlest pony for grownups or children anyone ever saw. . . . "

The horse got the most publicity, but Jim, Will's "cowboy son," tagged after his father around the horses and barns, learning to ride, rope and brand cattle. Because of their common interests, Will was closer to Jim than to the other children.

Finally, the young couple was getting ahead financially. After ten years in vaudeville they leased a nice house in Forest Hills, Long Island, bought a new car, and had a stable of horses and five mouths to feed. They could live like a real family.

Their fourth and last child—a son whom they named for Fred Stone—came along July 15, 1918. Even though he was a healthy, happy, normal child, he died just before his second birthday of diphtheria, in California. The family was so bereaved they put away all his pictures and almost never spoke his name. To this day, not a picture of him can be found.

In September 1915, Will opened in *Town Topics* at the Century Theater in New York, "where he wears a dress suit, stores his rope under his top hat, and captivates with his looped-in-dance with the charming Lois Josephine." He was congratulated by the *Times* and by the many friends who sent telegrams. The week Will turned thirty-six, the Harvard football squad visited the show and 3,000 persons employed in various capacities in theaters of the city attended a matinee. On November 17, he quit the show to begin rehearsals for the new Ziegfeld *Midnight Frolic* which was to be presented atop the New Amsterdam Theatre early in the year. On Christmas Eve and Christmas Day he was in the Ziegfeld show, where he introduced "some novel features" for the holidays. Stone had been right to insist that Rogers belonged in New York. He played before Cornelius Vanderbilt's party, Mayor Jay Gould and his party and others of the sophisticated crowd.

February 1, 1916, Will registered his new car, a Willys Overland, and he started a new piece of business in the show—rolling a cigarette and roping at the same time. Rogers did not smoke, but the trick was something he'd seen cowboys do, and he practiced hours to perfect it.

Will continued his climb—in the *Follies*, in films, as a lecturer, newspaper columnist, radio commentator—reaching the top in every medium he tackled. He later told reporters he was an oddity in Hollywood—he had the same wife he started out with.

And, after his death August 15, 1935, Betty Blake Rogers never sought a replacement for the "Injun-Cowboy" who for almost a decade had courted her by mail and by whose side she had lived happily for nearly twenty-seven years.

If Will had to die so soon—at age fifty-five—he might have picked just such a time and place.

At the peak of his popularity, he still looked for fresh material for his lectures, his radio shows and his newspaper and magazine articles. And as always he searched for new mountains to climb and new experiences to share.

He was flying with his friend Wiley Post, a fellow Oklahoman and one of the finest

Once the fence broke down and the horses got away. . . . Teddy could not be found. . . . Will took this as a personal tragedy and sent instructions to [Herb] to spare neither time nor expense [to get him back]. . . . Several months later, Teddy, who had been the idol of boys in the streets of America, the music halls of Europe and before the king of England, was in the hands of an old full-blood Indian, who was working him in his cornfield, hitched to a plow. The horse was brought back, put out to pasture again, and lived a long life.

~Betty Rogers

aviators in the world. He was seeking adventures at the top of the world among his kind of people.

They were within sixteen miles of Barrow, Alaska, when the plane sputtered, then dived nose first into a lagoon near an Eskimo camp. Both Wiley Post and Will Rogers were killed instantly.

The whole world mourned his passing. The great and the small—cowboys and hardened newspapermen, movie stars, presidents and kings—they couldn't hold back the tears. They cried for the loss of a friend named Will Rogers.

And Betty Rogers was left to cope. She lived nine more years and saw the three children become adults before she joined her "Billie" on the hilltop overlooking Claremore, Oklahoma. They had, in the end, settled down together.

INDEX